1971

W9-ACP-456

3 0301 00008261 6

THE APPROACH TO
METAPHYSICS

THE APPROACH TO
METAPHYSICS

by

E. W. F. TOMLIN

KEGAN PAUL (LONDON)

First published by

KEGAN PAUL, TRENCH, TRUBNER & CO., LTD.,

Broadway House, 68-74 Carter Lane

London, E.C.4

1947

PRINTED IN GREAT BRITAIN BY
CHISWICK PRESS, NEW SOUTHGATE, N.11

"*A philosophical problem can be resolved only when it is set and dealt with in relation to the events which have made it arise, and which have to be understood in order to understand it. Otherwise the philosophical problem remains abstract and gives rise to those inconclusive and interminable arguments which are so frequent with professional philosophers that they seem to have become a natural element in their lives, where they come and go lazily and in vain, always agitated here and there and everywhere, but always at the same stage of development. If philosophy has been, and is, the subject of a special mockery which has never been aimed at either mathematics, physics, natural science, or historiography, that mockery must have a special motive which is the one we have described. If we can seriously render it historical, we shall win respect and, if we like, fear for it.*"

Benedetto Croce, *History as the Story of Liberty.*

"*If any man makes search for truth with all his penetration, and would be led astray by no deceiving paths, let him turn upon himself the light of an inward gaze, let him bend by force the long-drawn wanderings of his thoughts into one circle; let him tell surely to his soul that he has, thrust away within the treasures of his mind, all that he labours to acquire without. Then shall that truth, which now was hid in error's darkening cloud, shine forth more clear than Phœbus's self. For the body, though it brings material mass which breeds forgetfulness, has never driven forth all light from the mind. The seed of truth does surely sling within, and can be roused as a spark by the fanning of philosophy.*"

Boethius, *The Consolation of Philosophy.*

"*Almost all things have already been found out, but some have been neglected.*"

Aristotle, *Politics.*

"Metaphysics . . . is no futile attempt at knowing what lies beyond the limits of experience, but is primarily at any given time an attempt to discover what the people of that time believe about the world's general nature; such beliefs being the presuppositions of all their 'physics', that is, their enquiries into its detail. Secondarily, it is the attempt to discover the corresponding presuppositions of other peoples and other times, and to follow the historical process by which one set of presuppositions has turned into another."

R. G. Collingwood, *Autobiography*.

"The noblest of all studies is the study of what man should be and what he should pursue."

Plato, *Gorgias*, 487.

TABLE OF CONTENTS

Preface

In introducing this book, I must record my debt to three modern thinkers from whose works I have derived unceasing profit over the past ten years. They are R. G. Collingwood, A. N. Whitehead, and A. E. Taylor. To the first, I owe not merely the awakening of my own interest in philosophy both before my undergraduate days and at Oxford, where I established an all too fleeting personal acquaintance, but also the theme which runs throughout the present work, which is that metaphysical thought is concerned with presuppositions, and that presuppositions are at the basis of what is called civilisation. Anybody who had the good fortune to listen to Collingwood's brilliant lectures (particularly those entitled "Central Problems in Metaphysics", to which I owe much of the substance of Part I) and private conversation, will never be able to judge to what extent, in later producing anything of his own, he is echoing his master's voice. I am not even sure that in acknowledging my debt to him in the following pages, I am not paying in currency from his own mint. At any rate, he would have appreciated the compliment. England has not produced so fine a mind for many a long day, whatever certain philosophical opponents might declare. To the second, A. N. Whitehead, my debt is more easily discharged, as I have repeatedly acknowledged it in the text and in footnotes, with special reference to what, in common with many others, I regard as his greatest work, *Adventures of Ideas*. In the course of that work, incidentally, Whitehead states a view of metaphysics very similar, and no doubt paternal to, the one expounded in Collingwood's *Essay in Metaphysics*; and his statement that "an attack upon ordered thought is an attack upon civilisation" might well be taken as a motto for the latter.

A*

Finally, I could not leave unmentioned the work of the late
A. E. Taylor, especially *The Faith of a Moralist*, undistinguished
title of a most distinguished book, which, if I have not cited
it in any place save here, has not for that reason been without
direct influence upon most of what I have written.

It might justly be said that most people go for their philosophy to almost every place save philosophical textbooks; and
that is not necessarily an unhealthy sign. The seeker after
truth and certainty wants a living system of belief, a faith that
works, rather than a collection of dead precepts, a charnel
house of wisdom. But there is danger in this increasing neglect
of the actual work of philosophical writers. Philosophy comes
to be identified with specious profundities or portentous
maxims, to be culled from the pages of highbrow or middlebrow novelists, from leather-bound poets, or even from the
smart aphorisms of columnists. From the historical development of philosophical thought little is expected. The purpose
of this book is to provide a necessary corrective to this common
attitude. What follows, therefore, is neither a chronological
history of philosophy nor the exposition of a complete system
of thought; it is an essay in philosophical tendencies designed
to throw light upon our present perplexities, and directed towards the removal of certain misconceptions about the purpose
of philosophical enquiry and the relation of such enquiry to
the problems of civilised life.

In short, the present work (for which I claim no great
pretensions) is designed to send the ordinary reader, the
reader whose needs and interests I have had in mind throughout, to the study of the actual works of philosophical writers.
These writers, with a few well-known exceptions, make far less
difficult reading than is commonly supposed. Consequently,
there is no attempt here to "write down" to any so-called
"popular" level. The habit of keeping the reader at a respectful distance by thrusting at him innumerable "introductions",
"guides", and "keys" has been responsible for identifying

veneration with unreadability. "Let me tell you what I think this extremely abstruse thinker is about", the introducer says in effect, "and you will not need to bother your head with what he actually said". This kind of thing has been going on for so long that it has become a scandal; and meanwhile, to complete the absurdity, a school of "philosophy" has arisen which endeavours to relieve the serious reader's conscience still further by assuring him not merely that he need not bother himself about the actual works of philosophers but that he need not consult the commentaries either, since the whole subject has finally been shown to be a lot of nonsense, and now at last we have an infallible technique for exposing its extravagant pretensions.

In these circumstances, it seemed useful to present to the public a book in which this tendency, among others, was subjected to examination; and it seemed useful that this book should be written as far as possible in untechnical language by someone who has no vested interest in the perpetuation of metaphysical studies, either as nonsense or otherwise; and it seemed useful to entitle it *The Approach to Metaphysics*, because, as the professional philosopher will be only too ready to point out, I have again and again left off just at the point where the fun is due to begin. If, therefore, such experts, perusing what I have written, are moved to exclaim—"this is all very elementary"—then I shall indeed know that I have accomplished my purpose.

I wish to thank the Editors and Publishers of *Scrutiny* and *The Dublin Review* for permission to reproduce in Part IV some brief extracts from material that has already appeared in their pages. My warm thanks are also due to Dr. A. H. King and Mr. M. F. Cullis for their kindness in reading through the proofs and making many valuable suggestions; and finally, to my wife for her great assistance in compiling the index.   E. W. F. TOMLIN.

Chorley Wood, *June*, 1946–*February*, 1947.

Introduction I

The Use of Philosophy

The kind of questions which we propose to discuss in this book and with which, it seems to us, all introductions to the study of philosophy should begin, may be stated briefly as follows.

Are we right in regarding philosophy as having a definite and recognisable function to fulfil: a function, that is to say, as definite and recognisable as that fulfilled by art or science, and as little capable of being fulfilled by any other intellectual discipline? Is the philosopher, in so far as he is true to himself, engaged in the kind of enquiry which can be shown to be both profitable and necessary? What, in other words, is the philosopher trying to do which is not being done already by the artist, the scientist and the theologian?

Such questions as these—the reader may be able to think of several others equally relevant—need to be answered, because they are the natural questions that anyone coming to the study of philosophy for the first time feels impelled to ask. Before I begin to take up the study of philosophy, the beginner is likely to say to himself, I want to be sure that I am not about to lose myself in a miasma of speculation from which nothing positive seems likely to emerge. Unless I am convinced that I can get from philosophy something that I cannot get elsewhere, I see no reason why I should sacrifice my time and energy for what at first sight seems a task as thankless as it is laborious. Tell me, in short, what philosophy is and does, and I shall then be able to decide whether or not I think it worth pursuing.

Such doubts and indecisions on the part of those about to take up the study of philosophy are wholly reasonable and legitimate; and if we are tempted to wonder why the beginner in philosophy is so much more doubtful of the value of his subject than, say, the beginner in science (who is usually overwhelmed with the importance of his studies) or the beginner in art (who is usually convinced of the unimportance of everything else), and are thereby led to draw the hasty conclusion that the study of philosophy is less urgent than that of other subjects, the answer is that such doubts and indecisions, far from being incidental to philosophical enquiry, are something essential to it, that, in fact, they belong to the first stage of that enquiry. Why should this be so? What kind of study is philosophy that our first reaction to it should be one of complete scepticism as to its necessity and value? Is there anything peculiar to the nature of philosophical enquiry or, better still, is there anything distinctive in philosophical *method*, that will enable us to explain this apparent idiosyncrasy? Let us see if we can answer this question.

Theory and Practice

The first part of the answer we propose to offer may appear, at first sight, to have little enough to do with what most people have been led to expect of the nature of philosophy. Nevertheless, it is to be hoped that in the following pages the importance of the argument will become increasingly apparent. If we think for a moment of an art like music or a science like economics we perceive, whether or not we are trained musicians or economists, that between the subject itself and the theory of the subject—between the theory and the practice—there is a clear distinction.

A successful artist, for example, need not be acquainted with theories of art or æsthetics—he need not even be aware that such theories exist—any more than a successful business-man need be acquainted with theories of economics. To put the same point in a different way: reflection upon the practice of music or business is not, as it were, an item on the agenda of these subjects themselves. Naturally musicians discuss questions of art and technique, and business-men debate questions of commercial policy; but a man can be a perfectly good artist or a most successful man of business without bothering his head about these theoretical questions from one end of his career to the other. The theory of music is no doubt a part of the world of music, just as economic theory is, in a certain sense, a part of the world of business. But, to put the matter in a somewhat paradoxical form, it is no more necessary that the theory of harmony shall *sound* well than that the theory of money shall be expensive or the theory of humour a joke. We do not for a moment say that acquaintance with æsthetic theory will be a hindrance to the artist, though excessive concentration upon theories may well prove an unnecessary distraction. We merely say that there is no more necessity that the artist will paint better with the works of Clive Bell, Roger Fry or Wilenski before him, than that the business-man will become more prosperous as a result of studying the late Lord Keynes's *Treatise on Money*, or the comedian more humorous and entertaining as a result of reading the treatises on Wit of Bergson and Freud. The profession of the business-man, the musician, or the comedian can be pursued quite independently of the theoretical problems to which, in the course of their exercise, they are found to give rise. And this is true of almost every occupation we like to think of, whether it be cricket, the making of omelettes, or tap-dancing. But there is one subject about which it can be said without hesitation that reflection upon it is part of itself, and this is philosophy. For, among the initial tasks of philosophy is that of discovering what philosophy is and should be. To engage in the task of discovering what philosophy is, is to engage in a philosophical enquiry.

Philosophy, in other words, is a mental discipline which exhibits in its most complete form something of which we used to hear a great deal: namely, a unity of theory and practice. And this, incidentally, goes some way towards explaining the presence of those doubts and misgivings which, in approaching philosophy, we find ourselves encountering: doubts and misgivings which are now seen to be a condition of philosophical thinking in general. Unlike a game of cricket or hockey, in which we can practise without actually taking part in the game itself, we are compelled to think and to learn how to think at the same time. Although the best way in which we can learn how to play hockey, for example, is to play the game regularly and often, it *is* possible for us to train for the game by adopting other and perhaps more labour-saving expedients: we can develop our muscles by performing exercises in the morning or by going for runs at night. In short, there are other ways in which it is possible for us to acquire proficiency than simply that of taking part in the game itself. In learning how to reason or to think correctly, however, this is not the case at all. There is no sense in which we can practise how to think without at the same time thinking as completely and accurately as we can. We cannot, that is to say, practise at arriving at true thinking unless we do actually set out with the deliberate intention of aiming to think truly: otherwise we shall not be learning what we want to learn. Thus we can say with confidence that the only way in which it is possible to acquire proficiency in solving philosophical problems is in the attempt to solve them. The choice before us is not between solving such problems philosophically and solving them in some other way. The choice is between philosophising well and philosophising badly.

The Scope of Philosophical Enquiry

It is now time to tackle the second part of the question as to what distinguishes the method of philosophy from that of other branches of study. We must first make it clear, however, that what follows must not be taken as being anything in the nature of a rigid definition of philosophy. The definitions of philosophy, unlike those of science, are, as we shall have occasion to show, never rigid; and if, as we have seen already, the task of discovering what philosophy is occupies an important part of philosophical enquiry, it follows that the definition of philosophy can never be a final one. Nevertheless, the fact that it may be difficult to say in what the goodness of a good man or the beauty of a beautiful picture consists, does not necessarily mean that goodness or beauty is an unreal, indeterminate or even a vague quality. And similarly, the fact that philosophy is a subject that cannot be defined during the course of a chapter or perhaps even a book, implies not that philosophy is any less real or definite than other subjects, but rather that its nature is such that it cannot be adequately defined in a few sentences. Nevertheless, to issue a warning about the difficulty of reaching an adequate definition of philosophy is not equivalent to banning definitions altogether. All that such a warning implies is that we should be prepared constantly to revise our definitions as the occasion demands and in the light of new discoveries, and this is something that philosophers find themselves continually obliged to do. It might even be said that the whole history of philosophy from the time of the Greeks to the present day consists of a series of revised definitions; so much so indeed that Professor Whitehead has summed up the history of modern philosophy as a series of "footnotes to Plato".

We have deliberately issued this *caveat* on the subject of philosophical definitions because it is clear that if we say, as we may have to say sooner or later, that philosophy may be defined as the study of reality in general, we have only *begun* to define philosophy. It is because so many persons think that, having advanced this somewhat grandiose definition, they have *finished* defining philosophy, that the whole subject has acquired a reputation for intolerable vagueness and abstraction. Nevertheless, it is something at least to have begun to define philosophy. What we must do now is to work onwards from this point.

In the first place, why is it that we need a special form of enquiry for the study of reality in general? In what respects do the enquiries of the scientist or even the theologian fall short of providing us with all that we want in this respect? Physical science, for instance, appears to be as good an example of the study of reality in general as we are likely to find. In what way, then, does the work of the scientist, which takes for its province all the facts of existence, need to be supplemented by that of the philosopher, who does not seem to be concerned with facts at all but only vague ideas? What form of knowledge does the philosopher suppose himself to be seeking which the scientist has not already pledged himself to discover? These are the sort of questions that we all, at one time or another, tend to ask when confronted with this claim on the part of philosophy to be the true study of reality. How are we to answer these questions?

The best way to answer them is to improve upon our original definition. If it were said that philosophy is the study of what reality "really is like", our first impulse no doubt would be to regard the statement as a quibble. But if we reflect for a moment, we observe that the new form of the definition contains an implication which was not present in the old: the implication, namely, that some forms of reality are not always as real as we think them to be, but only *appear* to be so. And this implied distinction between "what appears" and "what really is"—this differentiation between appearance and reality—is in fact the starting-point of all genuine philosophical enquiry. Philosophy—and here we perceive our definition beginning to take on a firmer outline—is the study of *ultimate* reality, of "what really is" as opposed to "what appears to be"; and as this contrast between appearance and reality is the source of all that is self-contradictory in our experience, it follows that philosophy is the search for a reality which is coherent and consistent with itself. It is precisely because our minds are so constituted as to be incapable of accepting as real and true what is self-contradictory, that we first become aware of the distinction between appearance and reality and start "philosophising". For it seems highly probable that this fundamental distinction, which is so frequently bringing us to a standstill with an abrupt jolt, is responsible for the rise, not merely of philosophical thought or reflection, but of thought in general. We literally "stop and think", and we do so because something has forcibly held us up. All our thinking, in other words, is the result of some form of frustration in our experience—a knot or rift which arrests or disturbs the flow of our consciousness.

The Status of Science

Assuming, then, that we have provisionally defined philosophy as the study of ultimate reality, we have still to show in what respects science—whether by science we mean mathematical physics or even psychology—is unable to compete with philosophy on its own ground. After all, an objector might say, there can be no facts that science is prevented from considering, for the simple reason that science, being occupied with observing and analysing the real world, is concerned with all that there is. But such an objection needs only to be stated to reveal its unsatisfactory nature. For the question as to what is "real", what is a "fact", and what we understand by "knowledge", are precisely questions with which philosophy is occupied. Physical science *assumes* that it knows these things, and could not proceed with its task unless it made this assumption and a good many others too. Philosophy, perhaps somewhat arrogantly, asks what right science has to assume these things and lays bare, in so doing, the limits and restrictions of scientific knowledge. It is because the various sciences are concerned not with reality as a whole but with particular aspects of reality—or perhaps it would be more accurate to say, with the whole reality from particular aspects—that no science can proceed without a basis of presupposition. This is not to belittle science in the least. Nevertheless, the tendency is for the sciences to forget their status of dependence, even though the assumptions upon which they depend consist precisely of those aspects of reality with which they are not immediately occupied.

All that we have been saying on the subject of science can be summed up in the statement that the scientific view of reality is an abstract view of reality. But before we leave this subject, let us take as an example a science which, though highly abstract in its method, may seem at first sight to possess precisely those qualities with which we have been crediting philosophy. We refer to the science of psychology, the reputation of which is to-day very high. If philosophy is occupied with thought, so apparently is psychology. If philosophy is occupied with the powers of the mind, so surely is psychology. What, in other words, is the fundamental difference between these two studies, both of which appear to be directed towards the same end?

The Claims of Psychology

The difference, I suggest, is not one of subject-matter but, as might be expected, one of method. The object which psychology and philosophy are engaged in studying is the same: the human mind; just as the object which physiology and anatomy are engaged in studying is the same: the human body. But just as physiology is concerned with the *functions* of the body and anatomy with its *structure*, so psychology is concerned with thought as a mere *process* or series of events, and philosophy with thought as directed towards a particular end, the end of truth. Psychology, we might say, studies thought in abstraction from the end to which it is directed; it remains indifferent to the distinction between truth and falsehood. Thought, for the psychologist, is just a happening and man merely a creature in which this happening happens. Whether what happens ought to happen and to what end it is directed remain questions which are left for the philosopher to answer. Now it is easy to see that, once we consider thought apart from its truth or falsity, the mental process that remains is merely a kind of behaviour. And if thought is reduced to a kind of behaviour, it follows that psychology will tend automatically to become the study of behaviour—in short, Behaviourism, the well-known theory of psychology which regards thought as a form of suppressed speech, and therefore a kind of action or habit. So we perceive that because it is concerned with thought in abstraction from the end to which all thought is directed, psychology always has a tendency to degenerate into physiology; and there is no actual harm in this so long as it is content to stick to its scientific method. But directly psychology claims to exert authority over other spheres, as it sometimes does, the result is harmful and finally unscientific. For if the behaviourist, for instance, maintains that all thinking whatever is a form of behaviour, it follows that the behaviourist's thinking about behaviourism is behaviour too—that is to say, a series of "goings on" in the mind of the behaviourist. And if our thoughts are nothing more than just "happenings", "events" or "goings on" in our minds, without any "sense of direction", it follows that to describe a thought as either true or false ceases to have meaning. And that at once lands us in all sorts of contradictions and absurdities which need not for the moment claim our attention.

Philosophy its own Justification

Now what has been said on the subject of philosophy and

its relation to science in general and the science of psychology in particular, is, as we promised at the beginning, by no means all that there is to be said about it. What we have done is to try to direct the reader's thoughts to the kind of problem with which philosophy has to deal and to the kind of method which it uses. Once we have got our bearings we shall be better equipped to take our philosophical enquiries a stage farther and to outline, as clearly as we can in a short space, some of the chief problems to which philosophers of the past and present have in fact addressed themselves. In the following chapters we shall not be trying to present anything in the nature of a system of philosophy, because our aim is the very reverse of stuffing the reader's brain with a number of pet ideas of our own. Instead we shall be trying to follow the example of the philosopher Emmanuel Kant, whose aim (as far as his own students were concerned) was to teach not so much philosophy as *how to philosophise*. We shall be endeavouring to show that there is a particular attitude of mind, the philosophical attitude, which each of us may cultivate if we exercise sufficient patience, and in achieving which we shall be better equipped to face the problems of everyday life. The kind of reflection in which philosophical thought consists does not need any further justification or "*raison d'être*" than that which it provides in the course of its progress; for in the process of reflection we engage in thinking about thinking, with the deliberate object of trying to think better. Such an aim is clearly its own justification. To compare the functions of the mind with those of the body is proverbially dangerous; but this much we can say with confidence, that just as a muscle grows strong with temperate use and exercise, so the mind increases in power, in resilience, and in range in so far as it is free to pursue the activity proper to it, namely, thought. There is nothing upon which our reason cannot ponder, no sphere from which its entry is debarred, and no foreseeable limit to its capacities. Indeed, at no time has the world suffered from a superfluity of Reason. Even during the periods in history called Ages of Reason, Reason was deficient, because the faculty most in evidence at such times has been an abstract form of reasoning which falls far short of the rich and creative instrument that is man's highest endowment. Finally, to look to some other faculty for guidance, call it "intuition", "instinct", or what you will, is futile, because even the advice to follow our instincts is advice which, if we choose to follow it, must be based upon grounds which our reason provides and is to that extent other than merely instinctive.[1]

Introduction—II

Thought and Feeling

Hitherto we have been using the word "philosophy" to describe that form of enquiry which deals with ultimate questions about the universe. To this word there can be no objection except that it tends to be used somewhat loosely, and that in its literal sense it means no more than one who is attached to wisdom.

In the chapters to follow, though the words "philosophy" and "philosopher" will often be used, we shall be employing by preference the more exact, but unfortunately somewhat formidable, "metaphysics". If a distinction between the two words is asked for we might say without inaccuracy that a philosopher is a man who, seeing beyond appearances, becomes a metaphysician in his appraisal of that which he sees. Of the precise meaning of the term metaphysics and the reasons why it originally came to be used, we shall be speaking at greater length in Part II.

In the first section of this introduction we dwelt in very general terms upon the nature of thought and the main

[1] For the relation between philosophy and theology, see p. 125.

reasons for dismissing the claims of psychology to be the true science of thinking or reasoning. Before we embark upon our journey it will be useful to enquire a little more closely into the exact relation between thought on the one hand and feeling on the other, and into the whole question of the capacity of the mind to exercise its powers without let or hindrance from such things as "environment", "matter", "the brain", and so on. To institute such an enquiry is of vital importance for us to-day, both because of the tendency, common to certain philosophical schools and to certain imaginative writers, to deprive the mind of its primacy, and because of the frequent assumption, consequent upon this deprivation, that thought is by hypothesis "conditioned" by factors outside its control. That the less respectable or, at any rate, less reasonable philosophical theories—such as solipsism, determinism and pyrrhonism[1]—tend to get into the papers and to queer the pitch of philosophy from the start, we shall have occasion more than once to observe. But we must fight our battles where we encounter the enemy, and so it will be necessary to clear the ground of certain misconceptions with which we find ourselves directly faced, before proceeding to the exposition of the metaphysical ideas of others.

That a clear-cut distinction exists between thought and feeling is usually assumed to be a matter of common sense. Common sense, however, merely indicates that a distinction is present. It cannot enlighten us, except in a very indirect way, as to what this distinction is.

Once we begin to reflect upon the two faculties, however, several fundamental differences become apparent. While in both thought and feeling distinctions of great importance have their place, there is nothing in the sphere of feeling to compare with the most fundamental of all distinctions within thought, that between thinking rightly and thinking wrongly,

---

[1] i.e., the doctrine, first stated by Pyrrho of Elis (c. 300 B.C.), that certainty in knowledge is impossible for man.

between truth and error. This must not be taken to mean that feeling is merely passive: it clearly is not. What is meant is that thought, in contrast to feeling, is essentially *teleological*: an operation, as we have seen, in which it is impossible to engage without committing oneself to the pursuit of a definite end, the end of truth. Thought, therefore, may be said to contain within itself, or to be animated by, an effort or *nisus* (a word to which we shall return in Part IV) to achieve a certain standard of its own. Secondly, feeling, as compared with thought, is essentially a "private" possession. What I feel at this moment may bear a certain superficial resemblance to what you feel, but I cannot, even by the utmost stretch of sympathy, feel your feeling; I can only feel what I should feel "if I were you", i.e., if I were in just your circumstances, which I am not and never can be. Again, your feeling and my feeling, however much they may seem to be opposed, cannot contradict one another. If I happen to feel cold, no one—least of all someone who asserted that he, on the contrary, felt warm—can prove that I am under a misapprehension. And finally, there is nothing within the sphere of feeling to correspond to what may be called the "idea-reality" distinction within thought. What I feel can never be a mere "appearance", the deceptive screen for some more ultimate reality: not so much because appearance and reality are here identical, but because this celebrated distinction is one which, in the case of feeling, does not arise. When a man thinks wrongly, we say that he is mistaken; and in saying that he is mistaken, we imply that if he were to think more deeply or carefully—if he were to "think again"—he would perceive that his previous thought, being incoherent or contradictory, was erroneous. Such revision and reorganisation are impossible in the sphere of feeling. To speak of "misfeeling", in the sense of failing to reach a standard embodied within the idea of feeling itself, is meaningless. We do not re-feel an old feeling; we feel a new one.

The Sphere of Feeling

It is impossible to imagine such a thing as a mind that did
nothing but feel. In so far as it is functioning properly, the
human mind is engaged in thinking and feeling at the same
time. It would seem to be the case, in fact, that feeling and
instinct, though deficient in the autonomy and independence
of thought and will, are essential to the proper functioning of
thought and will, that their so-called "blindness" is the blindness of the chrysalis, which is a protective blindness; and that
they form, as it were, the irrational "slough" which, in order
to function rationally, the mind is perpetually casting off.
Such blind, irrational forces, which Freud has collectively
termed the *libido*, would seem to belong to a sphere intermediate between body and mind. Now the presence of a
sphere intermediate between body and mind has been suspected, if not openly recognised, since the time of the Greeks;
and characteristically enough the Greeks had a word for it,
and the word was Psyche. The human Psyche cannot, without falsification, be described as either mind or body. To
employ the orthodox philosophical terminology, it is the
sphere of neither conation nor cognition, and yet its function
is at once a kind of thinking and a kind of willing. Now the
only kind of human activity which, while not actually thought,
is more akin to thinking than to anything else (in spite of the
distinctions we have enumerated), is feeling; and the only
kind of activity which, while not actually will, is more akin to
will than to anything else, is instinct. In short, feelings and
instincts, to which the eighteenth-century philosophers gave
the general title of "passions", are the material which go to
make up what is called the Psyche; and it need hardly be
observed that the proper science for studying the Psyche is,
and has always been, psychology.

The various treatises on Human Nature which were published in the course of the seventeenth and eighteenth cen-

turies are found upon inspection to be treatises on the irrational or sub-rational side of human nature: or rather, in spite of the belief of their authors that they were discussing human nature as a whole, these enquiries boiled down in the end to a disquisition upon the "passions"—love, hate, pride, envy and so on. They are not concerned with reason in the highest sense.

Again, if an inspection is made of the ethical treatises of Kant, or of the "Treaties on Human Nature" of Hume, or even the "Ethics" of Spinoza, it will be found that after some initial philosophising, the authors get down to an analysis of the more common human emotions, which they tend to "personify" after the manner of the "characters" of La Bruyère and Vauvenargues. In other words, they are discussing in each case neither the mind nor the body, but the Psyche. They are engaged, not so much in philosophising, as in psychologising. They are endeavouring, somewhat fumblingly perhaps, to work out a science of the feelings.

Such a science of the feelings, which is both legitimate and necessary, must inevitably be an empirical science—that is to say, a science having for its data the observed facts of perception. So far as is possible it must endeavour to arrange these facts in order, and to discover the laws, if any, to which they conform. Thus far, and thus far only, can the science of the feelings expect to go. But however successful within its limited sphere this science may be, the human nature which it claims to analyse represents more than a bundle of passions or sentiments. Plato's famous simile of the charioteer controlling his unruly horses had no other purpose than to demonstrate that Man's highest possession is that of reason: and of reason there can, in the strict sense, be no science.

In view of the existence of several works purporting to discuss the "psychology of reasoning", this latter statement may appear unnecessarily dogmatic. But if we continue to bear in mind the essential difference between thought and feeling we shall not perhaps find the view expressed above so evidently preposterous. Thought, we have observed, has a definite object; and indeed the whole process of thinking is one in which it is impossible to engage without considerable effort, and in consequence one from which the human mind (not noticeably more active than the human body) has a tendency to shrink. Of such an activity, therefore, there can be no empirical[1] account, since an empirical account is concerned solely with observed facts, whereas the "object" of thought, being the goal which the mind sets before itself, is not in any sense an observed fact. Since there is no place in the scientific view of the world for what are called "final causes", "teleology" is something of which science takes no cognisance. In other words, the scientific account of an activity involving teleological reference, such as an activity of thought, is necessarily an incomplete or abstract account. It reduces thought to feeling, and feeling to "behaviour". We call a method psychological when the interest of the enquirer is centred, not so much upon the object in view, as upon the accompanying emotions which, in pursuing the object, he is found to experience. Hence the professional psychologist's preoccupation with "reactions".

The Mind and the Brain

Although we are occupied with thinking during most of our waking life and possibly in some degree while we are asleep, we do not, as a rule, spend much time thinking about thinking. If the ordinary man were to be asked point-blank what thought is, where it is, and how it operates, he would probably reply—after some little thought—that thought is an activity that takes place somewhere in the brain, that it is an activity which is "fed" or sustained by impressions received from out-

[1] The word is derived from the Greek *peira*, trial.

side, and that it operates by sorting out these impressions and working them up into ideas.

That thought and the brain are intimately connected one with the other is a fact which can be demonstrated scientifically. If the brain is subjected to certain forms of treatment our mental activities undergo transformations of a peculiar and sometimes grotesque kind. Moreover, mental states can be artificially induced by various processes which are being daily perfected and developed. Nevertheless, it is one thing to be able to prove that thought and the brain are intimately connected, though this does not tell us anything very new. It is quite another to assert, in consequence of this proof, that the brain is the cause, or even the seat, of our thinking. As a matter of fact, it is possible to remove by surgery certain portions of the brain without causing any changes in our mental processes at all. Such operations, in the present state of our knowledge, do not really prove anything one way or the other. What we are interested in at the moment is not so much the extent to which we can tamper with the brain without affecting our mentality, as the logical consequences or implications of the above-mentioned theory that the brain is the cause of our thinking. For what does this theory imply? If the brain is the cause of our thinking—of all our thinking—then it is the cause, among other things, of the thought that this is so. But, as we know perfectly well, there have been other theories concerning the relation between thought and the brain besides that to which we have referred. How are we to choose between them? Which ought we to prefer? All we have to go upon is the fact that some brains "produce" one theory about the brain whereas other brains produce another: a peculiar state of affairs, admittedly, seeing that one theory credits the brain with certain powers which, according to the other theory, are denied to it. With two (or more) conflicting theories about the brain originating from different conditions of the brain itself, what are we to do? The obvious answer is that we must choose which is the true, or at least the truer, theory. But what can we possibly mean, in discussing theories of this kind, by the words "true" or "truer"? The most that we know about such theories is that they are produced by certain conditions of the instrument with which they are conceived. And if this instrument and everything to do with it is material, there is no sense in saying that one or other of its conditions is "true". A material thing just is. The distinction between truth and falsehood is in no way applicable to it.

If, then, it is maintained that thought is the product of our brain, the whole edifice of philosophy collapses, and along with it—and this is a point of great importance—the whole of science.

Nevertheless, it is obvious that the brain and the nervous system in general play an indispensable part in the operation of thinking, particularly in that form of thinking which takes place in perception. In the first part of our study we shall, therefore, be discussing the problem of perception in all its aspects. We shall then proceed to enquire into the possibility of a form of thought exempt from material limitations, and after that we shall survey the history of modern philosophy with special reference to the nature of this higher form of thought. And finally, we shall conclude with some observations upon the "crisis of reason" at the present time and the part played by metaphysics in the defence of an ordered and sane view of man and his world.

In the following pages our treatment will be simple and straightforward; there will be nothing in our argument which the ordinary reader, if he is prepared to rid himself of prejudice and the deliberate resolve to be baffled (with which he so often approaches a subject like the present), cannot be expected to follow. The theme running throughout this book should not be difficult to grasp, though it is easy to ignore.

The novelist, Marcel Proust, once observed that "each of us finds clarity only in ideas which are in the same state of confusion as his own". That may be a cynical way of talking but it contains a substantial element of truth. Nevertheless, we must be for ever trying to reduce the confusion, to drive a path through the débris. For every obstruction is an opportunity, and victory is merely the perpetual staving off of defeat.

PART I

The Approach to Metaphysics
via the Theory of
Perception

I

The Object of Our Thinking

The Nature of "Meaning"

In the present chapter we propose to try to give a definition of a word with which every student of philosophy must sooner or later come to grips, namely, realism. In asking what the word realism means we are endeavouring to arrive at an objective definition—a definition, that is to say, that will give us a clear and distinct idea of the concept for which the word has come to stand. In philosophy such objective definitions are neither easy to come by nor identical with other definitions, and the difference between philosophical and other definitions is a difference to which we should pay particular attention at the outset. Words standing for concepts of this kind are not mere labels affixed at some remote time and adhering by accidental custom; they represent historic habits of speech with associations of meaning to which time and usage have given sanction. As applied to such concepts, therefore, objective meaning signifies not something given and unchanging, but something that has taken time, often amounting to many centuries, to come to be what it is. In other words, objective meaning is the same as historical meaning. A word means what it has come to mean. To ignore the process that has made up its present meaning is to involve oneself in serious confusion. Words can even hit back at those who thus abuse them, and at those who become the victims of such abuse; and on such occasions a man's conversation or written words may often betray loose thinking and falsification without his being aware of the fact.

To arrive at the correct definition of a philosophical term is therefore to pursue something in the nature of a historical enquiry; and such an enquiry, if faithfully undertaken, will reveal the literal or root meaning of the word beneath the variety of associations that have made up its development. Excessive concentration upon either the literal meaning or the later associations, in abstraction one from the other, will cause as much trouble and confusion as to deny that there has been any development at all. The correct procedure, then, is to try to understand how the various associations have come to associate themselves in the way that they have.

Literal Meaning of Real: (a) *that which Constrains Attention*

To tackle the literal meaning first: the word Realism appears to mean primarily a belief in that which is real, or in that which possesses the nature of a "thing" (Latin, *res*). Now what precisely do we mean by a "thing"? Curiously enough, the literal meaning of the word "thing" has no connection, except very indirectly, with a material body. On the contrary, if we consult the dictionary, we find that one of the original meanings of the word "thing" was "an assembly or court". Later, according to the same reliable source, the meaning came to include the actual business brought before that court. There we have a good example not merely of the way in which one meaning develops out of another, but of how the word comes to stand neither for one meaning nor the other, but for the unity of the two. Obsolete as this literal definition of the word may seem to us to-day, however, it is clear that such a definition is the reverse of crude and primitive. It represents a stage of meaning to which no word could (as it were) leap at one bound. And therefore we may legitimately probe for an even more original or "root" meaning, out of which the whole of the later meaning grew, and from which it has never been permitted to depart too far. This root meaning, if reduced to bare essentials, defines the word "thing" as that which succeeds in "claiming the attention" of something, not merely in the sense of attracting attention by the possession of certain characteristics but in the sense of constraining us to attend to it. What we should particularly note about this basic definition is that it contains no notion of any difference, separation, or even distinction between "things" on the one hand and "minds" or "ideas" on the other. To-day, the word "thing" has come to acquire a material significance to which the root meaning, if we have correctly isolated it, is a stranger. This is not the whole modern meaning of the word; but it is an association of very great significance, and we shall have much to say about it in the future. If we consider the root meaning in its essence, however, we shall find nothing preposterous in including under the heading "thing" the minds and ideas which are to-day so often regarded as entities of a totally different order. Originally, then, the term Realism implied not so much a belief in the reality of "things"—i.e., material things—rather than minds, as a theory whereby the mind concerned itself with those aspects of reality to which it owed particular attention.

At first sight such a statement may strike the reader as somewhat vague. If that is all the word Realism originally meant, he may say, it surely provided the most flimsy basis for subsequent layers of meaning. What is it but a mere wisp or ghost of a meaning? But that is a short-sighted view. We must think again. This notion of the mind as concerning itself solely with that to which it owes particular attention is not a meaning that has been obscured in the course of centuries; nor is it one with which the ordinary man is unfamiliar. On the contrary, it is that aspect of the word's meaning with which he is perhaps more familiar than any other. When, in common parlance, we talk of a man as being a "realist" or as possessing a "realistic outlook", we mean simply that he is accustomed to face facts as they are, and to act from such motives as a clear view of the situation dictates. And when the mind "faces facts" it faces that to which its attention ought primarily to be directed; it refuses to occupy itself with anything irrelevant to its immediate purposes and problems. On the one hand, that is to say, the facts of the case or the situation solicit attention. On the other, the mind turns its attention towards that which, by obtruding itself, must forthwith be reckoned with. Whenever we talk of a man (or of a policy) as being "realistic", we always imply some element of obligation whereby the man makes a deliberate effort to come to terms with things as they are. Coupled with this notion of obligation is one of sacrifice. In concentrating upon that to which it owes immediate attention, the mind identifies its duty with the renunciation of all imaginative flights and speculative visions. We are made aware of this in everyday experience. The constraint of duty, as we know, always implies the sacrifice of some luxury; and in the case of the mind, luxury is to be found primarily in the free exercise of feeling or imagination.

Literal Meaning of Real: (b) *that which is what it professes to be*

If we study the works of the earliest western philosophers we observe that while the root meaning of the word "real" is roughly that which we have stated, it includes also something more. What this something is can best be seen by examining the Latin word *realis*. Now the word *realis* possesses two distinct senses. First, there is the strictly philosophical sense, according to which it means that which possesses the nature of a "thing". Secondly, there is the legal sense, according to which it means that which is what it professes to be. This latter sense has come to assume great importance in the history of philosophical thought. According to one school of commentators, Plato (428-348 B.C.) held the view that the material world, the world of sense, was somehow not quite real. It was simply a tissue of illusion, a kind of dream, or at best a series of ideas entertained by the mind but lacking objective basis. That Plato meant any such thing by his famous Theory of Ideas is extremely doubtful. Plato was by no means a subjective idealist: i.e., one who, believing in the reality of nothing but his own ideas, holds that his mind, or Mind in capital letters, is therefore the sole creator of reality. What Plato meant to suggest was that the world of sense as we know it was not wholly *true*. And that was very different from saying that it was not real. Plato sought to demonstrate not so much that the natural world was illusory as that by contemplating it we were not put in possession of the whole truth of things. In short, it was not what it seemed or professed to be. If we develop this second meaning we see that Realism has come to signify a belief in that which is wholly rational or intelligible; and this implies that a world which is not what it seems to be is to that extent less than rational.

But what do we mean by rational or intelligible knowledge? How do we arrive at it? And how, having arrived at it, can we know for certain that it is what it is? The answers to these questions have been so numerous and frequently so involved that the ordinary philosophical student may at first sight be bewildered by them. And he may thereafter be tempted to regard the various solutions put forward as so many monuments set up to commemorate the collapse and expiry of the mind's efforts to settle the matter. Great as the temptation is to adopt a defeatist attitude, this is the most unprofitable way of regarding philosophical problems, and the one least likely to lead to a positive settlement in the present. Philosophical theories, especially those possessing the suffix "ism", are attempts to tie down problems and thereby to render their nature intelligible to subsequent thinkers. They are stakes driven into the soil to enable us to recognise boundaries, or what once were boundaries, and *culs-de-sac*. They are knots which we wish to keep tied rather than to untie, for it is impossible to liquidate philosophical problems completely, unless they happen to be purely verbal and therefore a mere loop of words, easily straightened out by a polemical tug. The main theories that have been put forward on this subject are therefore worthy of examination; for such theories represent stages along a road which we are still travelling. To these we now propose to turn.

Early Stages in the History of Realism

One of the problems with which the mediæval and scholastic philosophers were most occupied was that of Universals. How, they asked, is it possible to apply the same quality to more than one object? What, in other words, is it that remains common to a number of different objects so that the same term may accurately be used of each? This question looks easy to answer, but it is not. According to one school of philosophers who called themselves Realists, a similar quality must be present in (for example) all cats by virtue of which they are cats and not other things: this quality, they affirmed, must be something called "catness". According to another group of philosophers called Conceptualists, the identity resided not so much in the cats themselves as in the way in which we thought about them. Yet a third group, calling themselves Nominalists, advanced the view that, whereas an undoubted similarity existed between one cat and another, the identity about which the Realists and Conceptualists spoke existed nowhere but in the use of the word "cat": in short, the identity was purely nominal. There were thus roughly three schools of thought: one asserting that the identity existed in the objects themselves (*in re*); another that it existed solely in the mind (*in intellectu*); and a third that it existed solely in the name (*in nomine*).

Stated in purely abstract terms, these various theories on the subject of universals may seem to bear little relation to the events of the time or of any other time. Having been brought up in the belief that the "schoolmen" spent their lives debating how many angels could balance on the point of a needle, most people will be inclined to dismiss the quarrel between nominalists, realists, and conceptualists as belonging to the same category of frivolity. And when they are told that this celebrated quarrel, together with the numerous variations upon it, gave rise to bitter public controversy and even savage persecution, they will congratulate themselves upon the fact that Progress has meanwhile so changed the situation that they, exempt from mediæval prejudice, are able to blast each other's cities to pieces without any such preliminary logic-chopping. However that may be, the truth is that the problem of universals involved a number of concrete issues, which, if strangely unreal and remote to us, deeply affected the lives of mediæval people. Not that the ordinary man and woman could state these issues in terms such as we are employing here, or such as their own scholars and prelates employed: any more than the sufferer from a rare disease, then as now, would discuss it among his friends in terms used by medical experts. The problem of universals, however, could not but be of supreme importance for at least one great mediæval institution—namely, the Church, with its forthright claim to universality or, as it has come to be called, catholicity. For consider the nature of the universality to which that institution sought to lay claim. By the Church, the Fathers and their successors meant a great deal more than the mere aggregate of all the individual churches, such as those to which Paul and certain other apostles addressed their epistles. If the Church were nothing more than a collective term (a *nomen*), in this sense, the only true realities would be individual churches; and that would contradict the orthodox idea that the Church, as the mystical Body of Christ, was the one supreme reality, of which particular churches were at best imperfect embodiments. The Church's catholicity, in other words, was the logical consequence of its reality, not of its ubiquity; and we can trace the gradual emergence of this catholic idea (which did not pass unchallenged) up to the time when, allied to the Roman Empire under Theodosius, it became the idea of Christendom.

Not until the eleventh century of the Christian era, however, did the conflict come to a head, though the mediæval quarrel between the nominalists and the realists was, like other similar quarrels, in some ways a reopening of old wounds. In the year 1090, Roscellinus, a Bishop of Compiègne, challenged the accepted Realist view. It was his contention, in brief, that universals as such possessed no reality. They were simply names or mental fictions. The only real things, he declared, were individuals or particulars. Consequently, all theological and scientific discussion must confine itself to these alone.

The Nominalist Theory and Its Implications

Such a view, which may seem to us to be dictated by common sense, struck at the roots of orthodox Christian theology; and if we reflect for a moment we shall be able to see why. To accept this *nominalistic* interpretation of things was to deny reality not merely to the Church, as a corporate and yet single body, but to certain dogmas of the Church which had come to be accepted as fundamental. Among these dogmas was that of the Trinity, which had already survived the great Arian heresy of the fourth century, and that of Original Sin. If, as Roscellinus maintained, nothing but the individual possesses reality, the catholicity of the Church was merely a *vocis flatus*, an empty word. So, too, was the notion that three persons can combine or unite in one God, for according to nominalism all that can exist are the three persons as separate individuals, without a common essence or personality. So, lastly, was the idea of Original Sin, for the only kind of sin that can exist is my sin and your sin, and these are personal matters which partake of no common or essential sinfulness. Clearly, such revolutionary ideas were at variance with all that the Church had been striving to teach for six centuries; and so it was that Roscellinus, condemned for heresy at a Council held at Soissons in the year 1072, was obliged summarily to recant.

Although the nominalism of Roscellinus and his followers was formally branded as heretical, the champions of realism on their side occasionally tended, in an excess of ardour, to go to the opposite extreme. Thus William of Champeaux (1070-1121), Bishop of Châlons, reversing the nominalistic idea, maintained that nothing save universals were real, thereby relegating individuals to the realm of fictions. The only natural reality, he declared, was Man. Individual men were mere accidental modifications of this fundamental concept. A more profound and balanced theologian, Anselm of Aosta (1033-1109), while holding to the realist view, made a brave attempt to reconcile the conflicting doctrines of the schools, and pointed the way for the later synthesis of St. Thomas Aquinas. This reconciliation, or its anticipation, took the form of accepting each theory up to a point and showing how it could be made to throw light upon a particular sphere of reality, whether divine or human. The argument was as follows. God was to be conceived as a universal—a substantial universal—preceding all other beings (*ante rem*); the Holy Spirit as a universal infusing creation with God's preconceived ideas (*in re*); and finally Man, the creature, as a universal in which these ideas were embodied (*post rem*). Here realism, conceptualism, and nominalism found each its appropriate sphere in an intelligible and ordered hierarchy of being. And as God was conceived as a universal before all and above all, the doctrine of realism retained its supremacy, and orthodox belief was identified with its rational acceptance.

Conceptualism

Just as it is possible to obtain a reputation for cleverness
and originality by erecting rules upon a series of exceptions,
so there is a tendency to assume that progress or development
in thought is only achieved through the impact of heresies.
As we shall have occasion to see, there is a certain sense in
which this may be true; but we need to define with much
greater precision what we mean by progress or development
in thought before we say precisely how true. And we should
distinguish right away between the causes of progress and the
occasions of it. In the light of this qualification we may examine somewhat more closely the conceptualist theory of
which we have spoken; for this theory, first outlined by Peter
Abelard (1079-1142), who also got into trouble with the
authorities for this and other indiscretions, contained certain
philosophical notions which were to reappear much later on
in the work of thinkers of a wholly new type.

As regards this theory, what the modern philosopher is most
likely to object to is its name, conceptualism. A concept such
as a universal is something apprehended by our intellect; but
intellectual activity, though primary, is not necessarily the
sole faculty of the mind. There are others; and to deny the
existence and power of these other faculties or activities is to
entertain a very narrow view of mental operation. Such views
are held. Certain philosophers, that is to say, having passed a
kind of Self-Denying Ordinance upon themselves, find to
their dismay that they lack sufficient faculties to explain the
mind's complicated workings; whereupon they postulate a
single faculty or even substance—a "neutral stuff"—which
for some reason best known to themselves, proceeds to "sprout"
these faculties previously denied autonomy, so that they are
back where they started but with their philosophical licence
endorsed for reckless assumptions. If, on the other hand, we
recognise the mind to possess faculties in addition to those of

the intellect, and if we think of these faculties as forming a mental "sphere", we can provisionally accept the common distinction between what is in the mind (*in mente*) and what is *in re*—between our thinking and the object about which we think. Some may declare that this distinction is obvious. Perhaps it is. But we are still obliged, as philosophers, to enquire into its precise nature and to examine all its implications, some of which are not perhaps so plain as we may at first have supposed.

It is true that the whole question of what we mean when we talk of things existing "in the mind" is most complicated; but it need not on that account be abstruse. If language were always to be taken literally, we should have abandoned it long ago as productive of endless confusion, but language is an instrument which we are obliged to use at short notice for such a variety of purposes that certain metaphors are made to work overtime and to deputise for any number of more intricate expressions. The metaphors of prose are all utility-metaphors. Hence, while we may not be sure that we know what the phrase "in the mind" means when we consider it by itself, we find that its meaning is illuminated by juxtaposition with the phrase *in re*. To take an example from ordinary experience: supposing that we happen to think a certain man to be dishonest, it is clear that the "idea" of dishonesty is "in our minds" together with the activity of thinking the man to be so. It is equally clear that the object, which is the man, not merely enjoys an independent existence but possesses characteristics which our minds, in apprehending, judge to be of a certain nature. Thus we may venture upon the conclusion that our minds, in operating normally, contain both ideas and activities; but we must not forget that the distinction between what is *in mente* and what is *in re* is based upon a metaphor containing spacial associations which, unless we make due allowance for them, may involve us in unnecessary obscurities.

Greek Philosophy and the Subject-Object Distinction

Having introduced the distinction between two spheres, one subjective and the other objective, it may perhaps be disconcerting to remind ourselves that such a distinction is foreign to early Greek philosophical thought. What is the explanation of this apparent neglect? The *idea* behind such a distinction, and one of the chief motives for drawing it, is clearly to explain the existence or occurrence of errors, illusions, and misapprehensions. Now it would be absurd to suggest that the early Greek philosophers, in failing to make this distinction, showed themselves unaware of such things as errors, illusions, and misapprehensions. Far from it; they were just as acutely aware of them as we are, and as any human and imperfect beings must be. The truth is, however, that the nature of error and illusion represented a much less urgent problem to the Greeks than to the mediæval philosophers; it did not bulk so large in their general view of the world. Those problems about which an age appears to be silent are not necessarily those of which it is completely unaware; for what a thinker may seem to neglect, he may in reality be *assuming*. And if the Greek philosophers appeared to neglect the problem of error as the mediæval philosophers conceived it and as we conceive it to-day, they were preoccupied with a problem closely related to it: namely, that which Plato sought to tackle in his theory of Ideas. Plato's theory, in fact, was the nearest approach to the problem of error that the Greeks succeeded in making; but the illusions of which he tried to find an explanation represented, as we have already een, a great deal more than a few odd mistakes or misapprehensions. His illusions formed a whole sphere of reality: a sphere of reality intermediate between complete knowledge on the one hand and complete nescience on the other—a sphere neither of certainty nor of ignorance. And to apprehend this intermediate sphere of reality he endeavoured to find a faculty appropriate to its nature, namely Opinion (δόζα). The result was a most interesting and ingenious theory of knowledge; but it was not a theory intended to solve the problem of error. The latter problem was one to which the mediæval philosophers addressed themselves with vigour because the civilisation in which they lived was a Christian civilisation, and Christianity had meanwhile introduced a philosophical revolution.

Mediæval Philosophy and the Subject-Object Distinction

The distinction between that which is *in mente* and that which is *in re* is therefore the product of what we may call a new climate of thought. To the mediæval Christian philosophers the objective world was considered to be ordered and systematic and, within reason, knowable. The subjective world, on the other hand, was regarded as lacking system except in so far as system could be introduced into it by discipline. This discipline was logic—a subject upon which the mediæval scholars and teachers laid great emphasis. Thus the schoolmen advocated instruction in logic not because they believed that the mind necessarily worked in a logical way but because they recognised its frequent failure to do so. Logic propounded the laws of thought: laws that needed to be drummed into the student as a necessary preliminary to any other form of instruction and to any attempt on his part to indulge in private speculation. As a complement to this view of the human mind as incapable of reaching truth unaided, the mediæval philosophers and theologians preached the incapacity of the moral self to act rightly without the aid of divine grace. According to its own lights, that is to say, the human soul might as easily stumble upon truth and right as not, because the lights of the mind were as capricious as will-o'-the-wisps. Mind or soul possessed no inherent or natural capacity to think upon the right lines. Left to itself, in fact, it inevitably languished in a state of error. And a more fundamental error, namely, original sin, was the natural condition of fallen mankind. Hence the general view of freedom held by the mediæval philosophers was very nearly opposite to that held by the Greeks. To the Greeks, freedom in both nature and social life implied the ability to live in conformity with rules. The speech of Pericles in Thucydides is the most perfect statement of this attitude. To the mediæval philosophers, on the other hand, freedom implied very nearly the same as sin—it was a condition of lawlessness and chaos, of failure to obey rules. The free mind or soul was therefore a standing invitation to the powers of evil to enter in and corrupt. Natural freedom meant primarily the freedom to go astray.

At this point a word of warning becomes necessary. To assert that all the philosophers of the mediæval period—a period at least as intellectually alive as our own—entertained such a view of freedom as that which we have outlined, would be an error. Nor would it be true to say that Christianity preached freedom solely of a negative kind. Out of Christian theology and tradition grew a conception of freedom no less positive and concrete than that held by the Greeks; and the freedom about which so much is talked in the political sphere and for which men are supposed to be prepared to sacrifice their lives, is a value which, in the last resort, holds Christian credentials. For Christian theology contains, besides the notion of natural freedom, the conception of a higher freedom obtained through salvation by grace. Nevertheless, we are concerned here primarily with the development of one philosophical problem out of another; and in the history of thought, as we have already pointed out, it is possible for half-truths and even quarter-truths to propagate new problems with as much facility as more balanced ideas. There is a sharpness and aggressiveness about a half-truth that challenges argument and rejoinder. Moreover, the expression of any opinion, however mature and complete, is in constant danger of over-

statement and distortion, or alternatively of incomplete
appreciation by other minds: so that the re-statement of
philosophical problems becomes an inevitable task in every
age, there being new aspects to emphasise as conditions of life
alter and new difficulties arise. And just as the newspapers
confine themselves to information about what is out of the
ordinary and novel, until the world appears to be an arena of
endless squabbles and acts of violence and not (as it largely is)
a place in which most things go on pretty much as before and
people lament the monotony of their lives, so the history of
thought appears to consist of a series of extreme viewpoints
pitted one against the other and undergoing demolition at the
hand of theorists equally intent upon propounding extrava-
gances. Even if a modicum of this be true, yet it need not
deter us. The danger is not so much that extravagant views
shall arise as that they shall remain for too long unchecked.
And thus the activity of checking and curbing—the activity
of critical thought—needs constantly to be fed and encouraged; for philosophical enquiry is of value not because it provides each age with a neat system or scheme or recipe to live
by, but because it is an activity of thought which, cultivated
by the individual, enables him to order his life better than he
would do otherwise. The "systems" about which the textbooks speak and to which they insist upon giving impressive,
if somewhat obscure, names are merely records of past
attempts to think in a coherent fashion about a particular
problem arising out of a particular situation. Nevertheless, to
study these systems and to trace their interconnection is far
from being a mere antiquarian occupation. Such study is the
means whereby we become better acquainted with the situation in which we ourselves are placed.

The Subjective World as a Sphere of Caprice

If, on the one hand, we have a mental or subjective world

in which there is no apparent order, and on the other hand, an external or objective world in which order is present in the form of laws, or at least regularities, the problem of how the mind, unaided by some superior power, manages to discern such laws (the so-called "laws of nature") appears very formidable. For not merely have the two spheres become unequal and non-complementary, but the task of arriving at truth has become a matter of establishing a relationship between the mind and objective reality in such a way that the first somehow "conforms to" the second. This notion of how the mind arrives at truth is one with which the modern realist philosophers have made us familiar; nor is it an accident that the word realism to-day is still used of theories of truth and knowledge which, at least as regards the assumptions upon which they rest, descend from the realist views put forward in mediæval times.

Modern realism, in short, affirms that order and system reside in the objective world (*in re*); and it is so anxious that this world shall owe nothing to any other source that it deprives the mind of almost all character, until the latter becomes a kind of photographic plate passively receptive of outside stimuli. Nevertheless, there is one big difference between the outlook of mediæval realism and the outlook of modern realism, and it is that at which we have already hinted: whereas the mediæval realists were concerned, as we have seen, with the problem of "concepts", which is a problem for our intellectual faculties, the modern realists are concerned with the problem of "percepts", which is a problem involving other faculties than the intellect. What both mediæval and modern realists agree upon, or rather assume in common, is the existence of two distinct, if not separate, spheres. We may therefore sum up the realist position in general by saying that just as the mediæval problem was to determine whether the universals in our minds possessed any equivalent *in re*, so the modern problem is to determine how far our mental "percepts" possess any equivalent apart from our perception of them. Modern philosophy has been largely occupied with attempts to bridge this gulf, whether real or illusory, between two distinct spheres of reality. Needless to say, the "shift" of emphasis has been responsible for certain changes of meaning in the terms employed. That was inevitable, and may also prove instructive; but there is no question of the problem, or rather its setting, having altered in essentials.

The Modern Problem of Perception

The problem of perception, to which we now turn, has given rise to some of the most complicated discussions in metaphysics. Moreover, it has assumed such importance in modern speculation that it has tended to exclude from consideration many other problems of at least equal urgency. In addition to this, it is a problem which, stated in technical terms, strikes the student as so thoroughly arid and prolix that its presence at the very threshold of metaphysical enquiry has dissuaded many an amateur from pushing his researches farther. For it has tended more than any other problem to give rise to those superficial and factitious conundrums whereby the laity are first entertained, then exasperated, and finally disgusted. As a result, philosophy comes to be regarded, not without reason, as a mere matter of logic-chopping and quibbling, fit occupation for the subsidised inhabitants of academic institutions but not for the ordinary practical man. Hence the comparatively low esteem into which the pursuit of philosophy has fallen, in spite of the fillip given to it by such institutions as the Brains Trust; and hence the resolution of the ordinary man to have nothing whatever to do with it.

With this half-articulate distrust on the part of the great majority of people, the more serious exponents of philosophy are bound to feel a measure of sympathy. A great English thinker, F. H. Bradley, once protested that he had "no capacity for the abstruse"; and indeed the interested reader will discover, if he goes so far as to examine the classic treatises of philosophy, that the major contributions to philosophy possess a degree of clarity and candour proportionate to the depth and majesty of their theme. Obscurantism is not the privilege of the superior mind; it is the refuge of the impostor. If the thinker cannot express himself except in parables or puzzles, he had better think again.

One of the chief reasons, then, why the problem of perception is inclined to baffle the student is that, in most courses on modern philosophy, he is brought up against it too precipitately. There are several explanations for this. The division of thought into periods labelled "ancient", "mediæval", or "modern" has been undertaken for the sake of convenience; it must not be thought to imply a break or fission of philosophical activity at any point, still less an awareness on the part of past thinkers that they stood at the crossroads as pioneers of reform or harbingers of decadence, as the case may be. Remy de Gourmont declared that literary renown was invented for schoolchildren passing their examinations. He was right in so far as it is the case that all attempts to cut up past ages into periods of creation and criticism, of decadence and renaissance, of darkness and enlightenment, represent the degrees of insight or blindness in ourselves as students of the past, and not features of the periods themselves. When we look closer at any period, even the most obscure and apparently lifeless, we detect movements, currents, and struggles no less vigorous than those found in ages more celebrated for vitality and achievement: until, as our interest and understanding increase, the whole period assumes a vividness in our minds that may put into the shade those next before and after it, and our entire conception of historical development undergoes a distinct shift and reorientation. If, therefore, we bear in mind that the problems of the sixteenth and seventeenth centuries have a long and interesting ancestry, we shall be in a position to understand both how they came to assume such complication and why their treatment was regarded as a matter of urgency by philosophers and scientists. We shall be able to see not merely how the problem of perception presented itself to the philosophers of the sixteenth century, but how, as a result of their handling of it, it came to be what it is to-day. The continuity of philosophical thought can never be too strongly emphasised, even though we are bound from time to time to make use of such terms as "mediæval philosophy" and "the beginnings of modern philosophy", with their suggestion of breaks and divisions that have no necessary objective status.

Primary and Secondary Qualities

It was in the sixteenth century—and that is why the period is said to usher in modern philosophy—that a new and revolutionary contribution was made to the problem of perception by a man of science, Galileo Galilei (1564-1642). With Descartes (1596-1650) Galileo may accurately be described as the founder of modern philosophical method. Scientific progress is most likely to be advanced, he said in effect, if we abandon the emphasis on logic and syllogistic reasoning after the manner of the ancient and mediæval thinkers, and proceed by way of practical analysis. Above all, what is needed is the reduction of the facts of nature to their simplest components. By this Galileo meant that all the properties of nature save the purely mechanical were to be ignored, since all the properties of matter except shape and movement were subjective, i.e., lacking in objective reality. His new idea was not something that occurred to him independently of his work as an astronomer; it was formulated in the course of that work as a useful hypothesis. What Galileo sought to do, in other words, was to mark out a domain or sphere within which scientific investigation could operate most effectively; and the sphere or aspect of reality which he demarcated was that which showed itself to be susceptible of mathematical measurement. Science, he said, should concern itself exclusively with "primary qualities": that is to say, those qualities in nature which could be accurately measured. Such qualities (which should perhaps have been called quantities rather than qualities) were distinguished from others called "secondary qualities", or those aspects of nature of which accurate measurement was impossible. Incidentally, the very terms "primary" and "secondary" conferred upon the aspects in question a different degree of importance. What was primary appeared by implication to be more important, more ultimate, and more rational than that which was secondary; and, as we shall soon see, this difference in emphasis was to exert a most powerful influence upon the course of later scientific and philosophical thought.

How the Qualities were Distributed

To fit a new idea into a framework or context is the step which follows naturally upon its formulation; and even if the adjustment is neither immediate nor conscious, it will take place inevitably as the idea proceeds to work its fertilising influence, until, perhaps many years later, a completely new crystallisation of outlook has been effected. Such changes of outlook are not proclaimed to the world in a kind of official *communiqué*, or even to the learned world in a paper read before some society which listens to papers; they are perceived in retrospect to have taken place, without the conscious knowledge of the thinkers most concerned with their enunciation. What usually happens to a new idea, however, is that it is brought to birth, nurtured, and even for some time employed within a framework which, regarded from a later point of view, is seen to have been already growing out of date. And that is precisely what happened in the case of the theory of primary and secondary qualities. Having made the distinction between what was scientifically tractable and what was not— between the measurable and the irrational—the scientists of the sixteenth and seventeenth centuries proceeded to allocate, as it were, these two sets of qualities between the subjective and objective spheres into which it had become conventional to divide reality. In the work of Locke (1632-1704), for example, the distribution was done automatically. Since they were capable of being measured primary qualities were regarded as the natural inhabitants of the objective world; they existed *in re*. Secondary qualities, in their turn, were regarded as belonging naturally to the subjective world; they existed *in mente*. In other words, primary qualities were pronounced rational, because they were characteristics of a world of order and rationality; whereas secondary qualities were pronounced irrational, because, as Locke said, they were characteristics of a world of caprice and lawlessness. The problem of primary and secondary qualities was therefore solved, or considered to be solved, within the framework of a theory of reality at least as old as the mediæval thinkers. As in the mediæval period, the subjective world retained its character of irrationality, whereas the objective world preserved its reputation for being the realm of order and reason.

I I

Foundations of a Theory of Perception

The Elimination of Mind from Nature in Seventeenth-Century Philosophy

With the impressive scientific achievements of the seventeenth century and after we are concerned only indirectly. What chiefly interests us at the moment is the connection, in so far as it can be established, between this sudden outburst of scientific achievement and the "climate" of thought in which it took place. Every scientist, even the most practical, makes a number of assumptions into the credentials of which he neglects to enquire, sometimes because he lacks sufficient time to do so, and sometimes because he is unaware that he is assuming anything at all. Often the most important assumptions that he makes are of the latter kind. Thus, when we say that the growth of modern experimental science was due largely to the new philosophical outlook of the time, we must not for a moment suppose that every scientist was consciously striving to prove the practical truth of the new theories. Many scientists never gave the matter a thought. All we can legitimately say is that by concentrating upon the mathematical interpretation of natural phenomena, the scientists made such headway towards understanding certain processes of nature that they were instinctively impelled to neglect those other processes which, in resisting such treatment, they assumed to be outside the scope of science. The result was what Whitehead has called a "closure of nature to mind": not in the sense that nature represented a closed book to the minds of scientists —on the contrary, they had just begun to open it—but in the

44

sense that natural phenomena were held to be governed by laws operating independently of any influence the mind might exert upon them. The mind might, with application, come to discover the nature and working of these laws; it could not influence them or claim any part in their operation. They were characteristics of an "external world" in which mind exerted no authority.[1] The notion that mind could intervene in the orderly working of the natural world would have been considered to involve an inconceivable suspension of the laws of nature; for the intervention of mind implied, for reasons which we have explained, the intervention of an element both irrational and capricious. Needless to say, such a view of nature and mind is still held, or at any rate assumed, by many thinkers even to-day: which is the reason why we ought to examine it with some attention.

Berkeley's Counter-attack

In allocating primary and secondary qualities to different realms, philosophers such as Locke tended to overload one sphere—the objective—at the expense of the other—the subjective. In the objective or "external" sphere, all was order, regulation, precision. In the subjective or "internal" sphere all was vagueness, disorder, unintelligibility. The substance or body of reality, in short, seemed to have been emptied wholesale into a realm external to mind, leaving nothing behind it but a collection of nebulous "ideas".[2] Again, we must take care not to attribute too conscious an act of share-out to the philosophers of this time. What in fact happened was that,

[1] The word "mind" is sometimes used in this book without the article; but this does not necessarily imply any particular theory about the nature of mind, at least at the present stage.

[2] Locke defines an "idea" as "whatsoever is the object of the understanding when a man thinks", but he occasionally describes "ideas" as occurrences in the mind due to natural causes. This raises the question as to how we can become aware of the correspondence between our "ideas" and the unknown reality which is said to lie behind them.

in pursuing certain problems in connection with perception, they raced ahead without stopping always to perceive what they had done. It is we who, surveying the scene later, perceive what was happening and what was going to happen. At the same time the implications of this "bifurcation of nature" (another phrase of Whitehead) did not pass wholly unnoticed. At the begining of the eighteenth century a remarkable young man called Berkeley (1685-1753), who published his first book in 1709, not merely perceived the direction in which Locke's theories were leading him but himself took up the argument and gave it a novel twist.

Berkeley's contribution was to have the effect of altering, though not exactly redressing, the balance between the two spheres of mind and nature. But whereas Locke had drained the subjective sphere of almost all its properties, Berkeley, reversing the process, caused a wholesale evacuation of the external world. He was thus responsible for an overloading in the other direction. The argument he put forward was as follows. If secondary qualities, such as colour, taste, smell, etc., are held to be characteristics of the subjective world, the world of our own ideas, what right have we to assume the existence of a realm external to this world of ideas? If our minds contain nothing but ideas what else but ideas can exist? "A soul or spirit is an active being", says Berkeley in his *Principles of Human Knowledge* (Section 139), "whose existence consists not in being perceived but in perceiving ideas and thinking." To claim to know what is outside our minds is to claim to know what is not an idea: but if all that we know are ideas, such an external realm is inconceivable. If, then, there exist such things as primary qualities, these primary qualities must also partake of the nature of ideas in order that we may know them. There is therefore only one realm, the subjective realm; and within that realm both kinds of qualities must exist on equal terms. The distinction between primary and secondary therefore ceases to have validity.

What Berkeley Retained

From this brief outline of Berkeley's argument, it might be supposed that he succeeded, whatever his original intention, in finally abolishing the objective world altogether. Like Locke he found himself more or less with one world to spare; or rather he went a stage further than Locke, because Locke's subjective world was at least peopled by ideas. If we examine Berkeley's theory more closely, however, we observe that the old partition of reality into two realms has by no means completely disappeared. Under a slight disguise it is still present. Although Berkeley appears to have put the objective world out of commission he still preserves more or less intact a distinction between two kinds of reality: namely, minds on the one hand and things on the other. Instead of existing independently of minds, however, material things derive their existence simply and solely from their relationship to minds. Berkeley still believes in a sort of objective world; but it is no longer, as with Locke, objective in the sense of independent. Its dependence upon mind is a necessary condition of such objectivity as it possesses. In short, it is objective only in so far as it is the object of thought.

It is sometimes asserted that Berkeley, in dismissing the notion of a world external to that of mind, implied that the material or natural world did not exist. This is not the case. It is one thing to say, with Berkeley, that such things as colours, sounds, pieces of furniture, rocks and fields exist only as ideas or impressions of the mind; it is another thing to say that they do not exist at all. Berkeley believed most emphatically in a real world; what he denied equally emphatically was that this real world existed independently of our perception of it. "There is a *rerum natura,* and the distinction between realities and chimeras retains its full force" (*Principles of Human Knowledge,* Section 34). He may have been wholly in error, but he must not be accused of harbouring an error even more preposterous and one against which his whole philosophy was directed. For, as we have seen, his criticism of the theories of philosophers such as Locke was that, by postulating a world of objects behind or external to our ideas, they assumed as existent that which was by definition unknowable. We shall see in due course to what extent his criticism still remains valid in regard to theories propounded at a much later time.

Translating the problem into metaphorical terms we can say that for Berkeley the inhabitants of the subjective world are in great part refugees from an external realm which, through some cataclysm, has dissolved into nothingness. These refugees, though dependent for their support and subsistence upon a new authority, the mind, retain nevertheless traces of foreign origin. Instead of the mind being dependent for its perceptive material upon an external or objective authority, as with Locke, the inhabitants of the latter realm, becoming displaced persons, have been forced into dependence upon the mental or subjective authority. This attempt to make of the objective world a function of the subjective world forms the truly original and seminal element in Berkeley's philosophy. That was his fundamental contribution to the theory of perception. What Berkeley retained unmodified from his predecessors was, first, the distinction (admittedly now somewhat indeterminate) between two kinds of reality, and secondly, the view that the mental world was essentially a world of caprice. It is true that he did not go so far as to place great emphasis upon this capricious element. The point is that he said nothing to suggest that he repudiated what was a common notion among his contemporaries and predecessors.

Thus, Berkeley's counter-attack against those philosophers who preached the existence and intelligibility of a realm external to that of mind ended up by wiping out the objective world altogether. The realist tradition of philosophy seemed to have been liquidated beyond hope of restoration. And the problem for thinkers boiled down to the following: how to reconcile such extreme subjectivism or idealism with the practical achievements of physical science. Nevertheless, it would not be true, and it never is true, to say that in such circumstances science can look after itself. It manifestly cannot. Science or *scientia* is simply another word for organised knowledge; and organised knowledge is something that can exist only in men's minds—it is an affair of thought, not of material objects, whether machines, apparatus or precision instruments, for the latter are merely practical aids to such knowledge. A scientific investigator, even the most humble laboratory assistant, must know what he is doing, must relate it (in so far as he is able) to other things that he knows, and will find himself at every moment endeavouring to build up a theoretical structure, a world of ideas, which shall provide him with a clue not merely to the full meaning of his past experiments, but to the feasibility of future ones. The degree of articulation achieved will vary from person to person; and what in retrospect appears to be a rift or lag between practice and theory will at the time strike the practical investigator as merely another problem awaiting elucidation. However the small craft of practical achievement appear to forge ahead the flood tide of intellectual co-ordination must in the end turn and sweep round about them, thereby lifting them from the reefs that might otherwise compass their destruction. Now, if science (still using that word in its broadest sense) represents not so much an attitude as an activity—not so much a collection of inventions or "gadgets" as a way of thinking—it follows that the scientific tradition is upheld by people resolving to think in this particular way and to go on thinking in this way, whatever the difficulties. And one of the functions of metaphysics is, as we shall show, to see that such a form of thought is both upheld and respected. Thus, instead of science and metaphysics being at perpetual enmity one with the other, as both scientists and metaphysicians have sometimes imagined, the two stand or fall together; and the abolition of metaphysics (supposing that such a thing could be brought about) would mean the eventual abolition of science. Advanced even a few years ago, such a statement would almost certainly have brought down an avalanche of ridicule and abuse upon the writer. But to-day, with the release of forms of energy more potent than anything hitherto imagined, the problem of technical ethics, as we may call it, has assumed a new immediacy. The old idea was that science, with its control of nature, would be able to save us; now it is rather a question of saving science. And this can be done only by returning to the problem of what science is, both in the general sense and in the limited sense of physical science, and by examining the foundations upon which its authority rests. The theories of Bishop Berkeley brought this matter to a head at the beginning of the eighteenth century, and for this reason it will be illuminating to trace their influence upon subsequent thought.

The Modern Revolt Against Berkeley

We have already seen how Berkeley's philosophy, having effected something like an incorporation of the objective world within the subjective world, transformed the realism of Locke and his disciples into an extreme subjectivism to which we may give the name idealism. The terms realist and idealist have often been abused. In modern times these words have come to stand for two schools of philosophy, between which diplomatic relations have been very strained and sometimes for long periods severed. Even philosophers must have their vendettas, their platforms, their manifestos; but such clashes between the academic Big Enders and Little Enders belong to the politics of the profession, not to its disinterested pursuit. What we are concerned to do here is to use philosophical terms in the sense in which they have been handed down to us by the tradition of philosophical thought. Sparingly as we may try to use them we cannot avoid using them altogether.

If, at the conclusion of a study of philosophy, the student declares himself to be a realist, well and good; if an idealist, likewise well and good. But above all let him assume the one or the other title as the result of serious reflection upon philosophical problems, not as the provocative banner of a partisan bent upon waging guerrilla warfare against anyone rash enough to challenge its authority. We are concerned not with the defence of titles but with the defence of reason.

In bringing the argument nearer to modern times, as we now propose to do, we must dismiss at the outset any suggestion that between the eighteenth and nineteenth centuries Berkeley's theories were accepted without challenge. The reverse is true. In British philosophy we have the great name of Hume[1] and several other distinguished thinkers of a later date; and in Europe, particularly Germany, a succession of philosophers arose whose influence extended far beyond the academic field. As our object is to consider certain problems of philosophy, however, and not to write a chronological history of philosophical thought, we are under no obligation at this point to turn aside from our main theme, which is the problem of perception. The consideration of other systems must be reserved for a later occasion.

Berkeley's theory of perception received one of its most formidable criticisms in an essay of great interest written at the beginning of this century by G. E. Moore, called *The Refutation of Idealism*. Designed as the manifesto of a new realist school in England its lucid exposition and persuasive argument earned it a reputation in the philosophical world out of all proportion to its modest dimensions. Moore, it is interesting to observe, reinstates at the beginning of his essay the distinction already familiar to us between the subjective and the objective world. The realist stage is thus set afresh.

---

[1] Though Hume described Berkeley's rejection of abstract ideas as "one of the most valuable discoveries that has been made of late years in the republic of letters".

But the performers are given somewhat different rôles. In the subjective world, Moore places not ideas but functions: here, he says, we have nothing but "acts" of thinking and "acts" of feeling. The objects of these acts of thinking and feeling— that is to say, what we think and feel *about*—are constituents of the objective world. This was something new. For what had the former realists maintained? According to their view, the subjective world was the repository of all those immediate perceptions which, because they remained outside the scope of measurement, could not be classed as primary qualities. Naturally they had to be accounted for; and as they could not be dismissed as illusions, they were accorded the status of subjective impressions. And in this respect Berkeley fully agreed with the realists. Indeed, as we have seen, he went farther. To take a simple example: when we put our hand near the fire, we experience the kind of sensation which, if analysed, appears to be made up of several different components. We have first of all a sensation of placing our hand in a hot place. Then we become conscious of a special quality in the heat which gives rise to the sensation of pain. And finally, we attribute this unpleasantness to the place itself, which we regard as a painfully-hot-place. But in actual fact, as Berkeley points out, all we experience is a single sensation. The painfully-hot-place remains throughout the experience the sole object of our perception; it *is* the experience. Now it was Berkeley's contention that things possess reality only by being perceived: *esse est percipi*. And therefore since the general feeling of painfulness has no existence apart from its being felt at this moment and in this manner, the painfully-hot-place has no existence apart from our immediate sensation of it.

The Two Choices before Modern Realism

Moore and most realists after him are concerned to demonstrate the inadequacy of this view. But the matter can be approached from two angles. Either Berkeley's position can be demolished completely by showing that all the objects of perception exist apart from our acts of perceiving—if such a demonstration is possible; or it can be partially corrected by showing that only certain of the objects of perception depend for their existence upon our perceiving them—if the proper allocation between one sphere and the other can be accurately determined. Now the total demolition of extreme subjectivism means, as we have said, the erection of an equally intransigent objectivism, according to which we are invited to believe that qualities such as colour and sound, as well as pain and beauty, etc., can exist independently of our perceiving them; and that is a view to which it is difficult to subscribe without abandoning a great deal that is self-evident. Moreover, to hold such a view would be equivalent to adding a third category of qualities to those already distinguished by realist philosophers. First, there would be primary qualities existing independently of perception. Next, there would be secondary qualities existing during perception. Finally, there would be "tertiary" qualities which are secondary qualities as they exist apart from the act of perception. What kind of existence these latter qualities might be expected to lead is, to say the least, difficult to imagine.

Moore and at least two other modern realists, Pritchard and Cook Wilson, endeavour to evade these difficulties and ambiguities by abandoning the attempt to rest their theory of perception upon any metaphysical foundations whatever. The realist mind to-day tends always to distrust metaphysics and to confine itself to "facts". And the fact of perception is one about which they claim to possess enough reliable evidence to settle the problems arising therefrom without resorting to bogus metaphysical buttressing. It is plain common sense, they affirm, to hold not merely that the objective world is what we perceive but that secondary qualities are inherent in what we perceive: e.g., the sky *is* blue. For if, as Moore says,

C

the subjective world contains nothing more than "acts" of perceiving, it follows that everything else, including all secondary qualities, belongs to a world of objects independent of perception. Beyond this point, then, he and his colleagues feel unwilling to proceed. To make assertions about the metaphysical reality and status of secondary qualities is to embark upon the kind of speculation which, in their view, leads to a realm of fantasy and mumbo-jumbo. As to the second alternative to extreme subjectivism that we have mentioned, few realists have shown willingness to accept the compromise view which this entails. For it is felt, not unnaturally, that to admit into the subjective world even a very limited number of ideas dependent for reality upon perception represents the thin end of the wedge, and that before he knows where he is the realist philosopher will be back at Berkeley's position with the objective world collapsing like a deflated bladder.

The Revolt Against Metaphysics

There are periods in the history of philosophy in which certain thinkers, shying from the giddy heights to which the speculations of their colleagues appear to be leading, decide to jettison the traditional properties of metaphysics and to concentrate upon "what everybody knows to be true". Such reactions against flowery and heady intellectualism are often exceedingly healthy. And the trouble may lie as much in the words and phraseology used as in the thought itself. To the modern realist school of philosophy we undoubtedly owe a tradition of clear and sober statement which contrasts markedly with certain specimens of idealist philosophy both here and abroad. Of realist philosophy written in a rhapsodical style the only modern example is that of George Santayana, whose fate it has been to attack idealism in language scarcely less lyrical than that of Croce and Gentile. Nevertheless, it is one thing to wish to purge philosophical language of inflated material—to substitute precise terms for vague theorising; it is quite another to wish forcibly to limit the scope of philosophical enquiry to a particular field, labelled either "what everybody knows to be true" or "common sense" or "practical philosophy", and to continue to work on the dogmatic assumption that such delimitation is final. For metaphysical enquiry is precisely that form of thought which can acknowledge no restriction upon its subject matter. Its function is nothing less than to challenge the authority of sciences claiming to impose such restrictions. Admittedly, there are many people, including some philosophers, to whom the value of such a form of thought as metaphysics is not apparent, or at least to whom its relevance, if recognised, is not considered to amount to much. And certain other philosophers, however excellent their motives, have queered the pitch by adopting in retaliation a lofty indifference to the popular clamour, going so far as to claim that philosophy, like Oscar Wilde's Art, is essentially useless, and the more exalted a subject for being so. To such an attitude we may legitimately apply the epithet which Coleridge used somewhat uncharitably of the utilitarian philosophy of John Stuart Mill—"solemn humbug". Briefly, the justification of metaphysical enquiry—or one of the justifications—is that it forms a perpetual reminder, as well as a perpetual demonstration, of the unlimited capacity of human thought. It provides a declaration of the rights of the human mind. And the intimate relationship between such a declaration and the difficult question of liberty in society is something to which we shall have occasion to draw attention in later chapters. For all forms of freedom are ultimately freedom of thought, as countries deprived of their liberties are quick to discover.

Not without deliberation have we dwelt upon the subject of hostility to metaphysics, because, as we have seen, it is very relevant to, among other things, the modern realist attitude to perception. The fact is that the exponent of a theory, which is a philosophical theory, has no business to declare that he does not intend to pursue, or take an interest in, the metaphysical implications of his problem. It is not that it is not done. It cannot be done. Sooner or later, that which a philosopher excludes from consideration will come home to roost. If we examine any such "common-sense" theory in detail, and above all, if we try to probe beneath the surface of its argument, we shall find attached to it an immense packet of roots, firmly embedded in the traditional soil of philosophy. A sceptical theory is another word for an incomplete theory—incomplete not merely because it is unfinished, but because it repudiates the foundations upon which it is resting. In Part III we shall take up this matter again from another and wider aspect.

An extreme example of such scepticism is to be found in the ingenious theory of perception advanced by the modern philosopher, Cook Wilson. To Cook Wilson the essence of true or objective knowledge lies in the fact that a thing can be what it is independently of our knowing it. By this he appears to have meant that since knowledge implies the presence of an object—something definite to know—this object, if truly real, must be able to stand by itself and on its own merits apart from the attentions of any subject or mind. If we consider his claim, however, we find that it exceeds in scope any normal theory of perception. It is in fact a statement, and a highly dogmatic statement, upon the nature of knowledge in general. And, as so often happens, metaphysics is reintroduced in the act of its repudiation. For the statement is clearly a metaphysical one. It implies, in the first place, that our knowledge of what the object is includes a knowledge of it when it is in fact unknowable. But how, if this account of knowledge be true, can we ever be in a position to know it? The fact that we cannot know the unknowable is evidence that we cannot know what a thing is independently of our knowledge of it. So much for the logical defects of the theory. There is another objection scarcely less damaging. Cook Wilson is supposed to be expounding a theory of perception: i.e., a theory designed to explain the relationship between the mind and its perceptual object. But what has happened to this relationship? It has vanished. Just as the fact of being known is irrelevant to the existence of the object of knowledge, so the existence of the object of knowledge has nothing to do with the act of knowing. There is therefore no intrinsic reason why anything that exists should be known at all. Knowledge and the object of knowledge are united by no necessary connection. The relationship is not explained; it is rendered more mysterious than before.

That knowing makes no difference to the object known is a legitimate hypothesis, and one with which the realists make great play. But, as we have already said, there are few, if any, precedents for the view that the object of knowledge makes no difference to the *act* of knowing. Such a conclusion, however arrived at, is extraordinarily difficult to make head or tail of. Something must surely make a difference to something, or how can the act of perception possibly take place? A metaphysical assumption, concealed beneath the surface of the argument, has thrust itself between the subject and object of perception, with the result that communications one with the other have become totally disrupted. Whereas Berkeley, using the same sphere to accommodate both subject and object, asserted an intimate relation between the two by his axiom *esse est percipi*, Cook Wilson, still retaining the landmarks subject and object, fails to erect even the flimsiest pontoon between them. They remain like follies perched on opposite sides of an impassable gulf.

The Metaphysical Implications of Perception

With all its defects, the theory which we have selected here for consideration cannot be dismissed as the extravagant notion of an eccentric thinker. Cook Wilson possessed a remarkably acute mind and considerable powers of exposition, as his posthumous book, *Statement and Inference*, shows. What vitiates his theory is the general attitude assumed towards metaphysics, and in particular the belief that, in advancing a theory of perception, metaphysical assumptions can be dispensed with. As the type of theory put forward is not uncommon, however, and as there are philosophers who are prepared to accept without flinching the logical consequences of his argument—who maintain, in other words, that the nature of reality may well be such that discontinuities and dualisms occur in the natural course of things—it may be wise to look closer at the general picture of reality that emerges. To suggest, as Cook Wilson does, that there exists no intrinsic relation between mind and the object of mind raises the more fundamental question as to why, if the two are unrelated, they should both have come into being. Now the latter question raises problems that belong properly to the sphere of cosmology, or the study of the nature of the cosmic process, and we can do no more than touch upon them here. Nevertheless, the subject must be tackled, albeit tentatively, both because metaphysical enquiry can afford to stop at no point in its course and because our aim in this book is to permit one philosophical problem to develop naturally—which means logically—out of the other.

If we assume, as many thinkers have done, that the universe consists entirely of something called matter, the difficulty is to explain not merely the emergence of mind but the essential reason for such emergence. If, on the other hand, we assume that mind has always existed in the universe, we must likewise assume that it performs a function related to its essence. Now the essence of mind is to know; and the objects of its knowledge are clearly to be found in the universe in which it resides. From the cosmological standpoint, therefore, mind and its object appear to possess an obvious and indeed inevitable connection. Nevertheless, such a connection is not provided for in the kind of theory of perception that we have been analysing.

Granted, then, that the essence of mind is to know, the inference is that matter, having created mind, had every intention of putting its creature to some use. In other words, matter must have experienced a need to be known—or, as Alexander would say, to be enjoyed—so that in creating mind it satisfied at least this aspiration. Alternatively, if mind created matter, which is perhaps the more orthodox hypothesis, the inference is that it experienced the need to exercise its functions in ways that the presence of a world of objects best facilitated. At the moment, we advance these statements not for the purpose of deciding which is the truer or more plausible account of the nature of the universe, but in order to demonstrate that, whichever alternative is finally chosen, the relationship subsisting between mind and its object is a necessary, intimate, and inevitable one. And any theory of knowledge that fails to account for at least some part of this necessity can hardly be classed as a theory of knowledge at all.

Return to the Problem of Secondary Qualities

It is now opportune to revert to the problem of secondary qualities in perception, and to try to discover at what point the realist philosophers seem to have taken the wrong turning. We must bear in mind, during the following section, that this is a problem to which close attention has been paid by a succession of scientists and philosophers, and that it would be highly unwise to claim to have reached a final solution of a question that is constantly revealing new aspects. Indeed, it would be true to say that the problem to which Locke, Berkeley, and Descartes addressed themselves was a very different problem from that which faces us to-day. Not merely are our interests different, but important scientific discoveries have in the meantime altered the whole context of the question and in some respects vastly complicated it. The first task, therefore, is to provide a satisfactory restatement of those facts of perception for which any modern theory must be expected to account.

Faced with an ultimatum from some philosophical pundit to the effect that the sky is not really blue, or that water is not really cold or hot, or that a certain beautiful woman is not really attractive, the ordinary man is inclined to reply that the philosopher can think what he pleases but that he, the ordinary man, knows better. It is quite possible that he does. For while there is no inherent reason why philosophical theories should aim to justify the ideas of common sense, there is every reason to require that philosophical theories shall not outrage common sense. When, for instance, we say that the sky is blue or that water is hot or that that woman is beautiful, we certainly do not mean to pay the sky, the water, and the woman the elaborate but dubious compliment of attributing to them qualities that we know them not to possess. Nor have we the least suspicion, when we are moved to make these observations, that all the time we are simply commenting upon certain states within ourselves. At least we do not mean to mean these things, even if some philosophers insist that we do. And so, to put the matter in a nutshell, what the serious philosopher must undertake to explain is first and foremost how it is that secondary qualities such as blueness, warmth, and beauty are instinctively projected by us into the objects about which we are commenting. For in the last resort, even if the philosopher succeeds in proving that such qualities belong to the subject rather than to the object, he is bound to include in his proof an explanation of what it is about the object, and about objects in general, that so affects the mind as to evoke images, ideas, or sensations appearing to characterise the object itself.

Any satisfactory theory of secondary qualities, therefore, must provide us with an explanation either of how these qualities belong to the object or, alternatively, why we normally ascribe them thereto. Secondly, it must account for reasonable differences of perception among different persons. And thirdly, it must supply us with some means of determining the "norm" of perception or at least of concluding that some such norm must exist. For the difficulty in discussing perception is that of explaining not merely the differences between people's views of objects but the identity which persists throughout these differences. If individual differences of perception were too divergent, the proliferation of "objects" in men's minds would produce untold chaos in the world of action, and disputes between witnesses of events such as accidents would not merely be perpetual but insoluble.

With regard to the first and undoubtedly most perplexing condition, it must be emphasised that secondary qualities, even though ascribed to the object, need not be assumed to characterise the object otherwise than when perceived. Nor, in turn, must this same qualification be presumed to give rise to those popular conundrums of perception about which we have spoken: for instance, the question as to "what a rose is like when we are not looking at it", though that question is not altogether idle, as we shall have occasion to see. Many of the difficulties with which theories of perception become encumbered are due, in the first place, to the habit of regarding the act of perceiving as something that in the nature of things it cannot be—namely, passive. Perception, it must be stressed, involves action, initiative, attention; and it is surely no more preposterous to suggest that such a faculty exerts an influence upon the object (whatever the nature of this influence) than to suggest that the object exerts an influence upon it. Realism has tended to regard the mind in a purely passive sense or, to speak more accurately, to regard perception as essentially receptive. Hence, for most realists the objective world has come to include not merely most of the paraphernalia of reality but all the active mechanism associated with know-

C*

ledge. The perceptive world is held to "impinge" upon our sense-organs, and these latter are thought of as engaged in registering the effect of this impingement. In the next chapter we shall endeavour to show the extent to which this account of perception ignores certain important facts.

I I·I

The Limitations of Perception

Perception as the Servant of the Body

If perception involves the kind of active attention that not merely apprehends but somehow influences the object, the question that arises is how the object can submit to such influence. In what way, for example, can my looking at a rose affect that rose, or my observing a sky affect that sky? These are legitimate and indeed familiar questions, and we must now make some attempt to answer them. Nevertheless, before committing ourselves to a definite statement, it is important to make sure in what sense the question is being asked. When we assert that the perception of a rose affects that rose, we must not be taken to mean that the act of perception is responsible for "creating" the rose in the extreme idealist sense; nor must we be taken to mean that there are somehow two objects, the rose itself and that which we make of it in perception, because this proposition would be open to precisely the logical objections that vitiate the theory of knowledge put forward by Cook Wilson. A more reasonable suggestion, and one which we propose to elucidate, is that only in and through the act of perception does a rose become what we know a rose to be. What exactly do we mean by this statement?

Before answering the question directly, it would be as well if, in addition to bearing in mind the active nature of perception, we recognise its essentially *bodily* characteristics. This does not imply that the mental aspect of perception is negligible. On the contrary, it is of great importance. But because the perceptive process is geared to our five senses, and because

63

these senses and their operation are easily identifiable, perception shows itself to be as much a bodily function as a mental one, though it would perhaps be more accurate to regard perception as a function neither mental nor physical but psycho-physical. The extent to which perception resembles a bodily function may be judged by comparison with some typical bodily functions. In such purely physical activities as eating, for example, the object of nutrition undergoes a process of absorption within the organism as a result of which vitality is both sustained and enhanced. The organism, for its part, is careful to select such elements from its environment as it is able to take in; and as the evolutionary scale is ascended, organisms are found either to develop or to invent elaborate means of selecting nutritive material over wider and wider areas. To this complicated process of nutrition, the activity of perception displays certain striking resemblances. Common to both is the process of absorption or, as we might call it, ingestion. What chiefly distinguishes the activity of perception from that of eating or breathing, however, is the fact that the latter processes entail a breaking down of their nutritive environment, whereas in the case of the perceptive process such destruction is dispensed with. Let us consider the case of vision. In the operation of seeing, the eye is certainly engaged in taking in or absorbing something from its environment; but what it takes in is not a physical material but an image of the object formed by the retina. In viewing the object, it effects no such destruction or modification as are required in the case of a purely bodily function. The same is true of hearing. What the ear does is to take in vibrations from its environment and reproduce them in such a way that we hear sounds. At the moment we need not go into details as to how this reproduction takes place, because we shall refer to it later. The point to stress is that there is no breaking down of anything; on the contrary, there is construction. And this construction is nothing but the activity which, as we observed just now, forms the hall-mark of the process of perception.

If we analyse this activity, we find that it is of two kinds. First of all, there is the activity of taking in, of absorption, of ingestion. Secondly, there is the activity of co-ordination, of working up into an image or pattern, and finally of apprehending that pattern as a whole. The first is a physical activity; the second is a mental activity. These two activities, which operate in the closest collaboration, are responsible to both the body and the mind, and thereby serve to unite the two together. Even those philosophers and scientists who identify the mind with the brain must perforce recognise this important distinction.

The problem of perception, therefore, turns out to be crucial to metaphysical enquiry. Instead of forming a rather obscure corner of the cathedral of philosophy, it is nothing less than the latticed screen connecting nave with chancel. Unless we understand perception, we shall never be able to understand knowledge.

The Limitations of the Perceptive Process

The combination in perception of mental and physical elements represents a field of study to which insufficient consideration has perhaps been given in the past. As we have pointed out already, the preoccupation with logical difficulties —which are many—has tended to monopolise the attention of most enquirers, to the neglect of wider and deeper issues. In reality, however, the presence in perception of two distinct "planes" of activity is something with which we are made familiar—and therefore to some extent neglectful—in everyday language. And everyday language, though a dangerous criterion in matters metaphysical, may be a useful guide. Let us take a further example from the two faculties of seeing and hearing. Vision is a matter of seeing things; but the sphere of vision includes another faculty in addition to seeing, namely, watching. Now the activities of seeing and watching clearly do not fulfil the same function. Admittedly, the latter presupposes the former, or at least a certain amount of the former, because we can watch something without necessarily seeing every detail of it. And the latter qualification perhaps provides the clue to the functional difference between the two activities. We see the individual; we watch the whole. Nor is it possible to explain away the difference by saying that watching is merely a succession of seeings and lookings—a prolonged seeing, a "good look". Watching is a great deal more than this: it represents that aspect of vision which not merely takes in the whole but, as it were, constructs the general framework within which seeing can with best advantage be performed. We see the bowler bowling, the batsman batting, and the fielders fielding; but we watch the match. We see the villain grappling with the heroine, the hero grappling with the villain, and the heroine embracing the hero; but we watch the film. We see the acrobat performing a series of remarkable physical activities; but we watch his "act". Such examples could, of course, be multiplied *ad infinitum*. The temptation is perhaps to state the difference by maintaining that whereas we "see" individual actions, we "watch" a general pattern which remains static. But is this in fact the case? The pattern that we watch, and that we form in watching, is a dynamic pattern: a pattern composed of actions which, as we see from the theatrical use of the word "act", is itself active. And this remains true even where the object undergoing observation appears of necessity to be static. A detective engaged in "watching" a house, for instance, is watching not an inert mass but an object which, potentially at least, is instinct with movement. The house itself is the mere raw material of his vigilance. What he is waiting for is the opportunity to make it the pivot of a drama of action in which strange men enter and depart on sinister missions. The pattern that he weaves about it is a dynamic pattern.

In the field of hearing an equivalent distinction is present. We hear individual sounds; we listen to, or for, the pattern they make in combination. If we were not all the time engaged in listening to it, the notes of a symphony that we hear would fail to add up to anything significant. Not that listening is merely an affair of memory, of holding the individual notes in mind for long enough to allow of the emergence of a coherent pattern; the general pattern is being woven and completed at every moment, for although a symphony (to take but one example) is not fully intelligible until the end, our appreciation of it begins as soon as the pattern-quality begins to emerge, and this may occur very early in the performance. In a sense, too, the conclusion to such a musical work represents not so much the completion of a pattern—though a *coda* is very much like tying up the finished work with a neat ribbon—as the occasion for a new pattern-process, namely, the integration of the work into our general musical experience. Thus arise those paradoxes of æsthetic appreciation with which music-lovers—and art lovers, for that matter—are only too familiar: the paradox, above all, whereby the actual attention to the work of art is found to absorb such energy that the so-called pleasures of æsthetic appreciation only come afterwards, when we have an opportunity to sort out our impressions and form new alignments, with the result that we may find ourselves deferring our actual enjoyment until the journey home on top of the bus, surprised to find that such retrospective meditations demand a degree of self-communion that is resentful of interruption and impatient even of the presence of intimate friends.

Whatever the precise relationship between the body and the mind, it is obvious that they find the task of working together not so difficult as to have prevented them co-operating satisfactorily during the greater part of life: so that if we fail to understand the full intricacies of this, the most gigantic of all compromises in the universe, we ought not to be put off by the

complicated relationship subsisting between body and mind
in perception. Perception, as we have seen, is the servant of
our bodily life, the means whereby the organism adapts
itself to its environment and possibly vice versa. Consequently,
the contribution of mind in perception is limited to strictly
utilitarian ends. This limitation serves in turn to explain why
the kind of knowledge with which perception puts us in
possession falls short of being universal and disinterested and
unqualified, like that of metaphysics. It is concerned merely
with the particular and the concrete, as Berkeley said it was.
There are those who deny the possibility of universal and disinterested knowledge, and to whom the function of the mind
in perception is capable of being whittled down to something
that could be undertaken by an activity less than mental. We
shall have an opportunity of seeing later on whether such
extreme emphasis upon the physical nature of perception can
be justified. Hitherto, the analysis that we have made seems
to explain, at least in general terms, the facts as we find them
in everyday life; and, as we have pointed out, in discussing
perception it is to the experience of everyday life that appeal
may legitimately be made.

Variations in Perception

In laying down the essential conditions which any theory of
perception must endeavour to satisfy, we referred both to
individual differences in perception and to the idea of a
"norm" of perception around which such differences revolve.
It is now possible to deal with these questions, because the
material for answering them has in great part been assembled.

If perception involves the degree of activity that we have
seen reason to ascribe to it, the idea that the percipient *col-
laborates* with the natural or physical world by acting upon it
will seem less strange and obscurantist than might otherwise
be the case. Nevertheless, the caution will bear repeating
that, however much the act of perception may influence the

object, there is no reason to suggest, after the manner of the subjective idealists, that the object is created by the mind that contemplates it. Such theories involve imbecilities that bring metaphysical enquiry into disrepute, and the more solemn their enunciation the more baleful their influence. What we are asked to account for is a fact which needs to be explained, not explained away: the fact, namely, that people do differ in their perception of objects, and that these differences are not so much departures from a fixed norm as variations which, within obvious limits, can each be justified. Critics may possibly intervene at this point with the remark that, by emphasising the active nature of perception, the task of explaining such differences is rendered more difficult. On the contrary, it is rendered much easier. For the possibility of there being variations in perception follows inevitably from the fact of activity. Because perception is a practical process, a means to the better control by the individual of his environment, it proceeds by active selection from among the objects of that environment. In so far as our minds are individual, and our individual needs different, our perceptive selections are bound to vary one from another. This is true both of one individual as distinct from another, and of the same individual at different times.

Granted that our individual perceptions do and must undergo variation, however, it still remains to be shown how there can be such a thing as a "norm" of perception round which these variations are grouped. If there are variations there must be something to vary. In stressing variety, however, are we not coming dangerously near to adopting the standpoint of subjectivism against which we have issued repeated warnings? Are we not in danger of losing sight of the object altogether?

No; not if we know exactly what we mean by "object". And here we come to grips with one of the most complex problems arising out of the modern theory of knowledge, though a problem to which the philosopher must address himself if he wishes to give an account of certain facts elicited by modern physics. If we are not to fall into subjectivism and to conclude, with the desperation of the solipsist, that "all we know is our own ideas"—if, that is to say, we are to break out of Berkeley's mental concentration camp—we must be able to establish the presence and existence of some kind of object independent of perception, though not necessarily so independent as to form part of an objective world wholly cut off from the subjective world, after the manner of the extreme realists.

Sense-data and Sensa

The beginner in philosophy has to read only a few text-books on his subject to become thoroughly familiar with the term "sense-datum". Nevertheless, the indiscriminate use of this term has been responsible for much ambiguity. That a sense-datum must be "given" by something other than the subject that perceives it is implied by the meaning of the word. And it is because of this latent implication, embarrassing to those who are not altogether clear about what they mean by the objective world, that "sense-datum" is frequently changed to "sensum". The latter is certainly a more non-committal term, but the history of recent philosophy shows that its entry into circulation has not always made for clarity. The status of a "sensum" remains, unless carefully specified, extremely vague.[1] From our point of view, then, the word sense-datum may be allowed to stand: for the implication that all sensa are given, or given off, by something objective is an idea from which we have no reason to dissent. The proposition that "all we know is sense-data"—a phrase that is not seldom heard in philosophical discussions—is, to our way of thinking, nonsensical; nor is it any less nonsensical to say that the mind

[1] A. C. Ewing, in his book *Idealism* (page 366), speaks of the possibility of "unsensed sensa"; but this is surely an expression that ought to have been avoided, in spite of the author's plea that he could find no other.

"gives such sensa to itself", as if the whole business of knowledge were a game of patience played by the mind to keep
itself amused. Exponents of "philosophy" are constantly
getting themselves involved in intricacies of this kind, and
their gambits are sometimes mistaken for extreme subtlety.
Hence the polemic that goes on against "academic theorising",
as if our universities and colleges were concerned with nothing
but attempts to mystify the common man.

The idea that objects are perceived by us *through the medium
of* sense-data is less open to criticism. We must sense them
somehow, and clearly we sense that which the object makes
available to us. But here the complication begins. How much,
in actual fact, does the object make available to us? Surpris-
ingly little. Confronted with the statement that he has never
in his life seen a cube (for instance), the ordinary man may
protest that he is being trifled with. True, he may not have
seen every facet of a cube all at one time, but at least he knows
what a cube is and that is good enough for him. He does; it is.
But such dogmatism will not satisfy the theoriest. We certainly do know what cubes are, what chairs are, and what
mountains are, and the consciousness of this knowledge is to
all intents and purposes sufficient for our practical needs.
But the problem for the theorist remains: namely, how we
can know that which, from the perceptive point of view, we
have never seen. Let us pursue this point a little farther. We
perceive a cube in a variety of forms; but we can never, even
aided by reflective appliances, obtain a view of it in which
it is *cubicle*. In other words, what the object makes available
to us is never in any one position or for a single moment that
which we know it to be. How, then, do we arrive at the
knowledge that we claim to possess? The answer is by the
interpretation of sense-data. Now interpretation is a very
different process from trying to arrive at the idea of an object
diagrammatically, or by means of mirrors, or by collating the
impressions of persons observing it from all possible angles.

The process to which we refer takes place in every example of perception all the time, from the most cursory glance to the most concentrated watching brief. In short, it is another name for that activity of the mind in perception of which we have spoken. The activity is the activity of interpretation.

The habit of interpreting sense-data is so strong in all of us, and operates with such extreme rapidity that we tend normally to ignore its continuous influence. It is not that we first see things (or hear things) and then proceed to think or meditate on them; it is that we think how best to see them. And the kind of thought employed in this task has a more traditional title still, namely, imagination. The mental agency that "fills in the gaps" of a friend's conversation, supplies outline and finish to our visual impressions, or adjusts our ears to the distinct discrepancy of pitch between a violin and the piano that accompanies it, is not mere "afterthought"; it is imaginative interpretation working throughout the perceptive act, and helping to sustain that act as a unity. In any field of vision, certain objects, or patterns of sense-data, "stand out", while others, not necessarily smaller in dimensions, appear to efface themselves. Let our interest shift, perhaps in consequence of a sudden movement or the entry of another object, and the pattern undergoes transformation. The ear is equally selective, and so is our sense of touch and smell. Admittedly, the senses can deceive us; but the man who, feeling a scaly surface, believes that he is touching bark when in fact he is touching a snake, is not the victim of illusory sense-data; he is the victim, and no doubt the innocent victim, of mistaken interpretation. To miss a stair is rightly to miscalculate, because we were under the impression that there was "one more stair". To mistake a cat for the rug at the bottom is to misinterpret.

Interpretation, then, concerns itself not with a single sense-datum but with a whole field of data varying in extent and clarity. A "single" sense-datum is always a cluster of data selected from this field, and such selection is dictated, as we have already observed, by our individual needs both momentary and permanent. Thus, perceived objects do not arrive at the threshold of our minds complete and fully formed. We arrive at them. There is never a sense-datum unmodified by a context of other sense-data; nor is the field of sensation thus roughly demarcated capable of being analysed as a mere sum of distinct data. Such a picture of the world of sense (which, as we have seen, is not a mere world of sense) may be pronounced unduly vague. It admittedly is vague. Clarity and precision are introduced into this sphere of perception only by the mind-body unity that forms the perceptive apparatus. Our conception of the object is therefore widened to include the "field" in which every object is necessarily located.

Example from Audible Experience

Nevertheless, even if the individual sense-datum is an abstraction from a field of sensation, this very field is none the less itself a datum, a collective gift, in so far as there must be something from which it takes its origin. The problem is to establish the nature and status of this "something".

We can best illustrate what is meant by a field of sensation being "given" by taking a comparatively simple example from audible experience. With obvious qualifications, the same argument will apply to sense-experience in general. In the case of a musical tone the vibrations issuing from the instrument that produces it (say a violin string), together with the resulting vibrations in the air, must exist independently of any percipient. These vibrations are therefore properly objective and must be thought of as natural phenomena capable of existing in the external world. What, then, is the actual musical note that we, as percipients, hear? It is clearly not the vibrations, whether of the violin string or of the air; these vibrations can produce by themselves no such quality as *resonance*. The note that we hear is not a thing that can be imagined as subsisting in the objective world, waiting merely to be "picked up" or "adopted", like the children in Maeterlinck's "Where the Rainbow Ends". A musical note, rather, is the result of co-operation between the mind-body unity in perception and the raw material vibration-pattern belonging to the objective world. In short, mind and nature engage in collaboration to form a quality that would otherwise enjoy no more than potential existence.

In expounding such a view of perception, the danger is that we shall be content with employing metaphorical statements to account for processes requiring strictly scientific elucidation. To maintain, for example, that tone qualities or images or tactile sensations are produced in consequence of some "fusion" between mental and physical elements is seriously to becloud the issue: the word "fusion" will get us nowhere. If we speak of the process as one of collaboration, however, we at least imply that the two parties have separate jobs to perform, and the way is open for the precise assessment of what each job amounts to, and how they work together.

On the basis of what we have said the percipient *qua* body has, or more strictly is, a mechanism for reproducing in its own structure (which consists of the tympanum and aural nerves functioning in a manner which the physiologist or neurologist can explain to us in detail) a vibration-pattern identical with that which exists in the air. But, as the physiologist will go on to tell us, the vibrations in the air must impinge upon the ear in a special manner if the latter is properly to "hear" a sound. To be precise: at any given instant, there is no more than a single vibration impingeing upon, and reproducing itself in, our aural mechanism; and, as we shall be reminded, the so-called "pitch" of a note depends entirely upon the "frequency" of such vibrations. In other words, what we need to understand, if possible, is how the percipient can experience sufficient successive vibrations to establish a rhythm which, apprehended as a whole, enables him to hear the note. To effect this synthetic process is the task of the percipient *qua* mind. The mental activity in perception, in fact, synthesises a number of successive vibrations into one unified and simultaneous act. It holds together past and present vibrations in one experience, so that the different vibrations form a new and indivisible unity. Now the musical note that we hear (against a background of other sounds, of course) consists simply of the "quality" which these vibrations of determinate frequency possess as thus mentally unified. And in addition to being the product of synthesis, it is also the product of rigorous selection from within a field of vague sound. The conclusion follows, therefore, that the musical *note* is something that we create in hearing it; but it must not be forgotten that the particular note that we are thus responsible for creating—let us call it Middle C for the purpose of the present example—is also determined by certain objective facts: in this case the vibration-frequency, which, as we observed, must exist independently of our perception. At most we can say that, in the absence of a percipient, the musical note exists potentially in the objective world but not actually.

The "Norm" of Perception

This furnishes us with a clue to the so-called "norm" of perception. However much our individual perceptions may vary, we are determined to create the note as Middle C by certain facts—namely, the vibration-frequency—which exist in the objective world. Thus the pre-existing constitution of the object dictates a norm which pegs down, as it were, our various perceptions and maintains a kind of unity among them. It is the difficulty with some theories of perception that while they cannot admit that each individual perceives the object in the same way, they cannot conceive of variations except as departures from a norm which forms the "true" or ideal perception; and they have to postulate ideal "observers" (of whom God is usually made honorary president) in whose eyes each thing is seen as it ought to be. According to the idea expounded here, the norm provides not so much the ideal perception as the guarantee that our own individual perceptions contain sufficient authenticity to enable us to agree that we are perceiving a common object.

In that last sentence the professional logician will be able to pick holes and the ordinary reader ambiguities. How can we talk about guarantees and authenticity without knowing more about the object than we apparently do? The question ought to be answered, because there is a type of person who, in the course of an argument about perception, stumps everyone present by enquiring how a group of spectators are able to tell that they are looking at the same object. How do I know that my tree is your tree, and so on? What is the guarantee that I am seeing the ships in the bay as you see them? The answer is that there is no guarantee: no guarantee, that is to say, apart from that which emerges in the course of our comparing notes on the subject. We agree about objects of perception and their characteristics exactly as we agree about anything else: by pursuing our discussion until there emerges good reason to believe that we are not mistaken in our assumptions. And the criterion that emerges is not so much a body of evidence as the mere fact that we continue to talk at all. Nor need the language used be verbal in character. Our actions will often be sufficient to ensure our agreement. In short, if the sceptic likes to argue that without scrutinising each other's minds we cannot possibly know for certain that we are talking or thinking about the same things, the answer is that there is no way of scrutinising each other's minds but that which we have habitually used since the beginning of history: namely, by expressing our thoughts in language, using that word in its widest sense.

The scientist may find little or nothing to object to in the foregoing theory of perception except its reference to the synthetic activity of mind. How, it may be asked, can we form such syntheses of past and present experiences as we have presupposed? Is not this putting too great a burden upon even such a versatile instrument as the human understanding? The physical or "brain" part of perception is not merely easy to grasp; it is really obvious. With the mind we feel less at home, because here we are up against the problem of memory, and that is a problem to which we have so far paid no attention.

The problem of memory, we may remark, is one of the most fascinating as well as one of the most complicated in human thought; but it would be foolish, in a chapter on the subject of perception, to become too deeply involved in its ramifications. Nor is its consideration at this juncture so urgent as might be imagined. The problem of how the mind achieves unity between past and present in perception (and not only in perception) forms part of a problem that has already occupied us, namely, the problem of what we have called the perceptive field. Let us return to this subject for a moment. In describing the perceptive field we must be careful not to think of a complex of sensation distributed merely in space— a filigree network of sense-data. A perceptive field is also a field distributed in time. It is not a mere point, because a mere point would preclude complexity. Nor is it a mere "now", because a mere "now" would preclude succession. To hear, see, taste, or feel anything occupies a measure of time, for the apprehension by the mind of a pattern of sensation presupposes enough time for that pattern to establish itself. There is thus a synthesis between elements both past and present: and not only between past and present but also between present and future. Every act of perception involves an element of expectation without which it would suffer perpetual truncation. How this process of synthesis is achieved is difficult at the moment to explain; but this does not alter the fact that the mind is perpetually engaged in its achievement, and that knowledge itself depends upon it.

The Real World

The conception of a perceptive field, and the notion of "fields" in general, is of such fundamental importance for modern thought that the reader is referred to perhaps the best statement on the subject that has been advanced in recent years. We refer to that contained in Field-Marshal Smuts' great work, *Holism and Evolution*, especially chapters 1 and 2. The following passage (page 12), selected almost at random, will serve as an example of the approach to modern problems which the author, who is as distinguished a thinker as a man of action, recommends:

"A 'concept' ", he writes, "is not merely its clear luminous centre, but embraces a surrounding sphere of meaning or influence of smaller or larger dimensions, in which the luminosity tails off and grows fainter until it disappears. Similarly a 'thing' is not merely that which presents itself as such in clearest definite outline, but this central area is surrounded by a zone of vague sense-data and influences which shades off into the region of the indefinite. The hard and abrupt contours of our ordinary conceptual system do not apply to reality and make reality inexplicable, not only in the case of causation, but in all cases of relations between things, qualities, and ideas."

The chief criticism that we can imagine as being levelled at this kind of attitude is that it opens the floodgates to all the vague and woolly notions which serious thinkers are anxious to keep out. Surely, it might be said, the whole function of a philosopher is to concern himself, in Descartes' phrase, with "clear and distinct ideas", and not with the blurring of distinctions. If professional thinkers are going to start smudging the delicate blue prints of logic, how can we expect the ordinary man to think straight and to use his reason as he is con-

stantly exhorted to do? Does not this campaign of vagueness
amount to mental high treason, with treachery starting at the
top, where its appearance is most to be deplored?

Not necessarily: for what Smuts is trying to indicate—and,
to be fair, we must point out that he treats the matter at considerable length and with an eye on such objections as we have
outlined—is not that distinctions should be blurred or merged
or obliterated, but that they should be a great deal more
accurate than we have hitherto been accustomed to draw
them. Precision should be increased, not relaxed. The mesh
of our intellectual sieve must be finer. The instruments that
we have been accustomed to use to dissect a reality that was
comparatively "simple" must be discarded for others more
delicate in order to deal with a world of matter and life of far
greater complexity than we had dreamed possible. To quote
Smuts again: "the science of the nineteenth century was, like
its philosophy, its morals, and its civilisation in general, distinguished by a certain hardness, primness and precise limitation and demarcation of ideas. Vagueness, indefinite and
blurred outlines, anything savouring of mysticism, was abhor-
rent to that great age of limited exactitude. . . . Concepts
were in logic as well as in science narrowed down to their most
luminous points, and the rest of their contents treated as non-
existent" (page 11). Not merely our ideas of matter and life,
but of conduct, commerce and social organisation have
become far more complicated: compare, for instance, a nineteenth-century text-book of economics and one published to-
day, with its crowded statistical appendices. Granted the
present conditions of society owe a great deal of their notorious
complication to sheer muddle. That cannot be denied; but
if we are to introduce order into chaos we must abandon all
thought of simple and easily-applied remedies and devise a
more subtle approach, paying attention to much that was
formerly dismissed as of little account, and detecting connections between forces hitherto assumed to be unrelated.

Those who are prepared to accept the present position, and who acknowledge that our ordinary assumptions need to be revised to meet a new situation, will not pronounce absurd a conception of the objective world providing "raw material" which the mind uses and develops for purposes of its own. The old idea of the mind as a kind of box-camera taking accurate snapshots of a fully-formed "reality" must clearly go by the board. We know, as a matter of everyday experience, that what happens to interest us at the moment tends to assume greater importance—to loom larger—than at other times. This distortion or bias is not to be dismissed as an aberration; it is in fact a condition of our getting things done, of our carrying on the business of living. It is not an example of failure on our part; it is rather an indication of success. We isolate, concentrate, focus, not sometimes but always. The mind-body unity of which we consist could hardly be imagined as functioning in any other manner. And as with space, so with time. If we are in a hurry all 'buses are late, all our colleagues dilatory, all clocks fast. To say that such experiences are illusory is to beg the question; they are the inevitable consequence of concentration upon a special problem—in the case that we have taken, the problem of getting to a particular place by a particular time. That a similar selective process is operative in the case of memory has frequently been pointed out. If, for example, all our memories were present to our awareness simultaneously action would be frustrated by the plethora of images and impressions thus tumultuously assembled. The result would be not enlightenment but befuddlement. To explain how such mnemonic selection is achieved is the business of the psychologist, though philosophers themselves have advanced various plausible suggestions. Bergson, for instance, with characteristic originality, maintains that the selective process is undertaken by the brain, which he defines as "an instrument for forgetting".

The objective world, therefore, is real enough, and it exists in a sense independent of perception. To that extent the realist view is correct and indeed self-evident. Even those qualities to which the seventeenth-century philosophers gave the title of "secondary" are, in a sense, "there"; and instead of being falsified or distorted in perception, they are realised or actualised thereby. To put the matter in another way, the objective world as we perceive it is the result of co-operation between ourselves and nature; and this co-operation is both a condition and a consequence of the practical business of living. Hence, as we have already observed, the knowledge that we gain in perception, being practical, is less than the highest kind of knowledge that we can conceive. It is utilitarian knowledge, a means to an end: the rent paid by the mind for its tenancy of the body.

"When the soul uses the body as an instrument of perception", says Plato,[1] "that is to say, when it uses the sense of sight or hearing or some other sense, she is dragged by the body into the region of the changeable, and wanders and is confused; the world spins round her, and she is like a drunkard, when she touches change. But when she contemplates in herself and by herself, then she passes into the other world, the region of purity and eternity and immortality and unchangeableness, which are her kindred, and with them she ever lives, when she is by herself and is not let or hindered; then she ceases from her erring ways, and being in communion with the unchanging is unchanging. And this state of the soul is called wisdom".

[1] *Phaedo*, 79 f.

PART II

The Nature of Metaphysical Thought

I

Metaphysics and Civilisation

Philosophy and Science

In the course of the last three chapters we have traced the development of the idea of perception from the time of the Greeks to the present day. In so doing we have been obliged to omit reference to a great many more theories than we have been able to mention, and at the same time to simplify the latter considerably, though it is hoped without distortion. During the present century alone, a great many philosophical theories have been advanced to explain the "fact" of perception, and much scientific investigation has been devoted to the physical "facts" of the process. And there still remains much to be done. What some readers may be inclined to feel, as they begin the present chapter, is that the "fact" of perception is something which we shall come to understand better only as a result of the discovery of more "facts" in the scientific sense. Why philosophise, they will say, when the only profitable source of knowledge is scientific enquiry? Will not science, as it elucidates the facts, provide its own commentary upon them? What is the use of generalising upon inadequate evidence?

This attitude, which is not uncommon, contains much that is both reasonable and just. But it is not an argument against the pursuit of philosophical enquiry. It is an argument in favour of it. Those who harbour doubts as to the use and efficacy of philosophy are covertly assuming that, all things considered, science is better able to do what philosophy has hitherto claimed to do; that the only legitimate method of

D

enquiry is scientific enquiry; and that scientific enquiry is concerned both with the investigation of phenomena and with reflection upon their nature. In thus exalting the sphere of science and defining its nature however, these protagonists of "the scientific attitude to things" are not so much abandoning philosophy as indulging in a form of philosophical argument. They are guilty not so much of swapping horses in mid-stream as of covertly changing the name of the horse that they believe to be winning. To them philosophy is no longer philosophy, science is.

It is one thing to object to the practice of hypostasising or personifying a word like philosophy, as if it represented a kind of super-entity entitled to make pontifical deliverances upon the nature of things in general; it is another thing to proceed, after dismissing this venerable figure, to usher in an efficient young person called Science, who forthwith assumes the same comprehensive functions and generalises with even greater abandon. If one person is forbidden to generalise what right has another? The "science" to which so many people to-day look with a combination of reverence and expectancy is as often as not endowed with all the arbitrary powers that were formerly vested in philosophy and theology. It claims to tell us in what reality consists; it undertakes to prescribe our moral standards; it even attempts to prophesy the future. We are constantly being told "what science teaches" and "what science has discovered"; we are rarely shown the credentials on the strength of which these affirmations are made. And yet it is precisely the credentials of science that are most urgently in need of checking.

We shall do well, in considering the problems of thought, to rid ourselves of the notion that philosophy and science are competitors in a field of investigation of which one or the other must eventually acquire the monopoly; and this will involve the simultaneous abandonment of the habit of hypostasising subjects which are in fact not subjects but methods.

Part of the difficulty of so doing is due to the nature of language, which is a good servant but a bad master. The use of abstract nouns, often with capital letters, inclines us to impute a sort of fake "personality" to ideas which possess no such character. We speak of Philosophy, and Science and Mind, and also of Democracy, England, Honour and Evil, as if these concepts were figures or persons capable of behaving by analogy like ourselves and enjoying a kind of abstract existence in a sphere of their own. Some philosophers, as we have seen, actually go so far as to maintain that this is indeed the case. To suggest that we should discontinue the use of abstract terms altogether would involve us in a great deal of tedious explanation whenever we made a generalised statement; and indeed the whole purpose of language would thereby be defeated. The difficulty is that whereas most people know what they mean when they talk about England and Russia, and even Right and Wrong, they sometimes fail to make the same mental adjustment when they talk about Philosophy or Religion or Science. For the content of these notions are usually less familiar to them; and they tend to "fill in the blanks" with a vague imagery, just as primitive tribes are supposed to people the dark or remote places of nature with spirits. "There are fairies at the *bottom* of my garden", not the top.

In the course of our enquiry we have had occasion not once, but several times, to refer to periodical attacks launched against philosophy and metaphysics, even by those who, in the academic world, are known as philosophers and who are paid to give instruction in that subject. We shall do so again. This continuous sniping at the slow convoy of philosophy can never be wholly prevented. In short, there is an *anti-philosophia perennis* as well as a perennial philosophy; the one shadows the other, and in the no-man's-land between them lurk many sinister figures who, at certain periods, issue into the open and establish a brief authority. The ordinary man, busy with his every-day occupations, does not, as a rule, concern himself overmuch with such attacks upon reason and ordered thinking unless the danger becomes too acute to ignore: and then he usually conceives of the struggle in terms of economic and political issues, which are but its external manifestations. As M. Maritain has said: "The very crises in the economic order urge us to study metaphysics."[1] Not all of us, admittedly; but there will always be scattered groups of thinking men and women to whom the chaos in society is seen to cloak a more serious derangement, and for whom the pursuit of ultimate causes becomes an obligation which they cannot shirk, even if they are brought near to despair in their search for a permanent solution.

To acknowledge the legitimacy of metaphysical enquiry, therefore, is to realise that what the philosopher is trying to discover is the same pattern as we ourselves, at a somewhat lower level perhaps, are engaged in discerning. We want to know, as a matter of instinct, what kind of a world it is into which we are born and must live our lives; we want to discover our limitations, both of knowledge and of action; and, unless we are content to be incurably parochial, we are anxious to learn how other people, differently placed from ourselves in situation and in time, have tried to solve these same problems. A much-quoted and much misunderstood observation by F. H. Bradley is that "philosophy is the finding of bad reasons for what we believe upon instinct"; but he completes his half-serious statement with a remark that is not always included, namely, that "the finding of these reasons is no less an instinct". In other words, man has an itch not merely to eat, to build, to propagate his kind, but to *know*.

The purpose of this apparent digression is to reinforce a point made several times in the last chapter to the effect that the knowledge obtained in perception is conditioned primarily by our bodily needs. The thought with which metaphysics is

---

[1] *Freedom in the Modern World* (Eng. trans., 1935), p. 5.

concerned, however, is usually assumed to be of a higher kind, exempt from the trammels of physical nature and able to operate with complete freedom over the whole range of existence. It is now time to ask whether such a form of thought is indeed genuine, and what, if we may rely upon its deliverances, it can tell us about the nature of reality.

In order to answer these questions—and it will be agreed that upon the right answers a great deal must depend, since the whole possibility of ordered knowledge is at stake—we must face up at the outset to certain difficulties which past thinkers, in tackling analogous problems, have raised.

Plato and the Forms

In Chapter II we made a brief reference to Plato's theory of knowledge, according to which the world known to our senses was held to disclose only partial truth. This emphasis upon the limitations of perceptual knowledge is significant, and, as we have seen, it has been corroborated throughout the history of philosophy down to our own times. In fact, Plato's account of the nature of knowledge in general raises so many profound issues that Whitehead can hardly be accused of exaggeration when he describes modern philosophy as merely a series of "footnotes to Plato". If, however, the world of matter is only partially true, what can be said to be wholly true? Is there a sphere of reality apart from that of matter, by establishing contact with which we can arrive at truth itself?

Plato sought to answer this question by stating his theory of forms or ideas.

The Greek word for form, εἶδος, has the sense of "shape" or "structure", as opposed to ὕλη or "stuff", the material composition of that structure. If we study Plato's account we find that a form possesses certain characteristics by virtue of which it occupies a unique status in reality. In the first place, a form is something immaterial. This does not mean that a form cannot be embodied in matter; it means that whereas a form like "squareness" is nowhere to be found perfectly embodied in matter, there are many things that approximate to the idea of squareness. Secondly, a form is something both eternal and unchanging. If, for example, we consider an organism, we find that it consists of a number of parts to each of which is assigned a special function. The organism is in a constant state of change, taking in nutriment from its environment, expelling waste products, and, at a certain stage of maturity, reproducing itself. These changing elements are material; but that which survives the change and decay of the material parts is, according to Plato, the *form* of the organism, or the principle which enables it to maintain its identity. An organism is what it is and not another thing because of the form which it embodies. Moreover, since an organism is something that obeys a life-cycle which conducts it through the stages of birth, maturity and death, the form must be regarded as the ideal to which the material components are at each stage trying to approximate. The form is therefore already exerting its influence in the embryonic stage, and the development and reproduction of the organism is the striving towards ever more successful responses to this influence. From this follows the third characteristic of a form: namely, perfection. However nearly perfect a natural organism may be, or however near to dead accuracy may be our attempts to draw squares or circles or triangles, the natural manifestations of these things are bound to fall short of absolute perfection. Such perfection is to be found only in the ideal form to which these natural "essays", whether on the part of man or of nature, represent approximations. Now, whereas we can perceive these natural approximations and thus derive a kind of knowledge from them, we have no immediate perception of that of which they are striving to be the embodiments. And so we arrive at the fourth characteristic of a form: namely, the fact that our knowledge of it is obtained not through perception but through another faculty. This faculty is intellect.

While Plato held that our knowledge of the forms in or behind nature is derived solely through the intellect, he went on to point out that, as active beings, we were impelled, so to speak, to realise in practical life the perfection thus apprehended. The manner in which this realisation took place was by a process akin to reminiscence. Plato's master, Socrates (469-399 B.C.), had claimed that, instead of instructing other people, he was engaged in a task of drawing from them knowledge which, without realising it, they already possessed. Such knowledge was elicited by a technique of questioning which, if we are to believe Plato's various accounts, Socrates developed in the course of his self-imposed task of discovering what men really meant by their everyday expressions of belief about the world. Thus Socrates has been rightly described as "the first great expert in debunking".[1] Plato developed this technique, or rather provided it with a philosophical basis. In his view the mind of man possessed a number of innate principles which could be elicited by a process of dialectical argument. These principles represented the deposit, as it were, of previous incarnations; and among the tasks of philosophy was that of opening men's minds to ideas recognised not merely to be true but to be their own possession.

It followed from this argument—which, if not invented by Plato, was certainly elaborated by him—that man, instead of finding the truth about himself in the world of nature, found in himself the truth about his world. And, by developing this theme Plato arrived at a conception of philosophy or dialectic which, in spite of the wealth of new problems that have arisen since his time, is still regarded as the most fruitful and positive that has yet been put forward, and one that almost all the great philosophers of the western world have agreed to accept. Unlike the various sciences, which begin with a number of

[1] A. K. Rogers, *Morals in Review* (1927), p. 7.

axioms and work onwards to conclusions, philosophy, in the
Platonic view, is not merely continually justifying its own
starting-point, but telling us more about that which we know
in a sense already. As we saw in the last chapter, this does not
mean that philosophy is committed to justifying any particular
view of the world, least of all the "world of common sense".
Philosophy is committed to no view of the world but its own.
What it means is that the philosopher, following the Socratic
method, reflects upon experience as he finds it, and exposes,
often to the scandal of his fellows, the latent assumptions and
dogmatisms with which it is encumbered. Sometimes, as with
Socrates himself, the single-minded practice of his profession
lands the philosopher in difficulties with the authorities. But
the death of a Socrates or a Giordano Bruno represents not the
failure of the philosophical outlook but its triumph. *Eppure
si muove*.[1]

To return to the doctrine of ideas. Plato held that true
knowledge was obtained only through the intellectual apprehension of the forms. For this reason his philosophy is called
"idealist" after the Greek word already referred to. Plato's
idealism implied that, since the forms alone are immaterial,
unchanging, perfect, and intelligible, the world of material
things possesses what we may call knowability only in so far
as they attempted to realise the forms in themselves. This
attempt was made not merely by nature but by man.

As the word idealism has acquired various layers of meaning
in the course of time it is important to stress that, in Plato's
view, the forms were not to be regarded as anything *mental*.
Idealism is sometimes held to mean that reality is either
created by mind (or thought) or that things exist only in so
far as they are thought about. We have already come across a
form of idealism of this kind, namely, that of Berkeley; and we

---

[1] "And yet it does move": Galileo, after having been forced to with-
draw his claim that the earth moved round the sun, is reputed to have
murmured these words. The anecdote is probably apochryphal.

need not suppose, without due consideration, that it is entirely devoid of truth. But Plato's forms are not conditional upon being thought about. On the contrary, man's intelligence, so far from being able to create the forms, apprehends them only with difficulty and as the result of severe discipline. Among Socrates' words of farewell to his friends, as recorded by Plato, is a passage of great nobility on the subject of the kind of discipline needed. "Wherefore a man should be of good cheer about his soul", Socrates declares, "if in this life he has despised all bodily pleasures and ornaments as alien to her, and to the perfecting of the life he has chosen. He will have zealously applied himself to understanding, and having adorned his soul not with any foreign ornament but with her own proper jewels, temperance, justice, courage, nobility and truth, he awaits thus prepared his journey to Hades".[1] Socrates' emphasis upon the virtues that go to make a true thinker are a timely reminder that, merely by taking thought, a man cannot become a philosopher; other qualities are needed, and these must be perfected with as much care as that which is bestowed upon mind-training.

Aristotle's Criticism of Plato

Plato's disciple Aristotle (384-322 B.C.), while accepting much that Plato taught, introduced certain qualifications into the theory of Ideas, and thereby initiated what was virtually a new school of philosophy. Aristotle's approach to philosophical problems was in many ways more systematic than that of his master, though his early training, beginning at the age of eighteen and ending twenty years later with Plato's death, was acquired in the Platonic academy. Consequently, Aristotle was responsible for the partition of philosophical thought into a number of distinct, if not separate, studies, upon each of which he delivered exhaustive discourses. Some of his early works, consisting of written dialogues, have been lost, except

[1] Plato: *Phædo*, 114f.

D*

for various fragments; the rest, composed for the most part after Plato's death, are concerned with such subjects as logic, physics, zoology, psychology, metaphysics, ethics, politics, poetics, and rhetoric. The treatise on metaphysics was so named because Aristotle's editors, in collecting his writings, placed this particular work next after that dealing with physics. To be strictly accurate, therefore, the metaphysics of Aristotle represents the name not of a science but of a book.[1] Nevertheless, the subject-matter of this book—or series of books; hence the use of a plural substantive not merely here but in the case of "physics", "politics", "ethics", etc.—is concerned with matters for which a special and distinguishing name had to be found: and for this reason the title metaphysics has been retained, both from force of habit and because the word is by no means inappropriate to a study of matters more ultimate than those with which physics is occupied.

In postulating the existence of a world of forms or ideas apart from the individual things that sought to embody them, Plato failed to supply a really convincing explanation of how, if the material world was endeavouring to model itself upon the immaterial, the connection between the two was to be established. Time, he declared, was "the moving image of eternity": but how could a world of particulars, engaged in ceaseless flux, presume to imitate a timeless pattern of universals? The very notion that the universals could exist alongside, still less outside, particulars was extremely hard to grasp; and even with the aid of the most ingenious and brilliant metaphors, Plato never succeeded in making the relationship either clear or plausible. It is to this difficulty in Plato's otherwise most profound and exalted conception of reality that Aristotle sought to draw attention. His argument was, first of all, that if the ideas or forms of Plato were to exert the influence claimed for them—if, that is to say, they were to play a more convincing part in the drama of reality than that

[1] R. G. Collingwood: *An Essay on Metaphysics*, p. 4.

of a *Deus ex machina*—they must already be hard at work within the world of nature, exerting an immanent authority rather than a mere transcendent appeal to perfection.

Thus, according to Aristotle, that which gives truth and reality to the world of nature is precisely the form or idea that animates it. Without form matter possesses no reality. To conceive of matter without form is to think of something abstract. By form, we must emphasise, Aristotle meant a great deal more than mere shape, i.e., length, breadth, height, etc.; he meant to include the totality of the properties of a thing. In other words, Aristotle maintained that if we are to understand how natural things not merely come into being but preserve their existence, we must recognise the present of two principles: first, the form and secondly, the matter. The form is that which both causes the thing to exist and provides the ideal which it strives at every moment to realise; the matter embodies the form by providing the element in which it is able to work its influence.

Aristotle's Doctrine of God

Such a sketch of Aristotle's theory of form and matter fails to do justice to the depth and subtlety of his argument. To substantiate his contention he goes into great detail, especially in analysing the causes—material, formal, efficient, and final— which function both in the work of nature and in the work of man, e.g., in producing an artifact. Concerning some of his arguments there has been much dispute and a great variety of interpretation: and it would be exceedingly unwise to dismiss such obscurities without giving them serious and prolonged study. Nevertheless, the brief outline already given takes account of what is essential to his thought upon the particular question of Plato's theory of forms; and this is for the present sufficient for our purpose in tracing the development of the theory and its influence upon subsequent discussion.

Whereas Plato held that our knowledge of matter was imperfect knowledge, amounting to little more than opinion, Aristotle suggested that what we perceive is not matter at all but the *types of structure* that matter embodies. Perception is simply perception of form. And he went on to explain how it was that perception of form took place. We perceive the structure of natural things, he said, by actually taking the forms of these things into ourselves. This is done by a process which, to employ a word used in the last chapter, we may call ingestion. The same process is at work in the case of purely intellectual apprehension. The objects apprehended by our intellects are immaterial forms. Hence, in knowing such forms, the intellect, itself immaterial, becomes one with its object. Now at the summit of the scale of being is God, who is pure mind. And since mind at its most perfect development must be capable of complete knowledge of reality, it follows that God and the world of pure forms are identical one with the other. In other words, the forms are nothing but the thoughts of God Himself.

Although Aristotle had criticised his master for failing to show in what manner the world of forms was related to the world of nature, it has been pointed out, not inaccurately, that Aristotle's God was separated from nature by an even greater gulf. According to Aristotle, between God and the world, between pure mind and nature, there exists a relation, but it is not a reciprocal one. As the highest and most perfect being, God influences and even attracts the world to Himself; but towards that same world He evinces no corresponding attraction. He dissociates Himself from a world which is irresistibly drawn towards Him. We, as human creatures, desire Him; He remains indifferent to our desires. In this respect Aristotle's God is a purely metaphysical principle, deprived of all religious characteristics. He is not even the creator of the world. The God known to religion, on the other hand, is related to man and nature by ties of mutual love and desire, and no religion that does not insist on such reciprocity has been able to command attention. Aristotle postulates a God without a religion.

With whatever repugnance we may be tempted to view Aristotle's doctrine of God we cannot ignore the fact that his contribution to the theory of knowledge is of great importance. For one thing, it introduces a new and special sense of the world idealism: namely, that the function of mind at its highest development is to arrive at a knowledge of itself *by becoming that which it knows*.[1] When we have entered more fully into the nature of mind, and seen reason to suspect those theories which deny to it autonomy, we shall find such a statement less obscure than it may at first appear. Nor must we forget, if we are tempted to lose patience at such rarefied ideas, that the object we have set ourselves here is to examine, with the minimum of prejudice, what other people have had to say about problems admitted to be of capital importance. To dismiss the efforts of past thinkers as inapplicable to our own situation, however different it may appear, is to sink into the very attitude of dogmatism which, as independent thinkers, we ought most energetically to reject. There are so-called free-thinkers who, in an otherwise commendable effort to break down superstition—to *écraser l'inflame*, bid us forget about the past and concentrate upon the present. Would that such oblivion were possible! The past which these thoughtless persons would have us ignore, far from being banished by such impetuosity, menaces us even more directly in the form of a gathering darkness, which, as every moment sinks into it and is lost in obscurity, comes dangerously near to overwhelming the dissolving islet of the present. Nor is our precarious foothold lit by anything but a faint glimmer, like the sudden blue flash of the sun that sinks behind the Cape Point horizon. For with the future unknown and casting no reflection, we find ourselves deprived of the very light which we had hoped, in our innocence, to fan to brilliance. A past

[1] This point will be clarified later (p. 262).

banished as obscure returns to establish a reign of darkness
more impenetrable still.

The new idealist principle which Aristotle defined, and
which was to influence even thinkers to whom his conclusions
were antipathetic, may be illustrated by a simple example
from the sphere of conduct. In order truly to know goodness
we must ourselves become thoroughly good; for the process
of coming to know goodness is simply the cultivation in ourselves of good qualities. There is no question of contemplating the idea or concept of goodness from afar and then
proceeding to try to imitate it in our lives; the form of goodness is absorbed, as it were, into our very being, so that in
knowing it we become that which we know. The object is
thus incorporated within the subject. The form informs us
and we act upon its information.

Transition to Christian Philosophy

It is regrettable that most histories of philosophy, and many
of the academic courses on philosophy which students are
obliged to take, "jump" the early Christian and even the
mediæval period, limiting themselves to the philosophy of the
ancient world and/or something called "modern" philosophy,
which is held to have emerged suddenly in the sixteenth and
seventeenth centuries as a result of an equally sudden movement known as the Renaissance. Such mapping or classification of the past is a useful and indeed indispensable aid to
study and comprehension. But, as we have said before, it
must not be forgotten that these classifications are of our own
making; that the labelling of one age, or group of ages, as
"dark" and another as "enlightened", another as being
characterised by revival and yet another by decline or fall,
as the result of applying to the past a scheme or system of
interpretation based upon *the present state of our knowledge*; and
that the acquisition of new facts or the fresh interpretation of
old ones (which may come to the same thing) may lead us,

at first perhaps inadvertently, to find light where once was darkness and decline where once we claimed to detect rebirth. Not that we need, on making this discovery, sweep aside the old categories or dismiss them as mistakes. The rungs of a ladder which we have left beneath us are not thereby to be condemned as useless. They brought us here. They led us to our present eminence. The history of the past includes the attitude of former historians to their own past; and the understanding of this attitude will help us to understand them. If we would know the situation in which they were placed we must grasp their own notions of how they came to occupy it. Admittedly, they may have been labouring under certain misapprehensions in this matter; but that, too, instead of rendering their character unintelligible, may serve the better to illuminate it.

Only if we have attained to a certain degree of historical insight can we bring ourselves to realise that our antipathy to Aristotle's view that God did not create the world is the result not so much of instinct as of the deliberate modifications in Aristotle's conception introduced by the Christian philosophers at the beginning of our era. Whether we realise it fully or not, we of the Western world have all of us been brought up in the atmosphere of a particular tradition, the Christian tradition, which is the foundation and preserver of our civilisation. A civilisation is not a matter of material achievement, though modern civilisation is associated in the minds of many people with technical advances, and they talk of the "progress of science" as if this were the same thing as the development of civilisation. A civilisation is a way of life, which is a particular way of thinking about life; and this way of life is preserved not so much by scientific or technical inventions as by the very forces that brought it into being, which are intellectual, a matter of thought and will. The fact that this is so is demonstrated by the methods used by those who would destroy—knowingly or otherwise—the civilisation or way of life

that we have painfully and slowly built up through the centuries. Their first object, as we know, is to launch an attack
upon our minds by the aid of propaganda, and upon our wills
by the aid of a mixture of promises and threats. Only in the
last resort and after frantic efforts to break down our mental
resistance—or, as we are accustomed to call it, our "morale"—
do they turn to the more wasteful and expensive method of
attacking our bodies. Such "enemies of civilisation", as we
very properly call them, thereby tacitly reveal that they
understand very well what civilisation is. And although there
are many distinguished thinkers in the liberal camp who
maintain that religions (not necessarily the Christian religion),
instead of being the preserver of civilisation, represent an
obstacle to its further development, and that subjects like
metaphysics, being parasitic upon religion, or at any rate
concerned with matters equally "transcendental" and therefore illusory, represent an equally dangerous menace to rational
or enlightened thought, such persons soon discovered that,
once they have dismissed these things as outmoded or childish,
they are at a loss to justify, and so to find means of upholding, a
good many values—the liberty of the individual, the conception of justice, even the bare right to live—which, as so-called
champions of light against darkness, and as humanitarian
reformers, they claim to be most anxious to defend. Nor are
they able to show us, in their desperate effort to provide an
alternative foundation, that these elementary values are
innate or self-evidently valid: for their particular mode of
thought, which teaches that nothing can be considered true or
valid unless it be proved experimentally or from "experience",
cannot allow of such *a priori* demonstration. In other words,
the repudiation of the religious and metaphysical basis of the
civilisation which they wish to see defended and which they
believe can be defended upon purely rationalist, scientific,
humanitarian or positivistic grounds, results in their finding
that the cheques they still wish to draw upon its credit are

not honoured, since they have been responsible in the meantime for reducing the whole concern to a state of bankruptcy. Such bankruptcy, indeed, is often acknowledged, with a combination of indignation and barely concealed surprise, by the most successful exponents of this view. The latest and most striking case is that of H. G. Wells, who, after a lifetime of preaching the menace to civilisation of religion and metaphysics, has quite frankly and honestly admitted that the mind of man—that is, the mind of the sort of man that Wells is and would have all of us be—is "at the end of its tether": little realising, apparently, that the fault is in the nature of the tether and not the mind; and that its liberation from such constriction, long overdue, may be the first step towards salvaging those values (enshrined, for instance, in Wells's recent attempt to draw up a new table of the Rights of Man) which are rapidly suffering submergence.

Thus, to put this matter more bluntly, the question is not whether we care for religious or for metaphysical thought or feel that we have any particular aptitude for it, but whether we are prepared to put up with the inescapable consequences of allowing these things to decay or to be overwhelmed. If we acknowledge and honour certain values, certain human or natural rights, we cannot honestly or even prudently refuse to enquire how these values and rights have come to assume the importance that they have for us, and upon what basis their claim to our allegiance rests. Such an examination is at bottom a metaphysical one. As students of metaphysics, therefore, we are impelled to ask what confers upon a right the title of natural, and how such an idea of nature originally arose. And we shall find, as we have hinted already on more than one occasion, that the enquiry thus set afoot is also a historical enquiry, leading us to an examination of the thought of the men who first began seriously to debate these issues, and from whose conclusions or suggestions our common heritage of thought was gradually built up. Metaphysics thus turns out to be the history of metaphysics. That is why we must dwell at some length upon the work of Plato and Aristotle, whose systems, themselves constructed from material accumulated by previous thinkers, provided the basis upon which the philosophers of the Christian era built their own massive syntheses, within which in turn the thinkers of the modern world (from whatever time between the fifteenth and eighteenth centuries we choose to date the beginning of that epoch) have debated the manifold problems confronting them. Such a task is urgent today for many reasons, chief of which is that a tradition of civilisation is most in need of examination when its foundations are being threatened. And whether he welcomes the forces of opposition or resists them, no man in his senses can remain indifferent to the fact that the assault is in progress.

Now, if Aristotle denied that God made the world the question arises as to how he thought the world came into being. The answer is that he thought the world made itself, looking to God as a model upon which to work. In the same way Aristotle denied that God had communicated to the world the movement or *élan* which set it going; all he maintained was that the regularity and order characteristic of such movement was the result of imitation of God's supreme rationality. (Plato had held a somewhat different view. He, too, denied that God created the world; but he at least suggested that the world was *made* by Him, though on the model of the eternal forms which logically pre-existed even God Himself.)[1]

Now the point to which we must return for a moment is this: we at the present day, whether or not we consciously hold any dogmatic beliefs on the subject, find Aristotle's doctrine of the relationship between God and the world

[1] In the *Phaedrus*, 246f, Plato speaks of the Immortals, led by Zeus, standing upon "the outside of heaven" and contemplating the eternal forms which represent pure knowledge. This contemplation he describes as "The life of the gods."

mystifying and even repugnant, because we have been brought up upon a different view. And upon the view thus forming part of our mental make-up, most of our assumptions about life and society have been founded: which is the reason why, in the course of the preceding paragraphs, we have emphasised the drastic and far-reaching consequences of the demolition or slow undercutting of this foundation. The new view, introduced by the Fathers of the early Church as a result of reflection upon the Christian revelation, entailed the belief that the world of nature and men was in a very real sense the creature of God—a personal God, not an abstraction—thus establishing a more intelligible relation between God and the world than the Greek philosophers, not by any means as the result of stupidity, had been able to formulate.

Importance of Theological Issues

To some minds, fed upon the secular thought of the past century or so, this ascription to the Christian revelation of a deep-seated and revolutionary influence upon the history of philosophy may well appear fantastic and even unhistorical. They have perhaps been in the habit of regarding religion, and the Christian religion in particular, as a kind of mental fog through which man has groped his way for centuries, nourished upon chimeras and blinded to the true nature of the world, until, by some miracle or accident, the obscurity was lifted about the time of the Reformation and Renaissance, freeing the faculties of man for their true task of scientific and technical enquiry. The Dark Ages were thus followed by the Light Ages[1], in which religion and metaphysics survive as absurd anachronisms, unworthy of the attention of civilised and enlightened persons. This attitude was stated in more modern times with great plausibility by the French philosopher Auguste Comte (1789-1857); and it is to Comte rather

[1] Cf. the German "Aufklärung".

than to Marx that the modern secularist should rightfully attribute the paternity of much that he believes; but on that question we shall have occasion to speak at some length in Part IV. A century or two earlier Bishop Butler, in the preface to his book *The Analogy of Religion*, aptly summed up the attitude of many of his contemporaries and, did he but know it, his successors:

"It has come to be taken for granted by many persons", he wrote, "that Christianity is not so much a subject of enquiry but that it is now at length discovered to be fictitious. And accordingly they treat it as if in the present age this were an agreed point among all persons of discernment; and nothing remained but to set it up as a principal subject of mirth and ridicule, as it were by way of reprisals for its having so long interrupted the pleasures of the world".

Not to subscribe to the dogmas of Christianity is one thing; to deny that these dogmas have exerted a decisive influence upon western thought is another. In this book we are out to understand how the problems of modern philosophy have arisen, not to indulge in Christian or any other form of apologetic. And in concentrating for a while upon the work of Christian philosophers, especially those of the third and fourth century A.D., we are engaged in an enquiry that promises to throw light upon the origins of modern thought, including modern scientific thought; for it was in these early centuries of our era that the *presuppositions* of many of our most cherished beliefs were worked out in circumstances which, being disturbed and chaotic, made formal decisions imperative. In order to recognise the legitimacy of such an enquiry—which may at first be deemed by some to have nothing whatever to do with our own immediate problems—we must be prepared to adjust our minds to an atmosphere or climate of thought in many ways totally different from our own; to visualise, in so far as we are able, a time in which the correct formulation of a dogma was literally a matter of life and death for thousands of people, and in which men were ready, not merely to persecute, but to be persecuted for what they believed to be the correct interpretation of a theological or metaphysical issue. We may be tempted to regard all this, from our present standpoint, as the pastime, albeit somewhat dangerous, of childish or ignorant people, or alternatively, as one more example of the way in which priests and kings, intent upon maintaining their power and influence, have thrown dust in the eyes of the toiling masses. But that is to project the ideas of a much later time, and not necessarily a more mature time, into a period in which the stress and strains of society were due to other causes. And in so far as we are accustomed to conceive of social unrest in terms primarily of politics and economics, and to envy more stable epochs in which these forces exerted far less obvious pressure upon the individual, so we must be ready to appreciate the conditions of centuries still more remote, in which the conflict in society took the form of theological debate, equally fierce and dis ruptive, and conceived by the ordinary man and woman with as much and as little understanding as may be found to-day in the case of political and economic questions.

Granted that the practice of reducing problems to theological issues has long been abandoned, we must not forget that this applies only to the western world. In the East, even the Middle East, it is still very evident, and not merely among Moslems but among Christians. Accustomed to think of Western Europe as a norm we hastily assume that other parts of the world are primitive to the extent to which they depart from this norm. And we are especially prone to play down the Oriental origin of our religion, forgetting Disraeli's definition of the Christian Church as "a sacred corporation for the promulgation in the west of certain eastern principles". If we bear these things in mind we may be led to reflect whether our own attitude is necessarily so reasonable as we had assumed, and whether it might not be regarded from another point of view as a departure from standards of much greater antiquity. In spite of the influence of western materialism upon the Middle East countries and the formalism of much religious observance in these areas, the spiritual consciousness of the people is by no means stifled. Nor is it mere habit that prompts a man to be referred to as a Moslem, a Greek Catholic, a Druse, a Maronite, as the case may be: these designations being far more significant than his nationality. Furthermore, it must not be presumed that the adherents of these sects are ignorant of precisely what it is that differentiates them from their fellows. They are theologically as well as spiritually self-conscious. Even young children can explain, if challenged, what doctrine they are expected to adhere to and wherein it differs from that of another sect—as the visitor to Syria (for example) may discover if he is sufficiently curious.

In concluding this chapter it is important to remind ourselves that the above remarks about our indifference, as Europeans, to doctrinal subtleties may, after all, be more apparent than real. True, the doctrines to which we are sometimes invited to subscribe are not theological or even seemingly connected with theology. They are political or, to be more accurate, ideological. In England and America formal adherence to one or other ideological doctrine is not yet regarded as obligatory upon anyone; but a very different situation prevails in other areas of Europe and Asia, where the tests of orthodoxy are extremely rigorous and punishment for persistent heresy capital. In making this observation we do not wish to imply a condemnation of these other systems, among which is one of the most remarkable social experiments in history. Such a condemnation, even if just, would not merely be out of place in a book of this kind; it would be irrelevant to the point we are making. And the gist of the point is that, given a system of society such as that which is being established, the resort to tests of ideological orthodoxy is perfectly **legitimate** and necessary. For the system is based upon certain doctrines about man and his world which, differing as they do—and as they are meant to do—from that of western Europe, need to be carefully preserved from error and contamination. Where there is orthodoxy there is ever-present danger of heresy. If these doctrines are to be believed in by millions of people they must be inculcated by every means of persuasion: for the cohesion of society depends upon their orthodox acceptance. They are not doctrines which certain intellectuals happen to believe; belief in them is a condition of the masses working in community of purpose. It is sometimes assumed that the democratic systems of the west have succeeded in proving, whatever their defects, that no special theories or doctrines are necessary to keep society together; that democracy is a form of society in which everyone can believe just what he likes; and that only such a form of society is compatible with human happiness. This sort of notion is likely to win assent only so long as the democratic system appears to be winning all along the line—as it was, for instance, during the nineteenth century; though even so, it might be remarked that the American Constitution, setting forth the aims of democratic society, speaks not of the gift or possession of happiness but only of its "pursuit". When once there arises a formidable competitor to liberal or parliamentary democracy, and this competitor succeeds in enlisting the enthusiasm of millions of people in the space of a few years, the subject of doctrine and definition presents itself once more, and a return to first principles—which means always a return before first principles—becomes essential. And it will probably be found that the trouble starts not by both societies calling themselves different things, but by both societies calling themselves the same thing. The divergence first appears in practice, where it is soon realised that the words "democracy" and "freedom" can refer to quite different matters. That the examination of the presuppositions of our civilised life forms a metaphysical enquiry has already been pointed out; and it will bear repeating that the question before us at this stage is not so much whether these ideas are true as what they are and how they have so thoroughly entered into our consciousness.

The Origins of European Civilisation

Judaism and Hellenism

To return to the Christian Fathers for the origin of many of the beliefs which have sustained our civilisation may seem to be going back a very long way indeed: some people might maintain that we need not pursue the enquiry farther than the Renaissance or even the American Declaration of Independence. But, if we reflect upon the early history of Christendom we shall be surprised not so much that the systematic formulation of Christian dogma took place so early as that it was delayed for so long.

Although most of the important dogmas were elaborated in the course of the third and fourth centuries the urge to work out a truly Christian philosophy, and therefore to refute the assumptions of the classical philosophers, began to manifest itself within a few years of the death of Jesus. It would not be true to say, however, that the apostles and converts to Christianity, however much they wished to emphasise the novelty of their beliefs, tried to put forward a new system of thought in the void. As late as the third century, admittedly, there were Christian philosophers, above all Tertullian, Lactantius and Arnobius, who, dismissing the classical Greek philosophy as the product of heathenism, warned the faithful against having anything to do with such snares. The Greek and Egyptian Fathers, on the other hand, brought up as they were in a tradition of philosophising at Alexandria, continued not merely to study classical thought but to ransack it for evidence of divine inspiration. In this task they often exercised great ingenuity. Among the ancient philosophers Plato received particular homage at their hands; it was even declared that he had derived much of his inspiration from the Old Testament; and some apologists—Justin the Martyr, for example—went so far as to assert that Plato, Heraclitus and Socrates, by ordering their lives according to the Divine Reason, had deserved salvation as much as any Christian convert, and more than some of them. Nor must we assume that the classical philosophy ceased, upon the coming of Christianity, to play an important part in the speculations of intelligent men. It continued to undergo development; and one of the principal lines of this development, the school of Neoplatonism, founded by Plotinus (A.D. 200-289) of Lycopolis in Egypt, influenced Christian thought in the most profound manner. Of Neoplatonism it has been observed that it formed "the last will and testament" of pagan thought. Even so, its bequests were many and fruitful.

There was a further reason why Greek philosophy and the Christian faith tended to exert a mutual attraction. Of all the religions of the east, that of the Hebrews had been most permeated by the influence of Greek thought. And in certain respects the essence of Judaism and of Greek philosophy bore a remarkable resemblance one to the other. Common to both outlooks, for instance, was a very strong ethical leaning. The God of the Hebrews, as distinct from the gods of other peoples, even of neighbouring peoples, was represented as being great and deserving of worship, not because he was powerful but because he was righteous. As far as we can see, this conception of the righteousness and justice of Jehovah is as old as the Hebrew religion itself: but it acquired greater significance and dynamism in proportion as the material fortunes of Israel were brought low, as happened during the Assyrian invasions of the eighth to the sixth centuries B.C. Later, too, when other Semitic gods of Syria were being ousted by the Hellenic figures of Zeus, Athens, Apollo and Aphrodite, the reputation of Jehovah suffered no equivalent eclipse among his devotees;

the conflict with Hellenism served merely to strengthen their respect for the Divine Law. But, in spite of its multitude of gods, which contrasted sharply with the staunch monotheism of the Hebrews, Hellenism had likewise exhibited a concern, almost an obsession, with problems of human conduct; and thus the two currents of thought, the Hellenic and the Hebraic, ran parallel and sometimes even converged. For in spite of the popular idea of the Greek imagination as peopled with gods and goddesses, the idea of one supreme deity was as essential to Greek as to Hebrew thought.

In the second place, Judaism had evolved in the course of its history a highly specialised notion of Wisdom embodied in a sacred literature which originated about 200 B.C. and succeeded that of the Hermetic Books. In this literature the whole work of creation was pictured as having been achieved by a Divine Intelligence, which had communicated to every existing thing its nature, its laws and its goal. Such a creative principle of Wisdom (Sophia) is indeed hinted at in the last of the Hermetic Books (which were presumably written between 500 and 200 B.C.), where it is actually referred to as the "Logos", or principle whereby things are constituted as they are: "earth and water no one could discern, yet were they moved to hear by reason of the Logos pervading them"— "a Holy Logos descended on that Nature", etc. Here we clearly observe the influence of Greek thinkers; but although the use of Greek terminology was not unnatural at this time, the tradition which it clothed was authentically Hebrew. Finally, the task of interpreting the Old Testament in the light of Greek philosophy was undertaken by a contemporary of Jesus, Philo of Alexandria, a Jewish theologian whose doctrine of the Logos was far more elaborate than that of the Hermetic writings. Possibly under the influence of the teaching of the Essenes, Philo refers to the Logos as the "first-born son of God" or the "second God", thereby pointing the way to the "word made flesh" of the Fourth Gospel.

God and Man in Neoplatonism

The Greek word Logos, which first appears in Heraclitus, means a great deal more than just "word" or "principle". It carries with it the notion of a principle of reason or creativeness, whereby a multiplicity of things are able to exist in organic unity. To the early Greek philosophers the problem of how natural phenomena can be diverse and yet form a world—how unity can persist throughout diversity and diversity become articulate within a unity—was a very perplexing one: and they attempted to solve it in a great variety of ways. The problem is likewise present in the work of Plato and Aristotle, the word Logos being used by Plato to refer to that principle which, out of its own single nature, can produce the variety of creation, or at least its ideal counterpart. Now we have already had occasion to observe that whereas both Plato and Aristotle formulated exalted notions of God and His wisdom, neither the one nor the other was able to show satisfactorily how this wisdom became *incarnate* in creation. To Plato God was the servant of the Forms, and the Forms subsisted in a world beyond the reach of created things, even though the latter yearned in imitative passion towards them. As for Aristotle, God was a model of perfection, which compelled attention and notice from the world but remained indifferent to its own influence therein. Neoplatonism, likewise, conceiving of God in even more transcendental terms, located Him as far above the Forms as the Forms were located above man: so that man's apprehension of the Divine Nature could at best be dim and fleeting, and a process of intense self-discipline and purgation was necessary even to achieve the elements of sanctity. In the work of the successors of Plotinus, especially that of Porphyry, Jamblichus and Proclus, the Neoplatonic doctrines were used to sustain a desperate rearguard action on behalf of paganism against the increasing influence of the Christian faith, and during the brief reign of Julian the Apostate (A.D. 361-363), a Christian by upbringing but a pagan by taste, this reaction took practical form. Nevertheless, the Neoplatonic emphasis upon faith as that which apprehends the infinite, to be distinguished from perception or knowledge of the finite, was in a sense nearer to the Christian doctrines which it opposed than to the classical doctrines which it upheld. The Neoplatonic doctrine of divine emanations, however, encouraged the revival of polytheism and its attendant mysteries of sorcery, magic and the exorcism of spirits. With the details of these abstruse philosophies (which were summarily put an end to in 529, when Justinian closed the school at Athens where Proclus had lectured) we are not here concerned. What we ought to emphasise is the fact that the Neoplatonists developed the ideas of Plato in such a way that the relation between God and man, instead of becoming more explicable, proved increasingly mysterious. Jamblicus especially goes to great trouble to show that God, by reason of His utter supremacy, is a Being with whom we can establish no communication whatever. Such infinite aloofness was supposed to enhance His majesty. That mystical ideas of this kind should have been combined with dubious practices of theurgy, thereby suggesting a more material attitude to divinity, is not so paradoxical as might be supposed: for into the yawning gap subsisting between man and God the Neoplatonists projected a vast realm of spiritual entities or intelligences, through whose mediation some indirect contact could be made with the Most High. Moreover, these divinities, especially the lowest or immanent "gods of the world", were such as might be placated and prevailed upon by methods which, whatever their legitimacy, had not been found ineffective by man in his dealings with his fellows.

The Collapse of the Roman World

When historians and other writers, including some theologians, describe the first few centuries of the Christian era as dark, and represent the world in which the early Christian philosophers lived as a world rapidly falling into decay, they sometimes suggest that what was happening was a collapse of the Roman imperial system before the inroads of barbarians. In other words, they think of the Decline and Fall of the Roman Empire as due primarily to a failure on the part of the Roman legions to defend the *limes*, or imperial frontiers. Gibbon looked at the matter differently; for although he suggests, and does his best to prove, that the weakness was caused by the gradual triumph of Christianity, thereby implying that the Christian faith was the chief agent of corruption,[1] he at least recognises that what causes a civilisation to change its nature is not a material catastrophe, such as a series of military reverses, but the disintegration of a system of belief—in this case Roman paganism—and the will to sustain it. The so-called "barbarians" who overthrew "decadent" Rome were usually persons who had acquired, after many years' service in or at the head of the legions (which in Africa, for instance, knew no colour-bar), both a considerable smattering of Roman culture and a familiarity with civilised life. Rome was conquered by Romans, Romans in the sense in which Rome understood the term—Roman citizenship being conferred upon aliens as the result of distinguished public service (twenty years in the case of the army)—not in the topographical sense of modern times. Furthermore, it would be equally inaccurate to say that the "barbarian invasion" was something of which Rome was entirely conscious. There were occasions when she readily, and as it were innocently, came to terms with the invader, as when a treaty was made at Hippo with Genseric, the Vandal chief, in 435: but in the latter case she supposed herself to be making concessions to a somewhat impulsive rebel instead of conferring official recognition upon the aggressive designs of a formidable rival. Thus it may be said with truth that the

[1] His actual words are "the triumph of Christianity and barbarism".

Roman Empire, which had built up a political organisation stretching from the Atlantic and the North Sea to the River Nile, perished from forces at work within rather than without. The ancient world collapsed—if the rather violent metaphor may be excused—because the inhabitants of that world ceased to have faith in the way of life in which they had been educated. And a people ceases to have faith in the way of life in which it has been educated not so much because it dislikes that way of life as because it finds it inadequate to cope with the new problems that have arisen. It is gradually perceived to be impotent, and therefore no longer worth defending.

Now we have already observed that civilisation is both a matter of thought and a matter of will. As a matter of thought it provides a pattern of ideas which dictates the way of life a people shall endeavour to lead; as a matter of will, it provides the faith whereby that endeavour is sustained. This thought and this will need not necessarily be conscious in everybody, and certainly not in everybody to the same degree; the great majority of people will pursue their various callings in ignorance, or in only very partial knowledge, of what it is that they are engaged in upholding. A man may live a life of virtue without ever having opened a book on ethics or ever having known that such a subject exists; and conversely, a man may devote the whole of his life to the study of moral problems without in any way increasing in moral stature. Similarly, a man may prove himself an expert in financial matters and even acquire control of vast commercial enterprises without ever having acquainted himself with a single economic theory; and conversely, a man may write twenty books on finance without developing the smallest capacity to make money, least of all from his writings on the subject. These paradoxes are common in every walk of life, but they do not invalidate theoretical discussion, nor do they provide an excuse for us to renounce the attempt to systematise our experiences. In times of crisis—the word itself means "judgment"—the necessity for explanation and reflection becomes obvious; it is when the machine breaks down that we rummage feverishly for the instruction-book, which we thereupon regret that we had not kept by us or consulted more frequently. No one can learn to compose music as the direct result of studying harmony and counterpoint; but he can on occasion discover from such study where he has made mistakes and thereby equip himself to avoid future ones. And even if we feel able to carry on our particular line of action without understanding the theoretical basis of it, we are glad always to know that there are some people who have made it their business to examine this basis and to whom we may make application in case of difficulty. If, therefore, there is any justification at all for the existence and maintenance of a so-called "intellectual class", this surely is it. And if there is such a thing as "higher education," this surely is its primary concern.

The New Answer to an Old Question

Looking back upon the era immediately preceding the birth of Christ and comparing it with that which witnessed the gradual triumph of Christianity not merely as a privately-held faith but as the official philosophy of a new world-order, we are able to perceive how this decisive event caused what may be called a liquidation of the old order, especially in the realm of thought. To say that paganism was "going to pieces" may sound unduly rhetorical. But in a sense it was. There was a rapid multiplication of sects, a spiritual fission, and a proliferation of pagan deities which, had it continued at the same pace, must have produced untold anarchy and irretrievable disorder in both thought and action. Naturally it will be pointed out that such a vision of the disintegration of the pagan world is as "subjective" as those which we have ourselves cited for rejection. It is the point of view upon which we have been educated. It is the past seen from our standpoint. That is so. But it is more than that. It is the point of view upon which the whole of western civilisation has been brought up; and the question is whether we appreciate the consequences of its abandonment, conscious or otherwise. Let us repeat that we are not here asking whether Christ's claim to be the son of God was or was not true. We are approaching the problem historically: that is to say, we are pointing out that the early Fathers and their successors were convinced that the coming of Christ was not merely a new departure in history but the human manifestation of the Logos—the "word made flesh"—which "made sense" of the old Greek problem of the relation between God and the world, and which, on the side of Hebrew Messianic tradition, formed the culmination of all that the prophets had foretold. The Incarnation was the solution to a problem. By it man's salvation was achieved not only because his soul was given the chance of deliverance but also because his intellect was simultaneously liberated from an intolerable burden. Here, as we shall see, was the answer which Plato and Aristotle had sought but failed to give.

When we speak of "thinking historically", therefore, we are not engaged in an activity wherein truth has no place; we are engaged in an enquiry into the reasons why certain people thought as they did and how they came to think it. The conventional limitation of history to political, or, as a concession, "social" history, has tended to obscure the fact that thought itself has a history, which is precisely the history of man's thought about himself and his world. The "events" described in history books—the battles, Cabinet changes, legal enactments, and so on—are simply the "shell" of history, the outside covering which we must penetrate or interpret in order to arrive at the thoughts of those concerned in their making. A mere list of events, chronologically arranged, is, as the name would imply, a chronicle: a man who thus sets it

E

down, a chronicler. The true historian, furthermore, is not simply a man who interprets or vivifies a chronicle: he is a man to whom a chronicle is one among many other sources of evidence, all of which he uses as aids to a better knowledge of what men in the past have thought. Nor is the past to which he turns a world cut off or divorced from his own: it is that which, if properly interpreted, gives meaning to his present standpoint—a standpoint which, as we have already observed, is at every moment linking him with the past by becoming one with it. An historian is a man who is trying to make sense of his own present by apprehending that which has given rise to it.

What Was the Christian "Faith"?

To students of theology the resemblance—which is much more than a mere verbal resemblance—between the opening of the book of Genesis and that of the Fourth Gospel is a commonplace. "In the beginning God created the heaven and the earth" is paralleled by "In the beginning was the Word and the Word was with God and the Word was God". Separated by hundreds of years, these two accounts of what took place "in the beginning", or how there came to be a beginning at all, are not without profound philosophical significance. The first embodies the Hebrew creation-myth, making it clear that God created the world; the second, defining creation in a more specialised sense, appears at first sight to invest the idea with unnecessary complications. On the question of precisely how much is owed to Greek thought by the writer of the Fourth Gospel, experts have differed in the past:[1] but no one can doubt that the references to the Word or Logos are introduced not with a view to displaying the writer's learning or familiarity with current jargon, but because he wanted to interpret the Christian revelation in

[1] Cf. *The Gospel according to John*, by C. Campbell Morgan (1933), p. 20.

terms which his contemporaries might be expected most easily to understand. They had learned to debate the nature of the world and its origin in precisely such language; and it was to demonstrate the relevance of the Christian faith to an age-old problem that the writer, whoever he may have been, chose thus to introduce his gospel.

The Christian affirmation that there was one God, that He created the world, and that He had revealed Himself to men in the person of His Son, was therefore made the basis for a new form of thought. The gospel, or good news (announced as being imminent first by the angels to the wise men[1]), was something more than the formal answer to an abstract question that the pagan world had asked but failed to solve; it was the foundation of a new order of thought and therefore, in its practical bearing, a new order of civilisation. The author of the Fourth Gospel is quite clear about what he wants to demonstrate. Having outlined his thesis in the first twenty chapters or so he proceeds to make a statement (chapter 29, verses 30 and 31) which, though it resembles a parenthesis, is really an explanation of his aim in writing. He has already spoken of various "signs"—that is, proofs—which Jesus gave "in the presence of the disciples": and he goes on to tell us that he has selected these signs from "many others" in order that "ye may believe that *Jesus is the Christ*, the Son of God and that believing ye may have life in his name".

Cursorily read, it might appear that the first part of this statement is a tautology. But it is quite the reverse. What the writer is asserting is that in Jesus we have the personification or manifestation of the Logos: not merely the fulfilment of the law of the Hebrew tradition, but the incarnation, or living embodiment, of the Greek notion of a creative principle. The second part of the statement deals with the consequences which an acceptance of this belief must logically entail. To

[1] And announced in the same terms, if we are to judge by the Greek text.

believe that the Logos, having taken human form, has "dwelt among us" is to open the way to a new kind of life. In metaphysical terms this means that a new pattern of thought, accepted by our intellects, becomes the foundation of a new kind of civilisation—a new way not merely of thinking about the world but of living in a world thus made intelligible: "both a new world and an old made explicit"[1]. Henceforth, the writer seems to say, we shall think within these categories: our science, our art, and our conduct will be conditioned by the acceptance of certain dogmas, the truth of which we shall assume to be a matter of faith. This faith is open not to any one nation or people but to all mankind. Its thought will be catholic.[2]

The introduction at this point of the word "dogma" (to say nothing of "catholic") may be regarded as an ominous sign, indicating for some people that (to use the slang phrase) "the worst has occurred". The objection to the use of the word "dogma" in connection with religion may be voiced both by enemies of religion and by those who claim to be its friends. That religion becomes dead or pernicious as soon as it assumes dogmatic presentation is a view to which many people have subscribed: it being suggested by persons of considerable eminence, especially in the academic world, that a return to religion, if desirable, must be conditional upon the wholesale abandonment of what is called the "dogmatic element" in its make-up. To give but one out of many possible instances, we may cite a little work by Professor John Macmurray, entitled *The Structure of Religious Experience* (1936), wherein it is suggested that if religion is to be of any use to society it must become "empirically minded". "Religion", says Professor Macmurray, "stands at the crossroads", waiting

[1] T. S. Eliot: *Burnt Norton* (II) (from "Four Quartets").

[2] Cf. Christopher Dawson: *Progress and Religion*, Conclusion: "A new *kind* of life has inserted itself into the cosmic process at a particular point in time under definite historical circumstances and has become the principle of a new order of spiritual progress".

presumably for men like Professor Macmurray—who has been stationed on point duty near that spot for some years now—to wave it on to the main highway of science. This repeated emphasis upon *experience* is worth pondering; for the question that next arises is whether, in religion or art or indeed any sphere whatever, the experimental or emotional aspect can be enjoyed apart from the intellectual discipline that goes with it, for without this discipline it ceases to be an element in a coherent form of thought. This intellectual content is not to be confused with the "rationalisation" of the emotional element: it is that on account of which the emotion has been released. If the experience were nothing more than a matter of feeling, which no experience ever is, the subject would never have come up for debate: for, as we have seen already, my feelings *qua* feelings are private to myself—there is no sense in arguing about them or about anybody else's. The alternative to making religion (or science or art, for that matter) mean what you like is to make it mean what it has come to mean historically as a result of the decisions and speculations of those most concerned with its development. In the case of the Christian religion—or, as it is more correctly called, the Christian Faith—we must preface our generalisations upon its nature by enquiring what its earliest advocates thought about it, and how their pronouncements underwent modification or elucidation at the hands of successors. The phrase "return to religion", if it has any meaning at all, must be understood in this sense alone: not as a revival of the dogmatic element, still less as the abandonment of it, but as a research into the meaning of the dogmas themselves. This is a historical enquiry.

People who are quite content with asserting that they have "their own religion" would be highly indignant with anybody who was rash enough to maintain that he had "his own science". Of course, people may well have certain feelings as to what they suppose religion to be, as they have their own notions about "the glamour of the East" or "how the rich live"; but day-dreams are not realities, and we are concerned here with historical facts, not fancies. Reality is not the same thing as "the present", a mere abstract "now"; it is a "now" and a "then" united in an act of historical vision.

Why Religion?

Even if religion is admitted to be more than a private matter ("what a man does with his solitude", in Whitehead's unfortunate definition[1]), the objection may well be advanced that the public record of religion, however charitably examined, has left much to be desired. And there will be many who, while ready to admit that religion has "played a big part" in the events of the past, cannot see what light it has to throw upon the structure of civilisation, particularly civilisation as at present constituted. Why drag it in at all? Was not Comte right when he declared that religion was simply a "phase" through which humanity, struggling to free itself from superstition and unreason, had, or should by now have, passed? The problem for our time, it may be said, is surely not a religious problem but a political or sociological problem: how, among other things, to organise society on a basis of security and peace for all men of whatever race and creed. That, surely, is the kind of catholicism of which we stand in need today.

It will be clear from what has been said in the preceding paragraphs that this is a view to which exception is being taken. In the first place, it is based upon a misunderstanding, though an exceedingly common misunderstanding, of the nature of religion. Religion is a subject which lends itself to a variety of speculation not so much because men agree as to what it is as because they tacitly assume that, no such general agreement being possible, they are entitled to understand by

[1] See his *Religion in the Making*.

it more or less what they like. Thus it is easier to acquire a reputation as a publicist today by surrendering oneself wholeheartedly to one creed after another, than by adhering to the same creed: the former habit being called "the quest for truth" and the latter being regarded as equivalent to mental stagnation.

In rejecting the view that religion is irrelevant to civilisation and even inimical to its development, it is easy to fall back upon a conception of religion no less open to criticism. This is the view, advanced by certain disillusioned liberal thinkers, that religion—any religion, if it is sufficiently respectable—is "necessary to the maintenance of civilisation". The kind of religion which is "necessary to the maintenance of civilisation" usually turns out to be either a spiritual Stakhanov or Bedaux system, useful in keeping the machine and its minders going at full pressure, or the motive-force behind a cleverly organised "courtesy campaign", designed to smooth over the acerbities of industrial life and class-conflict, and to reconcile the badgered and lonely individual to his lot. Always we are given the impression that if things had been working as well as had been hoped, such first-aid treatment would never have been prescribed. It is the recourse to a desperate remedy, much as a chronic sufferer, despairing of medical practitioners, might seek the aid of faith-healers and spiritualists.

There is no doubt that it is sometimes easier to be lucid and expansive on a subject that one does not wholly understand than on a subject that one does: a series of abstract generalisations, provided that it is delivered in suitably solemn tones, can be prolonged almost indefinitely, winning respectful attention from thousands who, if challenged to explain precisely what impresses them, would be hard put to it to give an answer. Certain highly spiritual forms of religion, of which examples need hardly be given, have been kept alive more because the earnest devotee lives in hopes that they may eventually turn out to mean something coherent than because they have already afforded him enlightenment; they "have a message", but it has not yet been deciphered. Similarly, when people talk of religion as necessary to the maintenance of civilisation, it is clear that most of them possess no coherent notion of what the civilisation is that needs to be maintained. If it is material wealth or invention, how can religion sustain it? If, on the other hand, it is something immaterial or spiritual, how can it be dissociated from religion itself?

The answer is that it cannot. We have already spoken of civilisation in terms of thought and will; and it is now time to explain how the will to civilisation—or, as we have put it, the determination to follow a particular way of life—is sustained. It is sustained by the religious faculty of a people, which in practical terms means the institutions which religion creates for the preservation and furtherance of its ideals.[1] These institutions need not necessarily be churches, though it is with churches that the religious faculty is most often or most readily associated. Interestingly enough, the period in history in which religion was most intimately bound up with ecclesiastical institutions, namely the mediæval period, was also that in which it expressed itself in most other institutions as well. We talk of the "ages of faith" precisely because in such ages the faith was able to express itself through a greater variety of channels, and in more direct fashion, than at any time before or since.

To talk of a faculty of the mind as engaged in "creating" institutions through which to express itself may sound a trifle obscurantist. But what is here being asserted of religion is true, *mutatis mutandis*, of any other rational faculty of which we like to think. Man's political and economic activities likewise create the institutions through which to express themselves: for it is hardly necessary to point out that a social institution—such as a bank, a college, a club or even a State— is not the same thing as the personnel of which it is composed,

[1] Cf. Croce: *Philosophy of the Practical*, translated Ainslie, p. 542.

still less the buildings, the archives or the financial resources connected with it; it is the collective will of its members to associate themselves in this particular manner for this particular purpose, and to maintain that association in face of opposition from both without and within. From within, because an individual may try to cheat by permitting one loyalty to override another. To protest that the existence of fixed institutions is likely to do positive harm to certain activities, particularly religious ones, is usually to go off and establish other institutions dedicated at the outset to the propagation of a purer and less torpid faith, but doomed, from the moment this propagation becomes methodical and successful, to harden into organisations no less rigid and hidebound than those from which secesssion originally took place.

Nevertheless, the question remains as to why the way of life that we call civilisation should depend for its preservation and stimulus upon the religious institutions of a society—and not, for instance, upon the political or economic institutions? To express the point somewhat frivolously: why the Church of England rather than the Bank of England? The answer may seem slightly paradoxical: it is because religion is a matter of faith, and because religious institutions exist for the purpose of sustaining faith in a creed which, though couched in semi-symbolic terms, contains the principles whereby we propose to live. These principles, being metaphysical, are the foundation of ordered knowledge. Ordered knowledge is another word for science, and the corpus of science (manifested not only in technical achievement but in such things as codes of behaviour) is what we mean by civilisation.

Theology and Metaphysics

We are thus brought back to what was said above about the Fourth Gospel, and in particular about the necessity for understanding, if not necessarily endorsing, the views of the

E*

early-Christian theologians as to what they believed an acceptance of the Christian revelation to entail. Only those whose historical vision is restricted, or who understand by religion something for which history provides no sanction, are likely summarily to dismiss a view according to which religion is the sustainer rather than the enemy of science. Nor should it be necessary to stress that this broad use of the word science, to which we have several times had recourse, is not a wilful departure from established usage: it is a return, for purposes which should be clear, to the usage of the era about which we are speaking. The differentiation of science into autonomous sciences, each claiming its own "view of the universe", took place as late as the nineteenth century, and philosophers like Kant and Hegel knew of only one science apart from that of philosophy, namely, natural science.[1] The use of the word religion, however, calls for somewhat more considered treatment. To talk of religion inevitably means to talk of theology, and the reader may well be asking wherein theology, according to the system of terminology here adopted, differs from metaphysics.

For Aristotle, let it be said at once, there was no difference at all: no difference, first, because he did not call his book "metaphysics"—his editors did; and secondly, because the central theme of that book was God. Now we have already pointed out that whereas Aristotle postulated a God, he did not conceive of that God as a being to be worshipped; he constructed a theology, but he failed to create a religion. And therein lies the distinction between theology and religion: the one is primarily intellectual, the other primarily emotional. It is a commonplace that a man can be intensely religious without possessing the slightest knowledge of theology; and it is probably inevitable, as it is certainly desirable, that the average community should contain few

[1] Cf. A. D. Lindsay, *Kant*, p. 16, and Ruggiero, *Modern Philosophy*, trans. Collingwood (1920), p. 378.

persons capable of theological speculation, and these need
not necessarily be the most devout. Nor can a man be expected
to be a theologian all the time, whereas to be religious by
spasms is not usually regarded as one way among others of
being religious. An early distinction between religion and
theology was that put forward by Origen, who pointed out
that whereas the writers of the gospels had compiled in a
language that all could understand, their successors had been
gifted by the Holy Spirit with the wit to discover reasons for
these doctrines. The apostles were not theologians (though
the author of the Fourth Gospel certainly was); the Fathers
were. Metaphysics ceased to be identified with theology only
when the Absolute of the philosophers ceased to be identified
with God: and it is not without interest to observe that, once
this identity was questioned (as it was at the close of the Middle
Ages), metaphysics begins to lose cast in favour of physical
science, which takes as its absolute not God but Nature. Nor
has metaphysics, in spite of several minor "come backs",
ever succeeded in re-establishing the reputation which, as the
intellectual ally of religion, it formerly enjoyed. In tracing
the history of metaphysical problems, therefore, we trace the
struggle and partial failure of metaphysics to keep its end up
in a world salaaming before the technical achievements of
science. Although the reaction against science as a kind of
substitute for religion and philosophy set in among a minority
many years ago—chiefly when the idea of progress was first
questioned—public alarm has perhaps reached its peak with
the practical demonstration of the effects of nuclear fission.
It needs a jog, or even an explosion, in the world of action for
certain preconceived ideas to be discredited in the public
mind; and clearly this has happened in our day, so that 1945
may well prove to be as decisive a date in history as 1859, the
year of the publication of Darwin's theory of Evolution.
Hence the present-day public is likely to take kindlier to
metaphysics than the preceding generation, which was taught

by its mentors to believe that such a form of enquiry was non-sensical. It will then be realised that the distinction between metaphysics and theology is a distinction without a difference. And if the upshot of the philosophies of Whitehead and Alexander (to be discussed in Part IV) is not that these two forms of enquiry are at bottom the same, then it is difficult to see of what value their systems can have been.

The reader need not be put off with this conclusion on the ground that he, or the kind of philosophy to which he subscribes, leaves no room for a God and therefore cannot admit the possibility of there being such a study as theology. It is natural, though not inevitable, that we should think of God in terms of Christianity or at least of the so-called Higher Religions; but (to take a modern example) the materialist's Matter in which dialectical changes occur *ex nihilo*, is no less a deity—hence the immense bulk of the "theological" literature, suitably pontifical in expression and austere in tone, that has recently grown up around it. The appearance of dogma, however subtly disguised in scientific terminology, is a sure sign of the emergence of a new religion; and if the search is conducted with sufficient energy, the presiding deity will eventually be located even if, as happened with the Wizard of Oz, the approach is made by way of the effects-room instead of the sanctuary.

Religion and Society

To summarise what has been said in the course of the preceding paragraphs: religion is not something "necessary to the maintenance of civilisation", as so many modern apologists appear to believe, still less a useful weapon in the hands of the ruling classes, as the Marxians believe, and least of all a private consolation or sedative, as the crowding out of religion from public life has led many sincere devotees to believe, but rather the source of all civilised activity, the stimulus and inspiration of all reflective thought, the promoter rather than the enemy of science. And it follows in consequence that of all the solvents of society, hostility to religion is that which is least to be feared: what needs to be guarded against is indifference, that wrecker of dynasties. This is, no doubt, the reason why all the great social movements of the last 150 years—Fourierism, Saint-Simonism, Owenism, Marxism, Guild Socialism and even Fabianism—have been parasitic upon the religion which in most cases (there are exceptions like Christian Socialism) they pretended to attack: why, in order to maintain their vitality, they have themselves usurped the functions and even the terminology of religion; why, finally, indifference to religion has been accompanied by indifference to, and impoverishment of, the fundamental instinct of procreation, about which alarm is expressed by few save professional economists. To grasp the true nature of religion, therefore, is to perceive that human society, however "pagan" its government and governing classes, is essentially a religious creation, and that the attempt, so often envisaged, to construct what is sometimes called a scientific society, or technocracy, is to forget that creatures and not cogs will be obliged to live in it. It is to perceive, too, that there is no specifically "religious" form of government as opposed to a pagan form, except in so far as one form of government is better adapted to religious observance than another. But we must not necessarily assume that those nations in which such religious observance is tolerated (which may mean no more than that it is regarded as "harmless"), or in which an established church gives religion the stamp of respectability, are in fact more religious, in the sense in which the term is here being used, than those where, for one reason or another, it lacks these privileges. Man is a religious animal; he is religious even in his denial of religion; for you can fight religion only with its own weapons.

Religion is a stage in the development of self-consciousness—

the stage in which man first becomes conscious of himself as a thinking and acting being. Casting aside his dreams he becomes for the first time conscious of isolation; but whereas our artistic imagination urges us to dream and only indirectly promotes action in the social sphere, religion urges us to fulfil our dreams. Consequently the religious imagination provides the stimulus to forms of striving and endeavour that, but for its influence, would never have operated with quite that degree of intensity. If it is asked what keeps a society alive (a question that troubles most people but once or twice in a lifetime), the answer is the belief of individuals that their society is worthy of preservation; and this means not so much a positive and conscious volition as a reluctance to abandon without a struggle certain traditions, or (more commonly still) to see their abandonment by other people. To take a somewhat conventional example: a man may not go to church himself and may boast of his freethinking and broadmindedness; but he may insist upon his children going. Again, he will lie like a trooper; but he will thrash his child like a trooper for doing the same thing. This is not because he thinks he knows how to lie cleverly, whereas his children do not; it is because he knows in his heart of hearts that children should not be brought up to lie, at least while they are incapable of exercising free choice. They are not old enough. And this is an admission, or a recognition, that society cannot carry on without rules and traditions; and it represents at the same time an excuse for his own divagations, because a master of the art of lying is the least proselytising of men. It being to his interest that as much truth shall be told as possible by other people, he seeks no converts. Vice is not the enemy of virtue, but the speculator in it.

Conclusion

The point that we have been trying to make in the present chapter is that western civilisation in its prevailing form, assuming that it has not already turned into something else, derives its structure or pattern from a metaphysical decision arrived at after great labour and deliberation by the founders and fathers of the early Christian church. This metaphysical analysis, a specimen of which we have drawn from the Fourth Gospel, was not something worked out at leisure or in the seclusion of priories or monasteries; it was hammered out, as it were, in the market place. Nor did it go unchallenged for more than a few years at a time. It was always being challenged, as a study of the multifarious heresies of those and later times will show. And it is being challenged today: the ancient heresies are constantly reappearing, are indeed always operating beneath the surface, exerting a tension in social life of which men are unconscious only because they have become so accustomed to its pressure and strain. Now, in consequence of this new metaphysical view of the world, the scientific tradition of Europe was initiated and promoted, until, with time, this tradition became for most people the distinguishing characteristic of European civilisation, which was (and is) frequently contrasted with the inert and unprogressive civilisations of the East. And the superiority of the one over the others was regarded as having been proved by the fact that European civilisation, after a bad setback at the time of the Moslem invasions, began in the sixteenth century to expand with the rapid advance of its technical skill over a great part of the globe, thereby proving the truth of Bacon's statement that "science is power". To maintain that the civilisation of Christendom has been the promoter and guardian of science does not mean that the actual members of the ecclesiastical hierarchy have always been well disposed towards scientists. There have been notorious scandals in this respect, just as there have been similar scandals in the world of education and even in that of science itself; but, as we have already pointed out, the temptation to erect a rule upon the exceptions must be resolutely avoided. The reason why Greek science failed to achieve results beyond a certain point, or rather, why it failed to break out of its circle of theorising, is that it was based, as we have shown, upon an unresolved dualism between nature and God—a fissure which runs throughout Greek religion, giving rise to a continuous struggle between monotheistic and polytheistic conceptions (nature being either a living spirit or a world of living spirits, the Greeks were never quite sure which). The Christian faith in one God, who was also, through the medium of His Son, the creator of the world, cleared up not merely the religious dilemma but the scientific dilemma. The belief in one God entailed the belief that the created world was also One and not, as an element in Greek tradition had continued to assert, Many. Consequently, science, instead of being a series of unrelated "techniques" corresponding to the different rites associated with the gods of Greek mythology, became a unified system of thought. But not a system of thought alone. This thought was not abstract but concrete; the World had been made flesh. Hence the new science that sprang up possessed the characteristics not merely of universality but of practicality. The order of the cosmic process, which the Greeks regarded as mirrored in the movement of the heavenly bodies, became manifested in the historical process; and thus the Hebrew idea of history as embodying a moral purpose was vindicated, at least to those who accepted the Christian revelation: which enough people eventually did to unify so heterogeneous an area as Europe.

Some critics may affirm that the "oneness" of science (if not of God) is too obvious to need stressing; but the prevalence of this belief today means not that the early Christian theologians were talking platitudes but that their victory over pagan thought was more decisive than we sometimes realise. Not that it was final; no intellectual victory ever is. But, like the author of the Fourth Gospel, these men knew what they wanted to prove; and the principles they laid down in their day are still the basis, however threatened, of our way of ordering our thought and lives. Georges Sorel, the French writer, remarks in his forgotten book, *The Illusions of Progress*, that religions will always present a dilemma to the intellectualist or humanist because he can bring himself neither to accept them as true nor to deny their great historical significance. The historian—and every metaphysician must be a historian—is obliged to recognise the fact that particular religions have not merely influenced the course of history but actually changed it. As St. Gregory Nyssen declared: "The Incarnate Word unites the universe to Himself, bringing in His own Person *the different kinds of existing things to one accord and harmony*."[1] At the conclusion of Part III we shall take up this theme afresh.

NOTE.—Those for whom the trend of thought in the above section presents difficulties, by reason of its unfamiliarity, are recommended to read the excellent translation of the *De Incarnatione Verbi Dei* of St. Athanasius, published in 1944 by Geoffrey Bles, with a preface by C. S. Lewis. The following passage is especially relevant: "The objects of worship formally were varied and countless; each place had its own idol and the so-called god of one place could not pass over to another in order to pursuade the people there to worship him, but was barely reverenced even by his own. Nobody worshipped his neighbour's god, but every man had his own idol and thought that it was the lord of all. But now Christ alone is worshipped, as One and Same among all peoples everywhere; and what the feebleness of idols could not do, namely, convince even those dwelling close at hand, He has effected" (p. 84).

---

[1] *Cat. Discourse*, Cap. XXXII (my italics).

PART III

The Metaphysical Background of Modern Thought

I

The Rationalist Attack on Scepticism

Aristotle and Mediæval Thought

We now come to the third stage in our enquiry. In this section we propose to take up again some of the problems treated in Part I, and to examine them afresh in the light of the conclusions reached on the subject of metaphysics in Part II. It is because the metaphysical basis of such problems is seldom studied or even suspected that the theory of perception often strikes the student as uncommonly dull and abstract: whereas it should be the stepping-stone to all the major issues in philosophy, which are dull only to dull people and a matter of indifference only to indifferent people. In the meantime, however, we have learnt something of the nature of metaphysics and have agreed to define it as an enquiry into the presuppositions upon which men, and groups of men called societies, base their ideas about the world. This means that in our examination of the metaphysical background of modern thought we shall be trying to discern the pattern of modern civilisation.

It must not be supposed that this pattern, if we can trace it, will be clear and obvious in all its points, or that it forms a kind of static matrix in which man deploys his nature and pursues his various activities. The pattern is susceptible to strain and severe distortion, as the forces making for a different configuration perpetually work out their influence.

Thus it is not so much the "march of events" that the historian studies as a mêlée in which he endeavours to observe the directions in which the various combatants are moving, and who is on whose side. Such a task requires a particular kind of insight and training, because historical vision, far from being equivalent to watching a procession, is an imaginative reconstruction from evidence, every piece of which requires interpretation in the light of all that the historian knows.[1] To this characteristic of the pattern we shall return in Part III, Chapter III.

In our references to Plato's theory of the Forms we dwelt upon the apparent discontinuity between the world of absolute values and the world of sensation. Similarly, in our references to Aristotle's doctrine of God, we emphasised a similar discontinuity, namely, that between God Himself and the world that seeks to emulate Him. As pure intellect God can do what He likes; His activity is capricious. Indeed it appears that, for Aristotle, activity and caprice are bound up with each other. The philosophers of the later Middle Ages, while holding Aristotle in the greatest respect, inevitably interpreted his work in the light of their Christian theological prepossessions. And in any case it must be remembered that the Aristotle of the Middle Ages was very different from the Aristotle of ancient Greece. In some ways he was a new creation. At the beginning of the thirteenth century his works, when known, were little valued. And while in the course of that century a great revival of interest in them took place, giving rise to the production of numerous translations and commentaries, the gist of much of Aristotle's teaching— for instance, his views on physics—was conveyed indirectly by way of the East. Thus Avicenna in Persia (980-1037) and Averroes in Spain (1126-1198) had already written commentaries on Aristotle in the preceding centuries; and some of the first Latin translations of Aristotle were presented to the universities of Oxford, Bologna and Paris by scholars working under the patronage of Roger II of Sicily and the Emperor Frederick II, whose courts were thronged with Eastern scholars. At the beginning of the fourteenth century,

[1] See *The Historical Imagination*, by R. G. Collingwood (Oxford, 1936).

in fact, the Catholic Church, after some initial hesitation, accepted Aristotle almost as an official philosopher, by which time St. Thomas Aquinas (1224-1274) had integrated his thought into a gigantic synthesis of Christian apologetic.

Now the fundamental difference between the Aristotelean and the mediæval view of God was this: whereas the former represented God's activity as wholly capricious, the latter represented it as supremely rational. To Aristotle capriciousness was a characteristic of the subjective world in general—of mind as opposed to nature—and this included the mind of God, or Pure Mind, as well as the mind of man, or finite mind. The reason why the mediæval philosophers credited the human mind with so great a measure of capriciousness was simply that they regarded its activity as severely limited, being susceptible to sin and error, and deprived, at least in its natural state, of divine grace. Thus it was the *passivity* rather than the activity of the mind that made for caprice; and thus the least capricious of beings, namely God, was also the most active and creative. Now in addition to being the Author of the activities of the subjective world, God was conceived by the mediæval theologians as the direct originator of the objective world, or the Author of Nature. Nevertheless, this objective world was not objective in an absolute sense, because, as the creation of God, it depended for its existence upon something other than itself. In this way the only completely objective entity was God, Who was also the only completely subjective entity. The Christian revelation thus provided the world with a new philosophical idea: the idea that man and his natural environment were both necessary, if imperfect, manifestations of the same creative principle. In other words, the Christian, unlike the pagan ascetic, was intended to find his salvation not by renunciation of the world but—initially at least—by realising his kinship with it.

As stated above, the complete formulation of this philosophical view was advanced by St. Thomas. Rejecting the

extravagant fancies of the Neoplatonists St. Thomas sought
to demonstrate that the human spirit, instead of reaching
truth by direct apprehension, needed to "work its passage"
through matter by building up a hierarchy of systematic
sciences of which the highest, theology, should treat of God
Himself. Like the Jewish thinker, Maimonides, who was born
at Cordova in 1135, he sought to reconcile reason and faith
by asserting a reasonable faith; and, like Maimonides again,
he derived his inspiration from the work of Aristotle. By
emphasising man's place in both the natural and spiritual
order he showed how his presence in the universe had given
significance to matter and rendered it for the first time intelligible. The duty of man, he says in effect, is not to reject,
still less to deny, the imperfections and disorder of the world,
but, by using his divine gift of reason (his only authentic
"guidance") to bring it to some sort of order, to work in and
with it, and thus to redeem it along with himself. The Incarnation was a symbol of this idea. Hence the "realism" of the
Thomist philosophy, and the claim advanced that St. Thomas
achieved the final synthesis of Christian teaching not merely
concerning the relation between God and man but concerning
the relation between man and his fellows. This practical attitude to life and mind is something to which modern disciples
draw particular attention; but, by a paradox of history, this
very attitude was responsible for the neglect of certain aspects
of St. Thomas's teaching in the centuries that followed. For
it was during these centuries that Aristotle's views on physics,
which St. Thomas had accepted implicitly, received their
most effective challenge; and when the philosophers endeavoured to come to terms with the new discoveries they
tended to ignore the religious aspects of St. Thomas's teaching
while preserving much of its theoretical structure intact.

Descartes and the New Method

It is important to understand these mediæval ideas concerning God and nature because they set the stage for philosophers such as Descartes (1596-1650), whose methods are held to have inaugurated a new conception of philosophy. That the publication in 1637 of Descartes' *Discourse on Method* forms a landmark in the history of thought has become a textbook commonplace. Nevertheless, we should bear in mind that Descartes was a man of his time, which means a man inheriting a great deal from the immediate past; that the problem which he sought to tackle was set, as we have said, in a context which is recognisably mediæval in character; and that he still adopts much of the terminology of his predecessors, even where he least agrees with their conclusions.

Descartes belongs to the modern world, however, if only because he accepts as a kind of new gospel the doctrine of Galileo that "nature is a book written by God in the language of mathematics", and the similar doctrine of Kepler that "the human mind was made to understand Quantity, just as the eye was made to see colours and the ear to hear sounds". Why, we may ask, did he accept this view? Because he believed not merely that it served to make nature intelligible but that it was directly responsible for the wealth of new discoveries that the physicists of his time were making and were promising to make. In other words, the quantitative approach to nature recommended itself to him not so much on account of its truth as on account of its success. And, as Whitehead has pointed out, "if success be the guarantee of truth, no other system of thought has enjoyed a tithe of such success since mankind started on its job of thinking. Within three hundred years it has transformed human life, in its intimate thoughts, its technologies, its social behaviour, and its ambitions".[1]

In short, Descartes was a mathematician before he was a philosopher but also while he was a philosopher. Of the importance of systematic mathematical reasoning for the

[1] *Adventures of Ideas*, Part II, Chapter VII.

understanding of nature he writes in several famous passages in the *Discourse*: "Above all", he says, "I was delighted with the mathematics on account of the certainty and evidence of their demonstrations, but I have not as yet found out their true use; and although I supposed that they were of service only in the mechanical arts, I was surprised that upon foundations so solid and stable no loftier structure had been raised" (Part I, p. 10). To raise such a structure Descartes proposes to apply to philosophy the method employed with success in geometry; in short, he proposes to advance by the aid of axioms and definitions deduced by reflection not upon the nature of the world but upon the nature of his own mind. He is concerned to establish science not upon some outside authority but upon the inward authority of reason.

Why did Descartes put the problem in this particular manner? The answer has in part already been given: it was because, like the realist philosophers of whom we spoke in Part I, he inherited from mediæval times the distinction between the subjective world of mind and the objective world of nature, both of which were held to be the creation of God. Reflecting upon this distinction Descartes was compelled to ask himself how it was that our minds, as inhabitants of the subjective world, could legitimately claim acquaintance with any other sphere of being? How could we trust the reports and registrations of our senses? The latter so frequently deceived us that it was difficult to see how we could ever be certain of anything at all. The question asked by modern philosophy, therefore, is not so much, Where can wisdom be found? as Where can certainty be found? Philosophy becomes identified with epistemology.

In asking and trying to answer these questions Descartes adopted a method that has been given the name of "methodic doubt". Consequently, the idea has grown up that Descartes, though subscribing to the orthodox beliefs of his day, was covertly promoting scepticism. Nothing could be more untrue. He was concerned with attacking scepticism. Faced with the problem of how we could pass from the subjective world to a knowledge of the objective world, and from both to their creator, God, he set out to resolve the doubts that were growing up in his time—doubts as to the efficacy of both philosophy and science, to which the classic expression had already been given in the works of another Frenchman, Montaigne (1533-1592). And as we have seen from the passage quoted above from the *Discourse*, Descartes believed that he possessed the key to his problem in mathematics, or rather, in the method derived therefrom. But, again, why mathematics? Not simply because he was by training a mathematician, the inspirer of Gassendi, Pascal and Newton, but because this training had shown him, among other things, that mathematical truths were applicable not to one or other sphere of reality, but to all spheres; it was the one universal science. To quote from the *Discourse*: "Those long chains of reasoning, quite simple and easy, which geometers are wont to employ in the accomplishment of their most difficult demonstrations, led me to think that everything which might fall under the cognisance of the human mind might be connected together in the same manner" (Part II, p. 11). Thus Descartes lays bare the presupposition upon which all modern science is founded: the presupposition that, in Whitehead's words,[1] "there is an order of nature which lies open in every detail to human understanding", where, after "human", the word "mathematical" might perhaps be inserted.

The argument that Descartes put forward was that, by examining our minds and their capacities, we could arrive by a process of inference at the idea of God. Having reached this summit we could then descend by another route to the idea of nature. It will do no harm to stress once more the extent to which he accepts the mediæval "setting" of the problem: all he is doing is to suggest a means of finding a way round

[1] *Adventures of Ideas*. Part II, Chapter VIII.

it. He does not cross the stage: he mounts up into the wings.

The philosophical method to which he has recourse, however, occasioned a complete break with mediæval and scholastic tradition. Careful as he was not to lay himself open to the charge of unorthodoxy he was in point of fact challenging one of the fundamental tenets of orthodoxy, namely, authority.[1] To the scholastic philosophers the test of truth was something external: the fallible human mind assented to that which, being outside and objective, provided a criterion of truth more stable than any native powers the mind might possess. The mind's concepts were, in a sense, copies of objective reality: and, as we have seen, the problem both for the mediæval realists and for their later disciples was how this correspondence between ideas and reality could be guaranteed as genuine. Anxious to dispense with the idea of external authority Descartes assumes that the mind, if properly trained, can be shown to possess a kind of original capacity or inner light of its own. This emphasis upon training was important; for Descartes, no less than any mediæval philosopher, was appalled at the mind's tendencies to err. But whereas the mediæval philosophers preached a régime of self-discipline in a moral as well as a mental sense, Descartes advocated the application of a technique of self-criticism. This was a process of subjecting our everyday conceptions to systematic doubt—of calling in question everything that we knew, or thought we knew, both of sense and of reason, until we arrived at an idea which was at once clear, distinct and indubitable. Such a technique of systematic doubt was to be distinguished from what may be called "experimental doubt", which is a state of mind that we do not voluntarily originate.[2] In short, his method of getting rid of scepticism was not the

[1] In 1633 Descartes learnt of Galileo's condemnation and made up his mind not to risk a similar fate.

[2] Cf. *Descartes*, by S. V. Keeling (1934), p. 76.

mediæval one of condemning or excommunicating the sceptic —for that is to get rid of a material not a mental thing—but rather that of taking the sceptic's doctrines at their face value and seeing where an acceptance of them, pushed to the limit, leads you. It led Descartes to the conclusion that this very process of doubting must give rise in the end to a principle of certainty. For if we know that we doubt we are aware of ourselves as engaged in an activity of thought; and if we truly possess such knowledge we possess at the same time and with equal certainty, the knowledge that we, the thinkers, exist. This argument Descartes enshrined in a phrase that has become almost too well known to quote: *Cogito, ergo sum.* We have but to understand this proposition, he maintained, to know that it is true.[1]

In addition to the certain knowledge that we, the doubters, exist, the principle of the *cogito* discloses a further implication of equal, if not superior, importance. Thus a transition is effected from a mere working principle to a metaphysical truth. The consciousness of ourselves as assailed by doubts is also the awareness of certain imperfections inherent in our nature which, though they may be partially overcome, suggest that we are at every moment liable to fall victim to error. Yet, from another and more hopeful point of view, this very consciousness of imperfection, this obsession with our own limitations, proves that we have some acquaintance with perfection in another and superior form, namely, in the being of God. It is the consciousness within ourselves of the reality of such a perfect Being that enables us to appreciate, at least in part, the extent to which we fall short of His excellence. Did we not possess an idea of complete and perfect truth we could not know, still less regret, that we erred. With Descartes the most intensive process of doubt lifts us, by its sheer insistence,

[1] The proof that the criterion of the *cogito* is an induction from a single instance and not a deduction is well stated in W. E. Johnson's *Logic*, Part II, Chapter VIII, paragraphs 4 and 5, and also Spinoza's *Principia philosophiæ Cartesienæ*, 1.

to a conviction of God's reality. We doubt as far down as we can go in order to rise as high as we can conceive.[1]

Meanwhile, what of nature? What of that objective reality which is believed to lie outside the realm of mind? How can we claim acquaintance with such a sphere, seeing that up to now we have confined ourselves to purely internal and subjective speculation?

Unlike his predecessors, the scholastics, Descartes is obliged to deduce the existence of the world of matter from the existence of spirit. The scholastic method, often assumed to be the more "obscure" or "transcendental", started in a much humbler way: it began with the world of nature and then proceeded to work up, through a majestic hierarchy of entities, to a supreme Being. Perched up there in the wings Descartes could not tackle the problem in so pedestrian a fashion. He derives the idea of a material world from the existence of God, and not vice versa.

Of God, the perfect Being, we possess a knowledge as sure as that concerning our existence as thinkers. Now the perfection of God, being self-evident, implies the further certainty that He cannot deceive His creatures. Whatever we find to be clear and distinct in our minds is, in Descartes' view, stamped with God's signature; and therefore our knowledge may be regarded as certain and reliable so long as we confine our attention strictly to clear and distinct ideas. Now it was Descartes' contention that of all the ideas that the mind entertains the most clear and distinct were those of mathematics; and this is the reason why he regarded mathematical knowledge as at once the most certain and universal. One of Descartes' successors, Malebranche (1638-1715), who other-

[1] Descartes advances two other proofs of God's existence: (1) the "ontological proof" (originally advanced by Anselm) whereby God is credited with the quality of existence because a perfect being must necessarily possess every quality; and (2) the "anthropological proof", whereby the presence within us of the idea of a Perfect Being is held to establish the existence of a cause great enough to account for this presence. See his *Third Meditation*.

wise departed somewhat from Descartes' viewpoint, summed up the general Cartesian position as follows: "To reach truth", he wrote in his *Recherche de la Verité*, "it is enough to make oneself attentive to the clear ideas which each finds in himself".

Not merely does God undertake to guarantee the truth of our clearest conceptions of the world of nature; He likewise undertakes to sustain our powers of thought in forming these concepts. It is He, for instance, that guarantees the reliability of our memory, so that in intuiting the truth embodied in the *cogito* we are able to pursue its implications far enough to become assured of the existence of matter. In another sense, however, we are drawn to believe in the existence of a material world because God has already implanted the idea of it in our minds: i.e., it is an "innate idea". But the reports of our senses can never be used as evidence of the truth of our ideas about this world: such sense-impressions are merely the occasion, not the cause, of the operation of our thought in a certain direction. All knowledge is therefore *a priori*, i.e., derived otherwise than through experience. Upon God's guarantee alone can we rely for the certainty that our knowledge of the world external to mind is valid. He made that world and He also made us; and there is every reason to believe that He intends the two forms of creation to subsist together in harmony. To suppose otherwise is to deny God's benevolence: for how could He deceive a poor mortal so?

Just as Descartes thought of God as both guaranteeing our memory and setting His hall-mark upon our clearest conceptions, so he conceived of Him as communicating to the world the movement whereby the processes of nature are set going. This is reminiscent of the Aristotelean conception of the unmoved Mover. In order that a body may exist, it must be extended in space; but the idea of extension does not include the idea of movement. And what of the regularity that we find in nature? That is the work of God, too, since God's essence is immutable and hence His activity in the world must partake of the same quality. God is thus engaged in creating all the time, but creating in regular fashion: hence conservation is the same thing as perpetual creation. As for secondary qualities, Descartes followed Galileo in believing that these, being relative, lay outside the scope of scientific investigation.

From this brief outline of Descartes' philosophy (we have said nothing about certain aspects of his thought, e.g., his notions of physics and physiology) it is clear that the attempt made therein to demonstrate how we, as minds, succeed in attaining to a knowledge of that which stands outside mind is not wholly successful. Setting out with the best of intentions to press human reason to the limit and to show that man's intelligence, through its very admission of error, could attain to certainty without either experimental or dogmatic support, Descartes finds himself obliged at the last to call in the highest authority of all, namely, God, to "underwrite" the whole daring project. As M. Maritain has said: "Descartes . . . endeavours, by means of a flight of pure spirit, to raise himself to the sphere of pure intelligence without passing through the gates of sense-experience, which is the way that nature has ordained."[1] For (to quote from another work of the same author,[2]) "if the intelligence, when it is engaged in thought, reaches immediately only its own thoughts or its representations, that which lies hidden behind these representations must remain for ever unknowable". Maritain, who is the foremost modern exponent of neo-scholasticism or neo-Thomism, sums up his attack upon the Cartesian philosophy by observing that Descartes "philosophised as he might have prayed. He closed all the gates of experience and set himself to attain reality from within himself".[3]

[1] *Le Songe de Descartes.*
[2] *Three Reformers.*
[3] *Le Songe de Descartes.*

The Rift Between Philosophy and Theology

Thus the *rationalist* attack upon scepticism leaves us with the human reason just as utterly dependent upon something other than itself as it was for those whom Descartes criticised for relying upon external authority. Moreover, Descartes does little or nothing to illuminate the creative powers of God, however desperately he may invoke their aid. He left this task to theology: and consequently it is in the work of Descartes that we observe that cleavage between "philosophy" and theology which was to become so marked in the work of his successors. The separation was not always conscious; but once it was suggested that the task of philosophy was to employ a strictly mathematical technique, thereby approximating to an exact and universal science, the terms theology and metaphysics came to stand for branches of enquiry which had forfeited their claim to the respect of "progressive thinkers". Amid all the advances and achievements of man's technical powers they had conspicuously failed to get a move on. What were they, after all, but clusters of exotic verbal foliage, disguising a disused and crumbling mansion? Such an attitude, both contemptuous and cynical, was becoming common even before Descartes' time, and was shared by some who were almost his contemporaries. Thus it is scarcely surprising to find Francis Bacon (1561-1626) already referring to Aristotle—who had never before been so insulted—as "the vile plaything of words".[1]

The effects of this separation between a philosophy that aimed at scientific exactitude and the traditional theology may be studied to best advantage in the work of a philosopher to whom we have already referred as having much in common with Descartes, namely, Malebranche (1638-1715). The

[1] The separation referred to had an effect on spheres other than philosophy, of which literature was one. T. S. Eliot has shown in his essays on seventeenth-century poetry (see *Selected Essays*) how a "dissociation of sensibility" took place at this time. See also Willey: *The Seventeenth Century Background, passim*.

F

chief reason why Malebranche provides an even better illustration of these effects than Descartes himself is that Malebranche is the more anxious of the two to conceal them. It
is as if he knew what was happening and did his best to hush
up the scandal. To belittle the religious bent of Malebranche's
thought would nevertheless be unjust: he is genuinely trying
to reconcile certain consequences of Cartesianism with
Christian and also Platonic thought. Like Descartes, he holds
that we possess an idea of the infinite prior to that of the finite;
but in consequence of his view that "we see all things in God",
he makes the divine power directly responsible for everything
that occurs not merely in nature but in ourselves, claiming
that it is God that provides us with "ideas" of the world of
nature of which we should otherwise know nothing. Whereas
Descartes invoked God to "underwrite" our intellectual conceptions, Malebranche imagines Him as compensating us for
our ignorance in a kind of paper currency of "ideas". The
existence of a backing for this emergency issue of currency is
an article of faith. All we know is that we have the divine
"promise to pay"; and that, if we are devout persons, ought
to satisfy us. Here, therefore, more clearly than anywhere in
Descartes' writings, we are able to observe the *reductio ad
absurdum* of the assumption, which neither philosopher seeks
to challenge, that the subjective and objective worlds are
mutually exclusive: for what the Cartesians are all the while
implying is that, given this partition of reality, we have no
alternative but to trust that God will relieve us of the embarrassment of admitting that our reason cannot overcome it.
That our reason may have put it there in the first place was
something that occurred to no philosopher before Berkeley,
whose solution, as we saw in Part I, was not so much to
abolish the distinction as to incapsulate one realm within the
other.

In view of the fact that both Descartes and Malebranche
(to say nothing of several other thinkers whose works we shall

consider shortly) are continually calling upon God to make up the deficiencies of a Reason that was once held to be self-supporting, it might be wondered how the Cartesians ever came to be branded as enemies of theology. Did not they share—or come to share—the mediæval view that human reason, unaided by divine grace, can achieve nothing? Did not they believe, as the mediæval thinkers believed, that God, the Author of both mind and nature, was continually intervening in the one sphere and the other, communicating His rationality to His creatures and governing their lives at every moment of time? They most certainly did. But the point is not so much that they accepted the mediæval set-up as that they accepted it blindly. They objected to dogma; but they took this one over wholesale. They were enemies of theology precisely because they claimed to be its friends.

The consequence was, as we have seen, that philosophy came to be preoccupied more and more with what is called the theory of knowledge, of which the theory of perception is an integral part. Hence the circumstance, also alluded to earlier, that the modern student of philosophy, setting out to study the "origins of modern thought" and therefore beginning (for he must begin somewhere) with Descartes, tends to assume that modern philosophers, led by the Frenchman, are for the first time facing up to the crucial problem of how we can have knowledge of the "external world", as if the ancient and mediæval philosophers were too timid or too orthodox to tackle this question. This is to forget not merely that the problem was a very ancient one, but that Descartes' attempt to solve it involved far more reliance upon mysticism and even the miraculous than that of his "superstitious" predecessors. Having claimed that he had found a new device for getting round scepticism he still realised that it is of no value unless it is stamped with the divine patent.

A somewhat restricted view of God necessarily follows. Like many of his successors, Descartes devotes much space to singing the praises of the architect of the universe, but the result is that God's majesty is not so much enlarged as diminished. No longer, as with the mediæval theologians, is He the Creator and Saviour of mankind; he is rather the Guarantor of the reliability of our sense-impressions. This conception of God eventually became known as Deistic: a view according to which God is not merely the power that winds up the clock of the universe but the inspector that sees that it keeps time. And physical science was until very recently disposed to accept this as the proper rôle of God, assuming, for the sake of respectability, that it was necessary to bring Him in at all.

From the purely metaphysical viewpoint, however, the most significant feature of the thought of the Cartesians, especially that of Malebranche, was its insertion of entities called "ideas" between the subject and the object, thereby separating them by a semi-opaque or semi-transparent screen. Introduced at first as the mediator between the two realms, the idea eventually became lodged or jammed between them; and the reality of which it was supposed to provide a representation becomes an "outer darkness" that, as Maritain points out, cannot strictly be known at all. The theorists of the "idea" tended to forget that ideas are not merely things to think with but things to think through. To return to the simile of a paper currency, while they assumed that the money could always be cashed in an emergency, they hoped and assumed that such a crisis would never arise. With Berkeley it did: and he promptly "went off gold" by declaring the external object null and void.[1]

Spinoza

The philosophy of Spinoza (1632-1677) is often held to have departed from the traditional line of thought, possibly owing

[1] It must not be assumed that no one at the time protested against this abuse of the word "idea". Arnauld in his book *Des Vraies et des Fausses Idées*, published in 1683, subjects the Cartesian view to a most searching criticism.

to the Jewish blood and outlook of its exponent. With due allowance for differences of temperament, terminology, and methods of exposition, however, Spinoza is all the while thinking in Cartesian categories, though thinking with great originality and earnestness. Possibly Spinoza was one of the most earnest people that has ever lived. Common to the philosophy of Spinoza and Descartes is the idea of God as providing the link between the world of thought and the world of nature. With Spinoza, however, the two are not so much joined as identical: God and nature are simply two ways of conceiving the same unconditional substance. As extended, this substance is nature; as thinking, God. Nor is it true to say that such substance, *Deus sive Natura*, is the ultimate cause of all else in the universe. It is not a cause; it is what the logicians or geometricians call a "ground". And there we have a further example of the influence of the mathematical approach to philosophical problems that Descartes commended to his contemporaries. The consequence of a "ground" are not so much independent items as elements in the ground itself; they are the ground become articulate, just as the connections observed in geometrical problems may be likened to arteries or veins illuminating the propositions themselves. If we like, we can say that the relation of ground to consequent is a kind of "timeless causality". According to Spinoza, all that our understanding can expect to do, therefore, is to contemplate the logical nexus subsisting between grounds and their consequents, and so realise the degree in which all things are related and united in God. We human creatures, being merely modes (consequents) of the divine Substance, enjoy one kind of freedom only: namely, the realisation that we are eternally bound to God by the "fetters" of His love.[1]

It has been the custom to refer to Spinoza as "God-intoxicated", and there is no denying the deeply devout attitude with which he approaches the major problems of thought.

[1] Spinoza develops this idea of freedom in his treatise on Ethics.

Nevertheless, in identifying God with Nature, and in postulating the reality of one single and eternal Substance (thereby earning the title of monist), Spinoza attributes to God a much more rational activity than Descartes does. Setting out (as we saw) to explain everything in terms of reason, Descartes is obliged to summon divine assistance half-way through the journey. Spinoza *starts* with God; we are His children, not His wards. From Him we obtain the water of life; whereas according to Descartes, He provides us with stimulants to give us confidence in our own capacities and to keep off the vertigo. It is, therefore, Descartes who is in danger of becoming "God-intoxicated", not Spinoza.

Leibnitz

Yet a third name in the history of modern philosophy, Leibnitz (1646-1716), is associated with the approach to the problem of knowledge through mathematics. Though greatly attracted by the Cartesian system Leibnitz could not bring himself to accept all of Descartes' conclusions. Likewise he made a deep study of the work of Spinoza, even going so far as to pay the master a visit in the year 1676; but his dissatisfaction with current thought increased rather than diminished, and he resolved to work out the whole problem of the relation between mind and nature afresh. For this task he was exceedingly well-equipped.

With the details of Leibnitz's theories of mechanics, logic and mathematics (he was the inventor, among other things, of the infinitesimal calculus), we are not here concerned. Much that he has to say on these and related questions is extremely acute: indeed his works are crowded, almost choked, with observations and suggestions of the greatest profundity, not all of which he had time to develop in the course of his busy life. What we are concerned to do here, however, is to examine the underlying assumptions upon which his philosophy rests: and the most rich and certainly not the least interesting repository of these is a treatise written in 1714, entitled *The Monadology*, the work with which his name is popularly associated.

The germ of the ideas expounded at length in *The Monadology* is present in a voluminous correspondence which Leibnitz carried on for several years (1686-90) with Arnauld, the philosopher whose dissatisfaction with Descartes' theory of ideas has already been reported. At one point in this correspondence the two disputants engage in an argument over what is meant by the term "individual". Leibnitz, for his part, puts forward the notion that each individual thing in the universe contains within it all that happens to that thing. This is really a logical problem: the notion, with which Leibnitz concurred, that everything that can be said about a true proposition is logically present in that proposition. If, that is to say, we undertake to analyse any true statement, we shall find it to contain implications which are not so much other things—other notions—as aspects of the same notion. The conclusion may seem simple enough, and perhaps hardly worth arguing about; but the logician is precisely a person to whom such conclusions, however harmless, represent an invitation to argue further: which is to say that they do not strike him as final conclusions at all. If, for instance, the proposition in question is true, then its truth will (as it were) apply to itself: that is to say, the proposition that everything that can be said about a true proposition is logically contained in that proposition must, if true, contain everything that can be said about that further proposition, and this leads us to the conclusion that the notion of any one thing contains and implies the notion of everything else.

Developing this view more fully in the book already referred to, Leibnitz makes it the pivot of a new philosophical system. He maintains that nothing but individuals exists, and that to be individual is to be both active and unified: in short, to be a centre of activity or force. To each of these units of force he gives the name of "monad", and he conceives of monads as self-contained, self-developing individuals existing independently of all other monads. Since the monads possess this self-contained character they are to be regarded as having "no windows by which anything can enter or depart"; nor do they need any such media of communication, because each monad is "a mirror of the universe". Nevertheless, some monads represent the universe better than others, and therefore we must conceive of there being in nature a hierarchy of monads, at the summit of which is the human soul, which nevertheless has a body related to its nature. Moreover, the less perfect monads are dependent upon the more perfect, though the obedience of the lesser to the greater follows not from compulsion but from the mere fact of subordination. In this way the universe is harmoniously built up; and the edifice is formed because each monad, in mirroring the whole within itself, takes its place within the scheme spontaneously. It "fits in" not because it is a part, but because it is a whole.

That such a scheme presents numerous obscurities, some of which Leibnitz's contemporaries sought to point out, cannot be denied. To grasp what Leibnitz is trying to make clear to us entails a species of imaginative insight with which, it must be admitted, not everyone is endowed in equal degree. Among the chief difficulties in the scheme is that concerned with the relation between one monad and another, or to speak more accurately, between each and all the rest. The notion of a central force, or what Alexander calls a point-instant, acting all over the universe at once, seems to follow logically from the acceptance of certain theories advanced by modern physicists; but although Leibnitz anticipated some of these theories, we cannot be sure that this sort of pervasive activity was what he had pre-eminently in mind. Nevertheless, it is in this aspect of Leibnitz's theory that we are particularly interested. For here, as at roughly the same point in the thought of

Descartes, he is obliged to summon to his aid an external authority whereby the whole structure is enabled miraculously to hold together.

This is the notion of Pre-established Harmony. The fact that the movements of our bodies seem to be related to particular states of mind and *vice versa* is due, in Leibnitz's view, not to any direct or causal action of one upon the other—because monads cannot interpenetrate in this way—but to the fact that God, the monad of monads, has thus deliberately arranged matters. The harmony between the one and the other may be compared with that subsisting between two clocks which agree because a skilful mechanic has so adjusted them that discrepancy is impossible. The comparison is to be understood exactly, because Leibnitz is anxious to distinguish his idea of Pre-established Harmony from any similar notion of God's contribution to the working of nature, and especially, we may surmise, from that advanced by Descartes and Newton. He says so quite plainly. "Mr. Newton and his followers", he writes in his *Lettre à Clarke*, "have a curious opinion of God and His work. According to them God must wind up his watch from time to time: otherwise it would cease to move. He had not sufficient insight to make it run for ever. Nay, God's machine is so imperfect, according to them, that he is obliged to clean it from time to time, by an extraordinary concourse, and even to repair it as a watchmaker repairs his work: the oftener he is obliged to mend it and to set it right, the poorer a mechanic he is".

In other words, what Leibnitz is objecting to is the notion, clearly implied by Descartes, that God is at every moment and with perpetual solicitude intervening in the order of creation. To Leibnitz such interference would suggest that the mechanism could not work by itself. And that would suggest that God has made it badly. According to his notion of Pre-established Harmony, on the other hand, the universe is conceived as working perfectly well by itself, since God has so "set" it that, like an automatic pilot, it carries on in the same direction and without faltering for ever and ever. "According to my system", he writes in *The Monadology* (p. 81), "bodies act *as if* there were no souls, and souls act as if there were no bodies, and both act *as if* each influenced the other" (my italics). Obscure as this statement may appear on the surface, Leibnitz is not suggesting that the universe and its constituents are made up of illusion, or that we can understand it only by analogy; he is trying to drive home the point that, as a result of Pre-established Harmony, everything carries on precisely as it was "set" to do at the beginning, with the result that the interaction between one thing and another is due, not to their working together or "upon" one another, but to their working separately. It is God that thinks their togetherness, not they that consciously will it.

If, therefore, the harmony, order and essential togetherness of the universe are due to an initial arrangement on the part of God, He has nothing further to do but to let it continue to function on its own; and since He has clearly arranged things as well as he can, the world as we find it must be acknowledged to be the "best of all possible worlds". It could not well be otherwise, given an architect of such supremacy. Readers of Voltaire's *Candide*, with its portrayal of that assiduous Leibnitzian, Dr. Pangloss, will be able to judge the extent to which this belief is practical or even edifying. Naturally, if the universe works as Leibnitz says it does, there is no question of the intervention of God at any point. Intervention is possible only in a process that has already started; whereas the God of Leibnitz, having arranged everything before the beginning, needs simply to sit back for all eternity and contemplate his own ingenuity. The heavens do not "declare" the glory of God: they are a silent witness to it. The silence of the infinite spaces that terrified Pascal fills Leibnitz with exultant optimism. The slightest creak would betoken incompetence.

From this brief sketch of the philosophy of Leibnitz one

thing clearly emerges. Even if God should refrain from perpetual intervention in the working of the universe, He it is
that assumes final responsibility for its cohesion. "A miracle
that endures ceases to be considered as such"[1]; but it is a
miracle all the same. In other words, the relation between
mind and nature is no more convincingly explained in the
philosophy of Leibnitz than in that of Descartes or Spinoza.
Leibnitz's monads may be "without windows"; but that is
because they have no need to look outside. They mind their
own business, while God looks after public business. Yet the
problem was precisely to show how the "private" world of
mind communicated with the "public" world of nature.
Leibnitz, for all his ingeniousness, has not really succeeded in
overcoming scepticism at all. He does not really answer our
question. Let us then see how his successors tackled it.

[1] Jean Cocteau.

I I

The Empiricist Attack on Scepticism and Kant's Answer

Locke's Account of Knowledge

In the last chapter we examined the philosophical theories of a number of thinkers whom the textbooks group together under the title of rationalists. We now come to a group of philosophers, most of them English, who attack the problem of scepticism from a somewhat different angle. For the sake of convenience they have been labelled empiricists. What chiefly concerns us is the general problem which they are attacking, and in particular the fact that, in common with the rationalists, they assume to begin with the mutual externality of the world of mind and the world of nature. It will be recalled that in Part I we referred on more than one occasion to the theories of these thinkers, above all, those of Berkeley. Our object in the present chapter is to show how, in spite of apparent divergences, the metaphysical background to their work is the same.

In his *Essay concerning the Human Understanding*, which was published in 1690, John Locke (1632-1704) set out to examine the nature and extent of human knowledge. This problem was, as we have seen, very much in the air at the time, not because it was the fashion to discuss such questions, but because, as a result of breakdown of much traditional belief,[1] it had become an urgent necessity to face up to them. Just as

---

[1] As early as 1611, John Donne wrote of "new philosophy" as calling "all in doubt" (*An Anatomy of the World*).

today the writer on social questions finds himself obliged to face up straightaway to the economic aspect of his subject, so the speculative thinkers of the seventeenth century found themselves obliged to face up to what, in technical terms, is called the epistemological aspect. Locke's primary concern, therefore, was to show not merely how the mind comes to possess its "ideas", but how, having acquired them, it proceeds to use them. It may be thought that this statement of the problem makes a great many covert assumptions about the nature of knowledge, thereby rendering the philosopher's task obscure and his conclusions suspect. Of some of these assumptions we are already aware, while later thinkers, especially Kant, drew attention to others. But such assumptions are precisely those elements which make the problem what it is, difficult or otherwise; and the conclusions that the philosopher draws are suspect only if we do not follow the process which led up to them. It rests with us, as later observers, to perceive the stages of this process.

Developing certain ideas already formulated, or half formulated, by Bacon and Hobbes, who are the forerunners of English empiricism, Locke set out with the intention of putting knowledge on a firmer and more intelligible basis than that which the rationalists had provided. He starts off with a comparatively simple principle, which he, incidentally, applies in the course of his own work: namely, that no idea entertained by our minds in the course of reflection is too complex to be reduced to simple elements. This principle deals a blow at rationalism at the start; for the simple elements to which Locke claims that our most complex ideas are reducible, are the elements of immediate sensation. The rationalists had strongly denied this. Their contention was that our universal concepts, or general ideas, were not to be derived from sense experience at all; they were already implanted within our minds, being there from the beginning. Consequently they may properly be called "innate". In order to prove his case that there are no such things as innate ideas, and never have been, Locke cites evidence, both from primitive peoples, the study of which (anthropology) was becoming popular about this time, and from civilised peoples in their most primitive condition, namely, childhood. Far from possessing ideas that are innate, the human mind originally possessed no ideas at all. How could it? For if, as Locke proceeds to argue, all our ideas are derived from experience, and therefore from outside, the mind in its primal state is nothing but a blank sheet, a *tabula rasa*. To change the metaphor, the mind originally formed an empty room into which furniture had to be imported from outside. It was not, like the Cartesian mind, an apartment to be "let furnished".

Of Locke's theory of ideas we have already spoken briefly in Part I. What we said there need not be repeated; but it must now be taken a stage farther. Ideas, according to Locke, are produced in two ways. First of all, they may be imprinted on our minds by the senses; these are called ideas of sensation, or simple ideas. Alternatively, they may be manufactured by the mind itself from the material gathered in the first process; these are ideas of reflection. It follows that the mind possesses two distinct capacities; an external capacity which is concerned with reality outside the mind (or as much of it as we know), and an internal capacity (reflection) which is concerned with organising our mental life proper. These capacities, which must not be confused one with the other, are almost to be regarded as two kinds of perception. The first, engaged in perceiving the external world, reports back its findings to the second. This latter, which is engaged in an interior perception, collates these findings, observes the relations between them, and works them up into new combinations. To employ a rough analogy, both faculties are concerned with "news" of outside reality: but whereas the first is a routine reporter, the second is a sub-editor who makes the story coherent and intelligible.

Nevertheless, when we speak of the external sense or faculty as perceiving "outside reality", we must beware of supposing that it establishes direct contact with this reality. As we have just seen, the external sense reports back nothing but sense impressions—stimuli, that is to say, derived from the material world but not identical with it. Of the material world as it exists behind these impressions, we have, with one qualification to be noted hereafter, no direct perception whatever.

Thus, as we saw plainly enough earlier on, Locke does not succeed in explaining satisfactorily either how the subjective world is related to the objective world, or how it can know that such a world exists. And his error has been repeated in various forms by the realist tradition of philosophy ever since. As it happens, Locke had a special reason, if hardly a reputable one, for abstaining from too great an emphasis on the complete and objective reality of matter. He wanted to avoid the charge of materialism, just as many philosophers of the present day are anxious to avoid the charge of idealism. Having seen and recoiled from the conclusions at which Hobbes had arrived before him, he was determined that his emphasis upon experience should not land him in a like impasse. The very force of his recoil against the threat of materialism, however, sent him farther back into the arms of subjectivism than perhaps he intended. Instead of demonstrating that we are in contact with something other than our subjective impressions, which is the obvious goal of one who starts out to prove that our minds derive their content from experience, Locke is unable to show that we have managed to contact anything but these very subjective states. We are not outside at all; we are merely in receipt of a series of dispatches from outside, the authenticity of which we have no means of judging. The sub-editor has no means of assuring himself that what his reporter says is absolutely true. Nor has the second or internal faculty of reflection any criteria from which to judge whether it is performing its functions well or ill, since the concepts or complex notions that it is engaged in manufacturing are clearly intended to refer to something which, unless it is shown to be of a different nature from them, cannot be cited as evidence that they are genuine. In short, the "truth" of our ideas and the ideas themselves are totally unrelated.

Locke's Dilemma

Although this dilemma was both noticed and criticised by later philosophers, especially Berkeley, it would be wrong to assume that Locke remained totally unaware of what had happened. He went so far as to take special measures to escape from between its horns. And the theory of primary and secondary qualities, already outlined, was the best solution that he could offer. According to this theory, a difference in *kind* was assumed to divide the data of sense, so that qualities such as extension, form, impenetrability, number, temporal succession and movement (i.e., primary qualities) were definitely held to constitute part, if not the whole, of the object itself. The rest was "secondary" and formed the mind's contribution.

From what has been already said about the manner in which sensations are received by our minds, it must appear that this attempt to identify and isolate at least *some* aspects of the world external to our minds, represented no more than a desperate counter-attack for the purpose of capturing lost ground. Nevertheless, Locke, like many another defiant commander, considered that it was an attack worth launching: and indeed such counter-measures are always useful, and even obligatory, if there is reasonable chance of joining up with forces known to be located somewhere in the rear of the enemy. In Locke's opinion this was indeed the case.

In expounding the essential features of Locke's philosophy we have, so far, omitted to mention two other notions to which he had recourse—notions which he shared equally with the rationalistic philosophers. These were the notion of

cause and the notion of substance. However "subjective" the
data of sense may be, and however much they may require
working up into new combinations by our reflective faculty,
they must (Locke recognised) clearly be the product of some
cause, even if we cannot say precisely what this cause is.
Now the only thing that can be imagined as lying beneath or
behind these sensations is the "substance" about which both
Descartes and Spinoza wrote. Instead of maintaining with
Descartes that substance is God, since He is the ground of
everything else, and with Spinoza that it is likewise God because there is no substance but that which is self-subsistent
being, Locke takes the more humble view that substance is a
kind of *substratum*, an "unknown somewhat", the presence of
which we can infer but not properly understand. There is
therefore no science of substance, for neither intuition nor
reflection can truly establish contact with it.

Such a view is clearly unsatisfactory. The forces with
which Locke has succeeded in making contact prove to be no
more than a ghost army. And being thus disembodied they
obstinately refuse to recognise his command; and yet, like
guerrillas or partisans, they continue to play a vital part in the
campaign. To drop the metaphor, Locke is reduced to asserting that the structure of the world of sense rests upon a foundation which, though he admits its necessity, he does not and
cannot understand. That such a foundation is indispensable
must be conceded in view of the principle, from which he
cannot depart without ceasing to be an empiricist, that all
knowledge is derived from experience. In the course of his
philosophical enquiry Locke maintains that we have a demonstrable knowledge of God; but it seems that the most potent
god in Locke's system is still this "unknown god" of substance.
Descartes and Leibnitz, seeking for a ground from which
everything else might be regarded as a consequent, pick on
substance without more ado. Locke, more guardedly, endows
substance with all the attributes of god except the name.

There is thus only one essential difference between the attitude to knowledge (if we can describe as knowledge that which is at no point more than perception) of the rationalists and that of such an empiricist as Locke, and it is as follows: whereas the rationalists maintain that the control and guarantee of our faculties is exerted from the side of the subjective world, Locke maintains that it is exerted from the side of the objective world. In fact, however, it makes little difference from which side it is exerted. According to what we have termed the traditional set-up, God, the creator of both worlds, forms the apex of a compass of which the two legs are mind and nature. It is therefore a matter of indifference which leg the philosopher chooses to make as his pivot. The compass can still be made to stand.

Berkeley's Challenge to His Contemporaries

The extent to which Berkeley succeeded in scrapping it has already been discussed. But the conclusion at which we saw him arrive, if only tentatively, was that the distinction between subjective and objective, though blurred, was by no means completely obliterated. In spite of being denationalised, the refugees from the objective zone continued to carry aliens' papers. As we saw, Berkeley did not deny the existence of a *rerum natura*; he merely contended, with unimpeachable logic, that such a realm could not be regarded as the ideal counterpart of some "unknown" realm external to it. There are not two natures. There is only one nature. And this nature is composed of ideas. What we see, hear and feel is real. It is not a "copy" of reality.

The aspect of Berkeley's thought to which we now wish to draw attention is that concerned with the reliability of our ideas. Granted that there is nothing objective but our ideas, what is to show that our ideas, as present to us, are true? We have already quoted Berkeley as saying that the distinction between realities and chimeras "retains its full force"; how can we be sure that this is indeed the case?

It was Berkeley's view that when our minds are presented with ideas in a certain order or series, we sometimes jump to the conclusion that this series, like its components, is objective in the sense of coming "ready-made" from outside. This, said Berkeley, is an error—the chief error in the thought of Locke and his disciples. An idea is not "of" anything else but another idea; similarly with groups of ideas. The "external" world itself is simply the particular way in which ideas group themselves together in our minds.

Berkeley goes farther. He maintains that this "association of ideas" in our minds, though often assumed to represent—if not actually to *be*—the manner in which things are connected, is in fact nothing more than the way in which our minds are designed to work. Between the ideas themselves there is no internal connection; what we experience at every moment of time is a unit, an individual, a particular thing, as we saw in the example of the "painfully-hot-place". What Berkeley is here stating is a new version of the nominalist theory of mediæval times; the belief, namely, that only individual or particular things enjoy real existence.

So far as it goes, this restatement of the theory of ideas is plausible enough. But the question with which we began has not yet been answered. If there exists no realm external to our ideas, where do these ideas come from, and what guarantees their truth? It was because he realised that he was bound to tackle this problem that Locke, with obvious reluctance, had recourse to the notion of an "unknown somewhat". To do likewise would have meant for Berkeley the collapse of his whole theory. He therefore seeks the solution along the road, or causeway, already travelled by the Cartesians. Our ideas, he declares, are not produced by anything at all; they are given, or rather lent. There is a Power in the universe which determines not merely how our finite minds shall work, but at what they shall work. If we were ourselves the author of our ideas, we should obviously be able to manipulate them at will; and this our finitude forbids us to do except in rare cases. "When in broad daylight I open my eyes", says Berkeley, "it is not in my power to choose whether I shall see or no, or determine what particular objects shall present themselves to my view".[1] The greater part of our experience is, as we know, received in this passive manner. Therefore we are bound to conclude, even if our religion did not expressly dictate as much, that the donor of our ideas is infinite in power, or in other words, God Himself. The divine Benefactor, who is at the same time a guarantor, operates once more from the subjective side of the picture; and in this respect Berkeley, having pushed the empirical method as far as it will go, finds himself joining hands with Malebranche, who, for somewhat similar reasons, subjected the rationalist method to an equal degree of pressure. Agreeing with Malebranche that "we see all things in God", Berkeley did not shrink from the conclusion that God's responsibility extended so far as to sustain the natural world in our "off" moments, i.e., when we were not engaged in perceiving it.

Hume's Reductio ad Absurdum

The truth is that the rationalist and empiricist philosophers, finding themselves locked within the subjective world, endeavoured forcibly to break out of it at either end. Descartes, Malebranche, Spinoza, Leibnitz, and Berkeley try, in their various ways, to climb out of the realm of mind to God, and returning, find themselves back in the subjective world once more. Locke rushes to the other exit; he tries to force his way out in the direction of the external world, but, the door being jammed, he is obliged to abandon the attempt as vain. Profiting from the experience of these pioneers, and resolved to liquidate the problem at all costs, David Hume (1711-76)

[1] *Principles of Human Knowledge*, 27, 89.

makes a kind of suicide pact with himself, and prepares to wreck the whole structure, if need be, rather than live in mental solitary confinement.

Gifted with brilliant analytical powers and a literary style of great charm and persuasiveness, Hume puts into operation his demolition tactics straightaway. And it must be admitted that, having begun in so negative a fashion, he seriously prejudices any chances he may have of reaching certainty, at least "by the way of ideas". Few thinkers have succeeded, as Montaigne had succeeded in a somewhat different sphere, in casting doubt upon *everything*[1]; but of all the philosophers of his time, and more successfully perhaps than his own disciples (of whom there have been many, not least in our own day), Hume took scepticism as far as it would go. Yet he still belongs, as we shall see, to the company of those whose original aim was the avoidance of scepticism, in the sense that he realises that his immediate predecessors, though right in intention, are exploring a blind alley. And he demonstrates this by resolutely penetrating to the end of it himself. His motto might well be summed up in the line of a modern poet:

"In order to possess what you do not possess you must go by the way of dispossession".[2]

The way in which Hume disposes of Berkeley's empirical "idealism" is by directing his scepticism upon the two elements in Berkeley's scheme which had survived the latter's own sceptical approach: namely, the belief in a spiritual substance as opposed to a material substance, and the belief in causation. And in order to expose the error that substance and cause are real things, Hume subjects them to precisely the same kind of

[1] Montaigne's famous query, "Que sçais-je?", was less perhaps a reason for doubting the human mind's capacity to arrive at certain knowledge than an admonition against fanaticism. Appalled by the readiness with which men indulge in mutual persecution and destruction, he invites his readers to consider whether truth can be reached with such ease, and whether, having been reached by us, its denial by others should justify our engaging in such ferocious reprisals.

[2] T. S. Eliot, *East Coker* (from "Four Quartets").

analysis that Berkeley used in disposing of the belief in a world external to mind. With regard to the spiritual substance of Berkeley, Hume points out that this is just as much a "figment of the mind" as material substance, since it is in no sense the object of perception. He turns the same destructive argument against the idea of the self. "When we turn our attention upon self", he writes, "what we are presented with is always some isolated perception". In other words, we never find *ourselves*, merely an impression or series of impressions of which the connection is not a logical but an associative one. "The thought alone finds personal identity when reflecting on the train of past perceptions that compose a mind"; but "all my hopes vanish when I come to explain the principles that unite our successive perceptions in our thought and consciousness".

Although Hume virtually despairs of ever adducing these principles, the union of one impression with another by means of association is still a principle of a kind, and one for which he claims the widest application. And an acceptance of the principle of the association of ideas raises the more ultimate question as to why we happen to associate some groups of ideas in one way and other groups in another. Forced to provide a tentative explanation of this fact of experience, Hume introduces a distinction of degree, if not of kind, not merely between one impression and another, but between impressions and ideas themselves.

Of what, then, is experience composed? It is composed, says Hume, of two kinds of mental entity. First, there are the direct data of sense: to these Hume gives the name of impressions. Precisely how they originate he declines to say,[1] perhaps because he cannot conceive that anyone should doubt their existence. Secondly, there are ideas properly so-called. These are copies of the original impressions. Not all impressions have ideal copies; but if they have the task of philosophi-

---

[1] In fact he says that their origin is "perfectly inexplicable by human reason".

cal analysis—or criticism, as Hume likes to call it—is to find the impression from which the idea is derived. Now ideas can be grouped or classed together in ways that do not correspond to the original groups of impressions; and this varied grouping of ideas, which may take many forms, is all that we really mean when we talk of reasoning, judging, supposing, and so on. The "powers of the mind" are simply its habits.

On other occasions Hume employs a somewhat different distinction within the field of our ideas. He describes them as differing in intensity or, as he puts it, liveliness. Such vivacity is the quality whereby true ideas are to be distinguished from those of a fictitious kind; but this is not a criterion of truth, merely a symptom. To speak of degrees of truth is simply to speak of degrees of vivacity. The same applies to impressions as well, so that an impression of a certain vividness is likely to graduate as an idea. To some extent this is a reversion to Descartes' principle of clearness and distinctness.

In Hume's language, therefore, that which we are accustomed to call the object consists simply of a "cluster of impressions"; and the mind that "knows" this object is itself no more than a complex of impressions or ideas formed by habit, which he calls our "second nature". Hume in one place likens the force of association to attraction. Our ideas literally gravitate together. There are no intrinsic relations discoverable in perception between them; and what is not discoverable in perception cannot, assuming our present constitution, be discoverable at all. In place of the image of the mind as knowing an object other than itself, Hume substitutes two groups of heterogeneous but partially caked particles, the one "mental" and the other "material", blending between which at certain points is held to constitute knowledge. The two worlds of mind and nature have been reduced to a shambles; and the constituents of both, being composed of uniform debris, are no longer clearly distinguishable.

Whether Hume's famous assault upon the notion of cause

depends wholly upon his theory of ideas and impressions is a question that has been much debated.[1] At least one connecting link, however, is to be found in the principle of association. In attacking the notion of cause Hume was, in effect, engaged in the destruction of the last secure bridge between the subjective world and the world of objects in themselves. Both Locke and Berkeley had depended on the firmness of this link in order to demonstrate that our subjective impressions, whether given or lent, must, in order to be here at all, have come from somewhere else. Dismissing the question as to how our impressions originate, Hume proceeds to an analysis of the supposed connecting link itself. The question he poses is how we are justified in assuming that a causal relation subsists between any two facts. Are we justified in believing such a thing from experience? Not at all. All that we are aware of in experience is that one perception, call it X, precedes in time another perception, call it Y. Except for this perception of *temporal succession* we observe nothing that would lead us to believe that the result Y is produced at the initiative or by the express operation of X. Nor can the mind ever find the effect in the cause, for the two are totally different. Experience teaches us—and we have, as good empiricists, no other teacher—that instead of there being any inherent connection between X and Y, the fact that one precedes the other strikes our attention simply because the observation of this succession has become a habit. All that we have to go on, in other words, is the fact that the succession has been repealed sufficiently frequently in our experience to have acquired a certain vivacity, though Hume has difficulty in showing how our idea of repetition is derived. Of objective status, then, the notion of cause possesses no element whatever, for nothing can be confirmed about it from experience.

It is easy to demonstrate the inadequacy of Hume's theory

---

[1] See Hume's *Theory of the Human Understanding*, by R. W. Church (1934), p. 85.

of ideas by pointing out that, in analysing the notion of cause, he is guilty of breaking at least one, and that perhaps the most important, of the rules he has himself laid down. Every simple idea, he has said, is a copy of a preceding impression. True, he cannot prove this rule; but like many another propounder of rules, he invites us to confute him by producing a glaring instance to the contrary. There is scarcely need for us to do so, because he does it himself. The idea of causality is a case in point. From what impression, we may ask, is this idea derived? From no impression at all. Hume thereupon proceeds to argue, in circular fashion, that because the idea of cause does not conform to his rule it cannot be regarded as a real idea.

Nevertheless, to pour scorn upon Hume by declaring, as many have done, that he has reduced the empirical method to a state of bankruptcy, is a work of supererogation. He is as well aware of that as we are. He expressly said that he was prepared to push the method to its logical conclusion. Well, he has done so. It is not that he necessarily approves of scepticism, though temperamentally he seems to find the results of his enquiry less depressing than some others; it is simply that he honestly sees no way out. If you propose to obey the rules, he says in effect (though, as we have seen, he breaks some himself) you cannot devote half your time to carrying on secret negotiations with occult forces, which, the moment the crisis arrives, intervene dramatically to restore the *status quo*, like Descartes' God. At the same time, he recognises that scepticism, as a permanent point of view as distinguished from a mere method of enquiry, is not natural to man, and for some men may be intolerable. He therefore does not resent their resort to fanciful illusions. For his part, he regards all notions of the supernatural as "sick men's dreams", or, with an anticipation of Darwin, the "playsome whimsies of monkeys in human shape".[1] As a philosopher, however, he

[1] *The Natural History of Religion.* § XV.

wishes to make it quite clear that the apostles of such illusions must seek to provide themselves with some other sanction than that of critical reason.

Hume possessed all the toleration that should logically follow from the adoption of an attitude of agnosticism. For it need hardly be said that an agnostic should be even less dogmatic than a believer.[1] It is perhaps the attitude displayed by Hume on the general question of belief (especially in his capacity as author of a Natural History of Religion) that has commended him to so many thinkers of the present century. For reasons which are not always clear, his modern disciples have adopted the name of positivists; and the attitude which they display towards metaphysics is something to which we shall be paying particular attention in a later chapter.

The Growing Hostility to Metaphysics

What is Hume's own attitude to metaphysics? In his *Enquiry concerning the Human Understanding* he speaks of it (the tone is familiar to us today, but it was not so familiar then) as "jargon, which, being mixed up with popular superstition, renders it in a manner impenetrable to careless reasoners, and gives it the air of science and wisdom". It is likewise significant that when Hume wishes to refer to, or to dispose of, a concept for which he can find no justification, such as that of spiritual substance, he is content to label it "metaphysical". This tendency is also visible in Berkeley, though the motives of the two philosophers, one a bishop and the other a sceptical scholar, are naturally very different. In other words, the term "metaphysical" is coming to be identified with two things, the Abstruse and the Unknown. And the question whether we are able to acquire knowledge of a world external to mind is being gradually merged with a much more funda-

[1] It ought to be pointed out that although in one place Hume maintains that reason cannot explain the origin of our impressions, he admits elsewhere the possibility that they might be derived "from the author of our being"—evidently an author less lucid than Hume.

mental question: namely, can there be such a thing as metaphysical enquiry at all?

Before we take up this question as it was itself taken up by Emanuel Kant, we must draw attention to a fact which the reader, whatever he may think of the various systems outlined in the foregoing pages, cannot have failed to notice. Not merely do the rationalists and empiricists remain locked up in the subjective world (at least in so far as they obey the rules of their respective games); the world in which they remain confined is still an irrational world. The ideas which this world entertains are ideas which are either given or lent in a fashion wholly arbitrary; nor, as we have already pointed out, is their truth regarded with the same importance as their origin. That admittedly was the problem: to deduce the origin of our ideas; and the philosophers of whom we have spoken are to be congratulated upon having, with certain exceptions, stuck to it. But in doing so they throw overboard a considerable amount of useful ballast; and along with this ballast vanish many of the most important possessions of the human mind.

Let us pause for a moment to scrutinise the inventory. Undoubtedly the empiricists were the worst offenders in this respect. Their distrust of universal principles is notorious. Unlike the rationalists, they do not ever succeed in showing how the truths of mathematics are derived, though Berkeley at any rate was a mathematician of a high order. In view of his extreme empiricism, Hume has the most difficult task in tackling this problem, and it must be admitted that he makes no great show of it. He maintains, for instance, that the truths of geometry are capable of being derived from experience, the truths of arithmetic not. A later empiricist, John Stuart Mill, took this line even farther, with what results we shall be able to see. Secondly, the empiricists of this time cannot make up their minds upon the subject of ethics, which they regard as a mere matter of feeling. This, too, is an atti-

tude which their successors are found to share even today
some of them, like Earl Russell, going so far as to assert that
ethics is not a subject with which philosophy is concerned
As for the rationalists, their sins of omission are glaring as well
Disgusted with the scholasticism of the Middle Ages, or rather
with that into which it had degenerated, Descartes adopted a
method of approaching philosophy that he had derived from
his understanding of mathematics. In doing so he finds that
he can say nothing about religion, poetry and history, except
what is pious and edifying, which is perhaps the most obvious
sign of poverty of thought. And in this way there grew up the
notion, which is still current in many circles, and has indeed
become almost a dogma, that the subjects already mentioned
were somehow not genuine categories of thought, but pseudo-
categories: the kinds of sphere of which the subject-matter, in
Aristotle's phrase, could well be other than it is. Of such
subjects there can be no science, and therefore, since science
is to Descartes the archetype of philosophical knowledge, no
philosophy. This did not mean that religion, poetry or history
could no longer exist: on the contrary, the century in which
this view was put forward was distinguished for its creative
achievements. It simply meant that they would continue to
exist in a kind of spiritual vacuum—religion and poetry being
regarded as matters of purely private concern and therefore
referred to, if at all, with all the delicacy and embarrassment
with which a private matter is conventionally invested, and
history becoming a diversion or entertainment, tinged with
nostalgia and sentiment for a past that was assumed to have
no significant relation to the present. This being the conventional assumption, it was to be expected that there should be
forces working counter to it. The contempt of religion produced great religious counter-movements; the contempt of
poetry (by which is meant imagination in general), the
Romantic Revival all over Europe; the contempt of history,
the beginnings of a wholly new and fruitful attitude to his-

torical investigation, at once theoretical and practical. And so the narrowing down of philosophical enquiry to which we have referred could not stem the creative powers of the mind; still less could it stem the impulse towards broadening the philosophical outlook. The urbane treatises of Locke, Berkeley and Hume are followed by the massive productions of Kant, Hegel and their successors.

The process whereby too violent a denial of a principle has the effect of raising up that principle in a new form is well illustrated in the conventional division of reality into two spheres. The chief objection to withholding recognition from one sphere and confining oneself to the other is the objection that it cannot be done. The knower and that which is known will always be distinguishable, however much violence is done to the structure of the theatre in which they are expected to perform their cognitive act. In maintaining that the knowable world consisted simply of the mind and its ideas, the so-called external world was not in reality abolished; it was, as we saw in the case of Berkeley's "refugees", merely forcibly incorporated within the subjective world. It had to go on breathing that rarefied atmosphere, to partake of that world's character, and to surrender to its whims. And finally, there being no other immediate problem involved but that which concerned the knowability of ideas, perception came to be regarded as the primary activity of the human mind, the be-all and end-all of its processes, to the neglect of thought and its universality. And this was the most serious of the losses inflicted upon philosophy by the jettisoning of valuable cargo by the rationalist and empiricist thinkers. Reason itself was deprived of its primacy, and in consequence the Human Understanding was that about which our understanding was least assured.

Transition to the Philosophy of Kant

The most satisfactory approach to the work of Kant is that

which makes clear at the outset the kind of problems that Kant intended to solve. To maintain that Kant merely "had another shot" at the sceptical dilemma at which the rationalists and empiricists had discharged all their armoury is not sufficient. True, he aims at a target already heavily marked with their fire; but such past efforts are a useful guide in his own marksmanship. As to how he came to interest himself in the problem at all, he records that it was a reading of Hume that first woke him "from his dogmatic slumber";[1] and the aspect of Hume's philosophy in which he found himself most interested was, as might have been expected, that of causation.

In maintaining that causation or necessary connection had no *a priori* basis, Hume had contended that experience provided us with nothing to observe save temporal succession. Let us take a simple example. We see one billiard ball hit another and the latter roll away. It was Hume's contention that on such occasions we were able to see no "force" whereby the movement takes place. All that we are able to see are a series of happenings, each distinct from the rest and related only from the point of view of time; one happens *after* the other. From nothing that our senses report, therefore, can we derive the idea of a necessary connection between one movement and the next. Kant, whose analytical gifts were at least equal to those of Hume, is not dismayed by the latter's destructive analysis. He has but one objection to it. It does not go far enough. Hume is supposed to be basing his denial of the causal nexus upon what he maintains he can see. Kant replies that, just as the believers in causal necessity claim to see more than is justified, and thus deserve Hume's rebuke, so Hume himself reads into the process a great deal more than observation warrants. For one thing, he claims that he sees the second ball move away from the first. But does he? To be strictly accurate—and that is what we are trying to be—his

[1] *Prolegomena to Any Future Metaphysic*, 260.

vision at any one moment is limited to seeing the ball in one particular position, and what he calls seeing the ball "move" is merely plotting the succession of static positions that the ball takes up. A Humian cannot logically claim to be seeing anything else, since all we are capable of perceiving are discreet impressions. We are no longer talking of habit now; we are getting down to that which precedes the formation of habit. Secondly, the analysis of movement into a series of different positions presupposes that the ball we notice to be in one position is the same as that which we notice in the next, and so on all down the line. If, as Hume contends, we "project" the notion of cause into the operations that we observe, so also do we project the notion of movement and the notion of identity. Now, to press the matter home, let us concentrate upon that which we assume to be the one stable sense-impression of the lot, namely, the ball at rest at any particular moment. Can we be sure of the absolute reliability of this particular sense-impression? Do we, in other words, really perceive the ball? It depends upon what we mean by perceive. We certainly do not see it. We have no perception of it as a ball, any more than we have a perception of a cube as a cube. We are obliged to imagine the back of the ball. We assume its spherical shape. We even credit it with uniform colour, calling "white" what is in actual perception no more than a series of patches of varying degrees of grey. The destructive power of Kant's analysis exceeds that of Hume almost as an atom bomb exceeds a pellet. Hume questioned one form of connection among objects; Kant disrupts the connections that enable the objects to cohere in themselves.

The reader may possibly have wondered why the results of the analysis pursued by Hume did not strike its author as leading to palpable absurdity. In the light of the much more vigorous analysis pursued by Kant, we can no doubt see the reason why. Hume's analysis stopped just short of absurdity. It was arrested at the stage which often precedes absurdity;

the stage of the intriguing and the whimsical. Normal people do not mind being told that they cannot see the causes between things; they mind very much being told that they cannot see the things themselves. They do not resent the accusation that their perceptions are often deceptive; they bristle up when they are told that their perceptions are wholly invalid. Hume concludes by telling us that scepticism is an attitude to which, if we are intellectually honest, we shall have to reconcile ourselves. It is a disappointment, but it cannot be helped. Kant begins by telling us that scepticism is an attitude which, faced in all its implications, can be shown to conceal more dogma than is compatible with intellectual honesty, and that therefore, to avoid not so much disappointment as disaster (i.e., intellectual suicide), the mind must help itself. The philosophy of Kant is a philosophy of mental self-help.

He begins his attack upon the problem of scepticism by applying the technique of intensive analysis to the concept of mind itself—not merely the Humian mind, but the Cartesian mind, for he soon perceived that the rationalist approach to scepticism was no better than the empiricist. Granted that our minds contain ideas, and granted that the problem of how these ideas originate has been temporarily shelved; granted, further, that Descartes was right to suppose that the idea of our self-existence is one of the few facts in the world of which we can claim absolute certainty—then it follows that the world with which we are familiar is made up of two things: ourselves, and the ideas with which we think or perceive. Suppose, however, for the sake of argument, that we agree to accept as true Hume's theory that, leaving out of account the power of habit, all that we know are discrete impressions. The inference is that what we know is always a "now"—or at best a series of "nows", which because they are discrete and separate, are never capable of being known by us as past or of being anticipated as future. For, as we have seen, Hume's account of how we can connect repeated impressions even by association is exceedingly unsatisfactory. Now, granted the situation thus created, what kind of a "self" can we imagine "ourselves" as possessing?

First of all, is it a self that we can recognise? Assuming recognition to depend upon the detection of familiar attributes, what are the attributes that a self must possess in order that we shall acknowledge it to be authentic? The first and most indispensable requirement is that it should endure through time. And if it endures it must also possess something without which its endurance would have no significance, namely, memory. A self that lacks consciousness of self-identity is not a true or reasonable self.[1] Hence our claim, in excusing a remark or deed that is out of character, that we had "forgotten ourselves"—a claim which, if sincere, should imply that we have now "pulled ourselves together" or reasserted our identity as responsible persons. Let us now go back to the self with which Hume appears to wish to credit us. This self cannot be anything but a present self, for we are able to know no other. Therefore it cannot be aware of any of its states except that which characterises it at this very instant. But what sort of states are these which exist solely in and for an instant? There are no such states. A "state of mind" or self is something that, in order to be known as a state, must persist through time. To be conscious of self-identity is to be conscious of this persistence. To be "in a state" is the same as to go through it; and the self which makes the passage must know itself as the same at the beginning as at the end. Moreover, the proper functioning of the mind throughout is conditional upon the remembrance not merely of past states of itself, but of past activities. This second condition is extremely important. For it may well be—and in most cases it must necessarily be—that the present act of perceiving and the

[1] Cf. Whitehead: *Adventures of Ideas*, Part III, Chapter XI: "What Hume, in his appeal to memory, is really doing is to appeal to an observed immanence of the past in the future, involving a continuity of subjective form".

G

memory of a past act of perceiving are concerned with one and the same object.

Our conventional set-up is beginning to break down. Here, apparently, is a new factor in the situation, the recognition of which is calculated to dispel the idea that the subjective and objective worlds are mutually exclusive. Apart from the knower and that which is known, there is a third thing not properly reducible to either, namely, the knowledge of ourselves and of other selves as engaged in the activity of knowing —in short, the knowledge of other knowers as knowers.

This idea as put forward by Kant was not wholly new. It was in part a development of Descartes' assertion that, as a result of the *cogito* we become aware of ourselves not merely as existing but as thinking beings. In other words, the subject or thinker is able, without ceasing to be subjective, to become objective—objective in the sense of an object to itself. Developing this idea, Kant contended that our notion of what is objective must therefore be understood to include not merely that which is external to mind, but in certain circumstances that which is internal. And not merely was Kant concerned to point out that the division accepted alike and without criticism by both rationalists and empiricists was an arbitrary division; he was likewise concerned to show that the breaking down of this division entailed the abandonment of the old idea of mental activity as essentially capricious. Owing to the failure to push Descartes' view of mind to its logical conclusion the rationalists and also the empiricists (who, like Berkeley, were not averse to taking a hint from Descartes on occasion) never gave sufficient attention to the fact that, if mental activity is to be regarded as autonomous at all, it must have its own rules. If it is an activity it must be a rational activity. Kant took this notion a stage farther: the activity of mind, he said, is not merely rational but knows itself to be such. Its rationality is the direct consequence of its self-knowledge. In other words, there is no need to drag in another agency, least of all God, to guarantee our credit. The mind must know, and not merely be told by supernatural means, that it is capable of arriving at truth. That is why, if it really possesses this degree of knowledge, it must also be in a position to know other minds as engaged in the same activity. There must be interpenetration between minds. There must consequently be a proper study or science of mind as mind.

With what measure of success Kant formulates this new science of mind—and we shall see later what exactly he means by science as applied to mind and not, as it usually is, to nature—cannot yet be stated. The point to which attention should be drawn at present is simply that Kant has opened up an alternative path for philosophy to the dead-end alley explored by his predecessors. The arch-apostle of the view that mental activity is capricious, Hume had thus been challenged to show good cause why, in proclaiming that such activity is purely habitual, he does not deserve the title of apostate. For, as we saw just now, the thing that he calls mind is in reality a parody of mind, and not too good a parody at that. The whole point of a parody is that we shall be able to recognise in it that which is being held up to gentle ridicule; and of such a view as Hume's the most complimentary as well as the most damning thing we can say is that we are unable to see in it the least resemblance to the mind of its author.

The Development of Kant's Ideas

To assert in text-book fashion that Kant aimed merely at the reconciliation of differences left outstanding by the two schools that had attacked scepticism, would be too simple a view. His general idea of the scope of philosophical enquiry was a great deal wider than that of his contemporaries; and it was wider because he was interested in matters to which, in his opinion, the academic philosophers had paid far too

little attention; the problem of natural science and the problem of conduct, for example. In the period spent in study at
the university of Konigsberg, where he matriculated in 1740,
Kant had made acquaintance with the writings of Isaac
Newton; and although he must have read Hume at some time
between 1760-70, the influence of Newton's writings remained
the more potent of the two, and the first publications which
bear his name are occupied chiefly with working out the philosophical implications of Newton's principles.[1] Constant
reflection on these matters throughout youth, as a Privatdozent
in East Prussia from 1755-1770, and finally as Professor of
Logic and Metaphysics at Königsberg (1770-1804), led him
to an increasing awareness of the discrepancy between the
metaphysical thought of his time (typified by the work of
Wolff) and the new view of the world presented, or rather
implied, by natural science. Nor was it simply with the welfare of abstract thought that he was concerned, as if he feared
that at the current rate of scientific progress he might possibly
soon be deprived of his job. He realised that if the Newtonian
conception of the universe were to be accepted, other things
than metaphysics as currently understood would need to
look to their laurels. The idea of freedom, for instance, must
be analysed afresh; and with freedom went free-will, and with
free-will, morality. The latter was everybody's concern,
whether they realised it or not. That moral convictions were
reducible to mere feeling, thereby ruling out objective standards of right and wrong, was a favourite contention of the
empiricist philosophers. But in 1762 Kant first became
acquainted with the work of Rousseau, whose identification
of duty with freedom made the profoundest impression upon
his receptive mind. To evolve an entirely new and comprehensive system of philosophy in which the world of Newton
and the world of Rousseau were rendered harmonious—in

[1] Kant was acquainted only with Hume's *Enquiry*, not his *Treatise on
Human Nature*.

which man's scientific genius was reconciled with his deepest moral conceptions—became his overriding aim over a period of many years of study and teaching. Finally, in the fear that advancing age would prevent him from arranging his thoughts in systematic form, he set to work in the year 1781 to write the great treatise with which his name, hitherto little known outside the town in which he was to spend the whole of his life, is associated: *The Critique of Pure Reason*. The composition of this long and extremely difficult work occupied a period of five months.

The fact that this first of the Critiques—for there were others—was put together at such speed, and as the consequence of a sudden urge to commit something to paper, suggests that it forms an interim rather than a final report. And the fact that its publication followed so many years of meditation, in the course of which changes of viewpoint were both frequent and to be expected, suggests that it forms, as it stands, a bundle of such interim reports. He meant to elaborate his final system later. Hence the great difficulty of reading *The Critique of Pure Reason* from end to end at a number of sittings, and hence the impossibility of expounding its contents piecemeal in a short space. It is not our intention here to embark upon such exposition, but rather to present as coherently as Kant's method of explanation permits, the essentials of his system and the conclusions that he claimed to have reached. For the problem of metaphysics assumes in his thought a guise that we do not find it wearing anywhere else, but which, having once been donned, has proved very difficult for his successors to discard, even when they wished to do so. And perhaps the reason why, after an initial surrender to the brilliance of his analysis, we find his conclusions somewhat disappointing, is that he asks too many questions at a time laying upon the reader the burden of fitting the right answer to each.

Of Kant's position *vis-à-vis* Hume we have already given

some illustration. We must now proceed to enquire farther into the new conception of a science of mind that he proposes to substitute for it. What was the reason for his dissatisfaction with the metaphysics of his day? And what had a subject like metaphysics to do with questions of the moral consciousness?

Kant began by pointing out that hitherto metaphysics had chosen to concern itself, no doubt rightly, with problems to which we usually give the name of "ultimate". To Kant these could be summed up in three words: God, Freedom, and Immortality. In the past, he points out, men have tried their best to bring these concepts within the scope of their reason. They have argued interminably about the existence of God. They have engaged in lengthy debates concerning the possibility of Free-will. Nor merely their intellects but their whole being has yearned, as it were, to acquire some degree of certitude upon the fact of immortality. What has all this apparently futile argumentation led to? In Kant's view, it had not led to anything; or at least, it had not led to any diminution in men's long-cherished belief in God, Freedom, and Immortality, for men are prepared to go on putting faith in these things, even though human reason, stretched to the limit of its powers, has failed to demonstrate their reality. Nor does Kant wish to suggest that such faith, however uncritical, is in any way misplaced or ridiculous. He shares it himself. The proper inference to be drawn from the failure of reason to produce positive results in this sphere is simply that it is not, in Kant's opinion, a sphere in which reason was ever meant to succeed. Such concepts belong to an altogether different order, the approach to which must be made by a new route. If, as has so often happened in the past, the attempt is made to confuse the first order with the second by applying principles valid in one but not in the other, the result is to produce contradictions of the most violent kind. With such painful contradictions the professional metaphysicians have in the past made us only too familiar; and where they have not confessed to find them inherent in the nature of their work, their critics have not been slow to expose their complacency. Every theologian has discovered, for instance, that to argue about the nature and existence of God soon lands us in perplexing questions as to how a God presumed to be omnipotent can be limited or obstructed by evil in the universe He created; that to pose the question of free-will is to ask how we, as finite and imperfect beings, can at the same time be free agents; that discussions of the conception of immortality escape all the categories of our intellect. As Kant points out in that part of *The Critique* known as The Dialectic, such perplexities are due to applying the idea of infinity to our understanding, whereas its application is legitimate in an entirely different sphere, namely, that to which access is had by our moral consciousness.

What, then, in Kant's view is the proper sphere of reason? The answer is—that sphere in which its operation has so far produced the most fruitful results. This sphere, as Descartes saw before him, is physical science. Such a conclusion, not in itself original, leads Kant to raise two further questions: first, by what procedure has reason achieved such success in this sphere, and secondly, how is it that questions are continually arising in ordinary experience which need to be taken beyond experience for their solution? The second of these questions may appear to contain an element of contradictions; but contradiction, as we have seen, is in fact the result of its denial. For Kant, a realm beyond experience is not a mere hypothetical figment; it is a fundamental reality. Such a realm is nothing but the ground of experience itself, the sole condition of there being such a thing. Of the nature of this world science can tell us nothing—hence Kant's otherwise rather puzzling assertion that it remains "unknowable"; but that which is unknowable to science need not for that reason be denied to our comprehension altogether. We may have, and in fact we do have, access to it in the way that we hinted above: through our moral will. The world that appears to us thus depends upon a world in which things are as they really are; or to be strictly accurate, the world of experience in all its variety—the world of phenomena—depends upon a deeper reality in which such multiplicity is resolved in unity. There are many "things"; there is only one "thing-in-itself".[1]

In the first part of the next chapter we shall be concerned with Kant's treatment of the two questions stated above; and the light that his answers shed upon the problem of metaphysics. Before undertaking this survey, however, we must again issue a warning that, in view of the nature of the enquiry here being pursued, our treatment will be confined to those aspects of Kant's thought which are strictly relevant to the discussion. An examination of all Kant's arguments would occupy a book in itself.

[1] This is because the category of "multiplicity" only refers to phenomena.

I I I

Kant and the Problem of the Thing-in-Itself

Knowledge a Joint-product

Whereas Hume did his best to show that, from the empiricist standpoint, the apparent necessary connection between things was an illusion, Newton had outlined a view of the universe in which cause and effect, far from being a subjective notion, represented a principle to which our reason could attain a vision in mathematical enquiry. Moreover, it was Newton's contention that physical science, being based upon mathematical principles and indeed approximating to the form of mathematics, assumed without question the universality of necessary connection. In other words, such a coherent structure as the universe derived none of its character from the human mind engaged in its contemplation. It was completely objective; and the fact that impressed itself most forcibly upon the young Kant was the absolute incompatibility between this mathematical vision of reality, with its objective conception of space and time, and the fractured and disparate cosmos implied by Hume. That is the reason why, at the beginning of *The Critique*, Kant asks how the judgments that we make in physical science can have acquired their character of absolute necessity and universality—in short, how they can be *a priori*. From this he goes on to ask a further question: namely, how can these truths, which are not learned from experience, manifest themselves in our common judgment of the world? How, in other words, is a *synthesis* possible between such truths and the raw material provided by our senses?

In the past, as we have shown, philosophers had been in the habit of assuming that the mind, in order to arrive at knowledge, must somehow "conform" to a reality external to itself. Examined and tested in all its implications, this assumption is found to involve numerous perplexities and contradictions, some of which we have pointed out in reviewing the thought of Locke and Hume. Kant proposes to act upon a different and very nearly opposite assumption. Having drawn attention to the fact that the truths of mathematics and logic are arrived at by the mind independently of reference to experience—for he is easily able to show that the empiricists were wrong to imagine that the proposition that $2 + 2 = 4$ and the processes of syllogistic reasoning are learned by us wholly in experience—he points out that the problem of knowledge has hitherto been misconstrued. What we wish to ascertain, and what must be ascertained if we are prepared to put faith in the deliverances of science, is not so much how our minds conform to reality as *how this reality conforms to our minds*. That, and not its converse, is the "miracle" of knowledge. Of the native ability of the human mind to reach certain truths unaided, we have demonstrable evidence. We have similar evidence, though more recently acquired, of the advance of the physical sciences as the result of the application to nature of the truths thus reached. As if we were in possession of inside information, we find that we can anticipate the workings of nature from an *a priori* knowledge of its laws. We can predict what has not yet happened in nature by reference to such principles. There is thus every reason to suppose that, in approaching nature in this manner, we are following the correct procedure. But how is it that nature is found to respond so readily to such treatment? How is it, in other words, that nature appears to apply itself to our minds just as actively as our minds apply themselves to it? If this *rapprochement* does indeed take place the inference is that what we call knowledge of phenomena is a joint-product: not necessarily a product of the combined efforts of mind and nature but a product of mind at work in the two spheres simultaneously.

To ask how this is possible is to repeat the question already asked about synthetic judgments: but to repeat it in another form and therefore to assist towards its answer.

Kant tackles the question in a manner that at first sight appears slightly odd. He maintains that the phenomena that we know must be distinguished from nature as it is in itself, which we cannot know; and that such phenomena are known to us by the combined efforts of perception and understanding —the one providing the material for the other to work upon. But this original material must not be thought of as mere raw material. It is sense-data; and Kant, following his predecessors in this respect, defined sense-data as that which exists only in perception.[1] Consequently, it must conform to certain conditions imposed by the mind in order that it may be perceived at all. It is already "stamped" with the forms inherent in our sensibility, among them space and time. Let us put this in another way. If this original perceptual material is sense-data, then it is something given. If it is given, it must be given not merely by something but to something. What gives it— nature—we do not know in itself, though we can think of it as necessarily existing. What receives it—the mind—accepts it on its own terms. These terms, as we have said, consist of laws that it has formulated independently of perception. Therefore nature is another word for phenomena, which, in so far as they are known, depend for their characteristics upon the character of that which knows them. This is the meaning of the passage (quoted here in part) with which Kant opens *The Critique*: "Whatever the process and means may be by which knowledge reaches its objects, there is one that reaches

---

[1] For convenience, the word sense-data is sometimes followed here by a singular verb.

them directly and forms the ultimate material of thought, viz. perception. This is possible only when the object is given, and the object can be given only (to human beings at least) through a certain affection of the mind."

Complicated as this explanation may seem, it provides a clue to the problem which Kant has raised. His question: how is it that the laws of thought, which are *a priori*, are obeyed by the world that we know in perception? His answer: because the mind that formulated them has taken part in the making of that world. His qualification: but this world is only the world of natural phenomena, not the world of nature as it is *in itself*.

Knowledge and Action

As we have hinted, there are many difficulties in Kant's exposition of his theories, due partly to his use of a rather forbidding terminology and partly to his tendency to modify his ideas as he proceeds, leaving the reader to make the necessary adjustments. His account of the thing-in-itself is not at all easy to grasp; and there has been a tendency to assume that his references to the part played in knowledge by our moral consciousness are dictated by an understandable, but illegitimate, attempt to introduce metaphysics by the back-door. But there was no need to introduce metaphysics by any door at all. It was already comfortably installed in the inner sanctum. The important thing was not to let it out. At the end of the last chapter we showed how in Kant's view the attempt made by metaphysicians to identify traditional metaphysical knowledge with scientific knowledge was not merely doomed to failure but fraught with disastrous consequences.[1] Science is concerned with the world as it appears,

---

[1] Kant sums up the error of what he calls the "dogmatic philosophers" by saying that they rendered "theology, morals and religion entirely dependent on the faculty of speculative reason". He, on the other hand, was concerned to give them a firmer basis.

with the surface of things; and *The Critique of Pure Reason* is an attempt to show both why and how it must be so concerned. The fact that this world of appearance or phenomena depends upon a world of reality or noumena does not justify us in assuming that science can either understand or assert this distinction. But the distinction can be understood and asserted to the extent that knowledge is understood and asserted to include, in addition to a knowledge of the world, a knowledge of *ourselves*.

Something of what Kant is getting at may be grasped by returning to his view of the mind as essentially a creative instrument. He insists, rightly or wrongly, that much of what we perceive depends upon what is happening in our own minds. In so far as we become conscious of what is there happening, we are in possession of a kind of interior knowledge, a knowledge of what it is that we are doing and a recognition that such knowledge is rational. Now to know what we are doing and at the same time to know that it is rational is to realise that we are endowed with a will that is at once free and creative.[1] In rational action, then, rather than in abstract speculation, we satisfy ourselves that the universe is an orderly universe, that the laws of nature are true and universal laws, and that we are at harmony with it. And it is this form of knowledge—or, if it is preferred, faith—which assures us of the reality of God, the author of the rationality of the universe; freedom, which endows our actions with responsibility, and immortality, the guarantee that this responsibility is a matter of eternal significance. In short, knowledge as a whole rests on faith, but a rational faith—just as scientific knowledge rests on perception, but a perception made rational by the union of sense-experience with the understanding that transforms it.

[1] Kant is concerned with the problem of the moral will in the second of his great treatises, *The Critique of Practical Reason*, and in several shorter ethical studies.

When Kant refers to questions arising in experience that need to be taken beyond experience for their solution, he has in mind this underlying or, if it is preferred, overriding unity in all knowledge, of which the particular form of knowledge called scientific knowledge cannot of itself provide an explanation. In the section entitled The Dialectic, to which we have already referred, he emphasises that such an ideal of unity is made manifest in every judgment to which we commit ourselves. For judgment is in part the work of understanding, and in part the work of a regulative Reason, which, as he admits, can be regarded as having as its subject matter ideas in the Platonic sense of the word.[1] The fact that both our minds and the products of our minds conform to certain laws implies, in Kant's view, the presence of a transcendental lawgiver: a figure that "surveys the whole scene", as it were, and knows that he is the monarch of all he surveys. And, if this be true, Kant has succeeded, where his predecessors failed, in overcoming the separation between the world of mind and the world of objects, not by the salvationist method of Berkeley, whereby the population of the objective world is accommodated within the subjective world, nor by the alternative method of mobilising a ghost army of ideas operating in the no-man's-land between mind and nature, but by the advance of the mind's forces right into the territory of the objective world, which they proceed to occupy and organise according to a code of law previously drawn up by them. Thus, to vary the simile, Kant regards nature as a counterpane of phenomena (or what Locke calls secondary qualities) draped over a framework of *a priori* laws: this framework being itself upheld by more fundamental laws, much as the totality of the regulations of a country are upheld by its constitution. Mind is no longer to be regarded as standing "over against"

---

[1] Cf. Kant, by A. D. Lindsay (1934), p. 135. This is admittedly a slight shift in the use of the word reason, which in earlier sections of *The Critique* is spoken of as the faculty of *a priori* knowledge.

nature; it is to be regarded as having "taken over" nature, cultivating its resources in order that it may simultaneously enjoy its produce.

Kant's "Copernican Revolution"

The reason why Kant wrote *The Critique*, and no doubt the reason why, on getting down to work, he wrote it at such speed, is that he considered that he had made a revolutionary discovery in philosophical thought. A discovery must not be kept too long unannounced, or a revolution from getting going. In claiming for his discovery an importance in thought equal to that achieved by Copernicus in astronomy, he may have been guilty of slight, though pardonable, exaggeration; but, as Professor Kemp Smith has shown, the comparison between the Copernican and the Kantian Theory is more exact than a good many such analogies, and illuminates Kant's procedure better than some of his other explanations. According to Copernicus, certain changes in the apparent position of the heavenly bodies may be accounted for not by changes in those bodies but by changes in the position of the observer caused by the rotation of the earth; part of what we see, in other words, is understood by realising what is simultaneously happening to us as observers. Kant for his part seeks to show that, in order to understand certain features of our knowledge, we must understand what is happening in ourselves as knowers.

The question to which we must now turn is that of Kant's contribution to metaphysical enquiry. As we have already pointed out, Kant held certain views about the "mission" of metaphysics, which he combined with grave misgivings about the way in which that mission was being discharged by his contemporaries. His avowed aim, therefore, was to prevent further abuses by instituting an enquiry not merely into the current state of metaphysics but into the conditions under which metaphysical thought was possible. How far did he succeed in realising this aim? To this question there have been contradictory answers. It has been said, for example, that in asserting that the subject-matter of metaphysics was God, Freedom and Immortality, and in proceeding to show that these matters lay outside the scope of reason, he was in effect proclaiming the complete incapacity of metaphysics to discuss that which it professed to study. This was the same as saying that the conditions under which metaphysics alone was feasible were conditions impossible of fulfilment. But under cover of asking whether metaphysics was possible, Kant was in point of fact asking another and more important question: namely, whether metaphysics could ever become a science of the same kind, and with as much overt success, as physical science; and in showing that it could not do so he was in reality demonstrating not that metaphysics was impossible but (as he had gradually come to assume) that the method of science and the method of metaphysics were different.

Did Kant realise exactly what he had done? It is not altogether clear. It is not clear, chiefly, because by calling his philosophy "critical", he had forearmed himself against possible charges of inconsistency. By giving it this name he presumably meant that he proposed to assess what had been done by others before undertaking to build a new system himself. But what, in that case, distinguishes the critical approach from the constructive? Nothing, we may surmise, except the consciousness that such an approach, rightly undertaken, is itself constructive. In trying and failing to demonstrate that metaphysics can be a science (if indeed he failed as certainly as he tried), Kant succeeded in showing, *malgré lui*, what metaphysics ought in fact to be, namely, an enquiry into the presuppositions of science. He did not arrive at this conclusion by a fluke. Granted the object with which he set out, the result was inevitable. In asking his original question whether or not metaphysics could become scientific, he was driven to examining what it is about a science that makes it successful in the way that metaphysics had failed to succeed; and this was an enquiry not into the bare idea of science but into the presuppositions of that form of science which had apparently been more successful than any other, namely, the physical science of his own time. He was thus engaging in a form of enquiry which is not merely permissible but obligatory to a metaphysician, and not merely conducive but necessary to the intellectual health of the age in which he lives. Kant, like a true philosopher, is elucidating the dilemma of his contemporaries.

What Are the "Eternal Verities"?

Borrowing an idea popular in the sphere of literary criticism, or what used to pass for literary criticism, it is sometimes asserted that the philosopher, like the artist, should concern himself not with particular truths but with eternal truths. If this were literally the case, philosophers endowed with normal ability and adequate learning would presumably all be engaged in saying the same thing over and over again. There is a sense in which such repetition is not merely desirable but inevitable. But it is not a mere marking time; it is simply another word for the continuity that runs through philosophical tradition, without which it would cease to be a tradition and cease also to be philosophical. Except in a sense that we shall discuss later, the eternal truths of philosophy are not elements within a whole—articles in a bundle called Wisdom, into which, if we are original, we can always pop a few extra pieces; they are the whole itself perpetually reasserted, the dynamic behind all thought in so far as it rises above mere feeling. That truth is to be pursued, that right is to be obeyed, that duty performed, are not separate pronouncements to be reiterated by all thinking people; they are characteristics of thought itself, ideals to the pursuit of which we commit ourselves at every instant of conscious life. We thus arrive at them not by but in thought; and within thought likewise we lose sight of them and retrieve them again. In this sense error too is eternal, eternal in being the shadow that necessarily accompanies the light of truth. To say, as a certain kind of sceptic says, that we can never arrive at truth is equivalent to saying that we can never depart from it; for to arrive at truth in the sense that is apparently intended would be to halt our thinking at a stopping place marked "Go". The "endless adventure" is thought: and we know from experience that adventure is always a plural thing (in novels it is always "The Life and Adventures of . . ."), each episode giving rise to the next, in an endless serial.

The purpose of the above paragraph is not to indulge in a lyrical digression, designed to give the reader a respite after the intricacies of Kant's metaphysics, or to persuade him that philosophers, instead of being kill-joy pedants, are in reality the most entertaining and public-spirited of men. It is to drive home a point upon which there has been much misunderstanding, and which, because it has been so frequently misunderstood, has led people to believe that metaphysics is a subject reserved for those who have a special aptitude for it— an aptitude which the ordinary person, on reviewing his faculties honestly, decides, perhaps with genuine regret, that he does not possess. The point is as follows. Metaphysics, chiefly as a result of Aristotle's definition or definitions of it, has often been regarded as a form of enquiry having for its subject-matter something called Pure Being. Whereas the individual sciences are assumed to have a definite subject-matter—a restricted area within which they may legitimately pursue their investigations, be it the processes of the mind or psyche, the characteristics of organisms, or the phenomena of the physical world—metaphysics (so Aristotle and many of his followers would seem to suggest), just because it is metaphysics, is concerned with that which is subject to no restrictions or limitations whatever: its work is to study Being in itself, or that which remains after we have stripped away everything that, by imposing a limitation or qualification upon Being, makes it less than pure. The process involved is thus the opposite of what occurs when we qualify a noun by "piling on" adjectives: a being, a human being, a male human being, a tall male human being, etc., etc. Reverse this process, it is suggested, and you arrive at something which is just Being by itself, or Pure Being. Study this residue and you are studying the subject-matter with which metaphysics has been traditionally concerned.

We have said that the ordinary man, presented with this information, is inclined to shy off. It is not that he entertains any particular prejudice against metaphysical enquiry—though very likely he does, because he knows others, endowed with the kind of intellect he respects, who have shied off too; it is simply that, as he puts it, he cannot imagine what Pure Being can be, and consequently he cannot imagine what metaphysics can possibly have to say on this, its supposed subject-matter, or indeed on anything else, assuming that it starts from such subject-matter. Now, this is too modest an attitude on his part. It is not that he cannot imagine such a thing as Pure Being. It is that he cannot think it either. For it is not a thing about which anything intelligible can be thought. If, therefore, metaphysics were, in fact, the study of this unthinkable "concept", metaphysics would exist as a study only in so far as, in apparently studying something, it were all the time engaged in studying something else.

To suggest that metaphysicians, in imagining that they were enquiring into the nature of Pure Being, have been either talking undiluted nonsense or talking sense of another kind without knowing it is to suggest that metaphysicians, beginning with Aristotle and working downwards, have been at best suffering from a long-standing misapprehension. A glance at the history of ideas will be sufficient to dispel this thought, be it a source of ribaldry or otherwise. If we were to suppose that the acceptance by an individual or a community

of mistaken beliefs on a certain subject necessarily implied
that that individual or that community were irretrievably
sunk in error, and that in consequence they were rendered
incapable of any form of rational understanding, we should
be condemning not merely the greater part of the human race
for the greater part of recorded time, but ourselves and countless future generations into the bargain. We should be implying, for instance, that all those who lived before the promulgation of the heliocentric theory talked nothing but nonsense
about astronomy; that all those who held the Phlogiston
theory talked nothing but nonsense about chemistry; that all
who thought that thunder was Jupiter's way of being angry
could have arrived at no truth respecting meteorology; and
that a man like Philip Gosse,[1] who believed that God planted
all the fossils ready-made in the course of the first week of
Creation, was not to be trusted upon anything connected with
geology. This is plainly false. It is not impossible, though it
is not necessarily desirable, to make important discoveries
while under the influence of assumptions which are wholly
erroneous: similarly it is not impossible, indeed it is common,
to arrive at perfectly valid conclusions about metaphysics
while assuming metaphysics to have as its aim something
which, like Pure Being, may not even be there to be aimed at.
The idea of the philosopher's stone was no doubt vain: the
search for it probably bore fruit in more than one valuable
discovery.

These considerations link up very well with what we were
saying just now about the rational pursuit of thought. As long
as something is being examined systematically and with disinterested motives, the so-called "eternal truths" will be
present, not as that which is discussed or pondered, but as that
which does the discussing and pondering. It is sometimes
enjoined upon those who would follow the mystical life, that
they should spend their time contemplating the "eternal

[1] Cf. *Father and Son,* by Edmund Gosse.

verities". If they are true mystics they should spend their time living them. For the truth is that to love God is not a form of crystal-gazing; it is doing His will. And that, and not any suggestion of trance-like perception, is the real meaning of the much-quoted line of Dante, "*La sua voluntade e nostra pace*".

In spite of this explanation the objection may still be advanced with good reason, that if Pure Being is an empty concept, no one could have aimed to study it even by mistake, because as we have said, there would be nothing there to be studied, and hence nothing to give rise to any initial act of enquiry. It is one thing, the objector might continue, to say that a mirage is not an oasis; it is another to say that it is not even a mirage. We say that this objection is advanced with good reason; it could have been advanced with a better one. Pure Being is the mirage on the horizon of abstraction, and it recedes as the process of abstraction is pushed to the limit. But in theory there can be no limit to the abstractive process, so that as long as we go on it is there, and as soon as we stop we find that, like a good many mirages, it has vanished. Like the recurring decimal, it represents a perpetual invitation to go forward, but an invitation that we cannot accept because we are unable to catch up with what we are seeking. Meanwhile we endow the mirage with what we believe to be the results of our pursuit. The desert traveller sees pure water. The seeker after reality sees Pure Being. For the latter the mirage is fadeless because his search is without end.

Metaphysics and the Sciences

In speaking of Kant's attitude to metaphysics we said that the proper rôle of the metaphysician is to examine the pre-suppositions of the sciences, and that Kant devoted much of *The Critique*, particularly the Transcendental Analytic, to ful-filling this rôle. By the sciences, it must be recalled, we mean any form of ordered knowledge concerning a limited subject-matter: and in this sense it is clear that there may be as many individual sciences as men like to invent. A science like biology, for instance, in which considerable progress has been made during the last century, will show its fecundity as much by the detailed discoveries that it makes as in the numerous subsidiary sciences to which it has given rise: histology, embryology, ecology, etc., and also in the rapidity—the increasing rapidity—with which these sciences "come of age". A younger science still, psychology, is already seen to be engaging in the same process of generation, though some of its offspring appear to have been premature. Now, as we remarked in Part I, each of these sciences is committed to various presuppositions in regard to its subject-matter which, in the course of its investigations, it may leave unexamined. This is not because it has no time to examine them; it is because it has no immediate occasion to do so. Nevertheless, as many scientists have interests of a more general kind, and as every intelligent person experiences an urge to unify his impressions, it is inevitable that there shall be a tendency in every science, particularly in the most young and vigorous, to apply its limited criteria to that which lies outside its boundaries. To talk of the existence of "boundaries" between the sciences, however, may be misleading: for it may give rise to the impression that reality is divided up into separate fields, like the squares on a patchwork quilt or the coloured counties on a map, and that each field is cultivated in a particular manner. The actual situation is very different. The sciences do not cultivate particular plots of reality; they cultivate the whole of it. But as they employ different methods in this cultivation they naturally arrive at different kinds of result. In asserting that individual sciences exhibit a tendency to go beyond their legitimate sphere, we refer to the tendency to assume that their particular technique is the only one that can legitimately be applied to experience as a whole. And, as a result, we find ourselves confronted with statements by scientists which, unless we are prepared for shocks, may cause us some embarrassment: such statements, for instance, as that since the health of Royal personages is the subject of more public prayers than that of other individuals, the fact that royalty are found statistically to enjoy no better health than other people is a proof of the futility of prayer,[1] or, to take a more common example, that since the beauty of a symphony or a landscape cannot be measured experimentally, it is on that account purely "subjective", or, finally, that since the activity of thought cannot be "located" anywhere in the human brain, it consists simply of a "laryngeal habit", or even a physical "secretion".

Now the question may at this point be raised: why do the sciences make these arbitrary pronouncements? They make such pronouncements because the basis of every science is itself arbitrary, since the basis of science is hypothesis. Unlike metaphysics, every science "commands" its starting point:[2] and having commanded its starting-point, it naturally finds, if it is successful, that all the "facts" obey it. This again must not be taken to mean that science deals only with certain facts; it must be taken to mean that science deals with all facts in a particular manner. Thus it is a mistake to assume that the science of psychology, for instance, "arrives" at the conclusion that the mind can be studied as a material thing productive of material events like thoughts; the idea of the mind as a material thing capable of such production was the hypothesis with which it started out. Similarly, it is a mistake to assume that physical science "arrives" at the conclusion that the universe is a constellation of atoms or electrical disturbances; the idea of the universe as composed of such material entities (some of them becoming distinctly rarefied

[1] See J. B. S. Haldane: *Possible Worlds*, where this observation of Galton is cited with approval.

[2] See Croce, *Logic*, V.

nowadays) was the hypothesis with which it started.[1] And if somebody, anxious to discredit this "scientific view of the world", points out triumphantly that the hypothesis with which it sets out is a false one, and suggests that science might more profitably start afresh by having recourse to one that is true, we must undertake to point out that a hypothesis, just because it is a hypothesis, is neither true nor false. But surely some scientific facts are true? And surely science is constantly enjoining us to "refer to facts" to test our hypotheses? Granted: but that is because true and concrete facts are not scientific facts but historical facts, and because the final appeal of science is not to other scientific facts but to history. Hypotheses are based not upon further hypotheses but upon that which is non-hypothetical or categorical.

Metaphysics and History

From what has been said above, and from what has been hinted on several occasions previously, the conclusion might possibly be drawn that metaphysics and history, though usually assumed to be as different as chalk and cheese, are here being identified one with the other; and it might be contended that such a conclusion, if intentional, is clearly preposterous. It is indeed. When it is affirmed, however, that the task of metaphysics is to examine the presuppositions of the sciences, and that scientific knowledge rests upon a foundation of historical knowledge, what is meant is that the kind of questions that metaphysics asks, in seeking to discover the presuppositions of science, are historical questions. Owing to an addiction for abstract and impersonal terminology, however, metaphysicians have often obscured the fact that this is so. From the time of Socrates to the present day, what metaphysicians have been asking is upon what *basis* men have

[1] It may abandon this hypothesis, as we see in the work of theorists such as Eddington.

affirmed what they do affirm; with what in mind have they arrived at this or that conclusion; from what premises have they argued to this or that result? What, in short, are the presuppositions of their thought, the foundations of their science?[1] And, in order to arrive at satisfactory answers to these questions it is necessary to examine such evidence as is available, i.e., the works of past thinkers or the reports of their beliefs. What Descartes, or Berkeley, or Kant thought about science and about metaphysics can be deduced only from a study of the works of Descartes, Berkeley, or Kant, and of the conditions in which those works were produced. Metaphysics as a methodical form of enquiry, therefore, is the fruit of a particular kind of historical research—a research into the question of what a past scientist, or a past group of scientists (not all working in laboratories and not all conscious of the fact that they were scientists in our sense of the word), in framing certain hypotheses about nature, presupposed by them. And a metaphysician who succeeds in elucidating the "matrix" of presuppositions entertained by scientists in the course of history—a task no less difficult than that undertaken by the historian, and therefore for practical reasons limited to the consideration of particular epochs, each of which is given a convenient label—will be elucidating the "pattern of civilisation".

Metaphysics as the "Pattern of Civilisation"

The idea of a "pattern of civilisation" has already been referred to (Part III, Chapter I), but we must here take leave to repeat that, in speaking of such a pattern, we do not wish to imply anything symmetrically perfect, still less anything static, as if civilised man were in the habit of acting in

[1] Cf. Plato, *Theætetus*, 150 f, in which Socrates declares: "My art is like that of midwives, but differs from theirs, in that I attend men and not women, and I look after their souls when they are in labour, and not after their bodies: and the triumph of my art is thoroughly examining whether the thought which the mind of the young men brings forth is a phantom and a lie, or a fruitful and true birth."

front of an elegantly designed backcloth, grown threadbare in places and even a little patched, but withal preserving a certain old-world dignity and charm. The pattern is a dynamic pattern. And this implies, as we went on to say, that at any one time there may be, and indeed there invariably is, more than one design in process of formation. We have to imagine something as little resembling a formal configuration as a shifting palimpsest of exfoliating elements, capable of being interpreted only by stereoscopic vision. And in each case such similes render the process more rather than less obscure, as so often happens in the effort to describe processes of thought, we may remind the reader that what is here being depicted is simply the kind of process which is at work throughout history, even the modern or stop-press history with which we are made familiar in the newspapers. To the superficial eye —and we mean that adjective to be taken literally—each epoch of history appears to exhibit some peculiar and unmistakable direction or trend, whether of thought or action: but if we scrutinise the prevailing ideas of that epoch—the art, the thought, and the customs or *mœurs* that we find there exemplified—we shall observe that this so-called "prevailing movement", which we had supposed in our innocence to permeate equally every level of social activity, is in reality perpetually engaged in combating, negating, and running counter to another and very nearly opposite movement; so that the former may be said to "prevail" not so much because its antithesis is "annihilated" as because this latter is perpetually rising up, like some mythological monster, only to be subdued afresh. This is true even of those epochs which in our relative ignorance we call "Dark Ages". For we are apt to think that what we cannot understand or grasp must therefore be unintelligible or beneath our notice (as indeed in a sense it is), and that those doors for which we have not yet discovered the key must necessarily lead nowhere, or at best into an unlit chamber. This is a serious error, for it is we, and not history, that are blind. One generation may be indifferent to the period be-tween A.D. 100-400 and call it "dark" while the next, perhaps our own, being somewhat preoccupied with ideas of decline and collapse, observed in this same period the small, if un-mistakable, beginnings of cultured awakening: and, as if a cataract had been scaled from our eyes, our whole vision of the past proceeds to undergo readjustment and refocusing. What was obscure becomes clear; what we had considered as mere archæology becomes a vital art;[1] what appeared neg-ligible becomes significant. This does not mean that past historians must be considered to have been sunk in error; it merely means that they are, as one day we shall be, past his-torians. Nor need we become involved in the quagmire of relativism and assert that in every epoch the past is turned upside down and inside out according to the angle at which the historian is looking. The changes in historical vision are less violent, more a matter of shifts of emphasis. No historian, however original, can alter the fact that Julius Cæsar, Napoleon, or Hitler lived when they did, or that the Reforma-tion represented a religious rift, or that the French Revolution altered the composition of French (and therefore European) society: all they can do is to deepen our understanding of these people and these movements. As far as the history of western civilisation is concerned, historians are bound to exhibit a measure of agreement simply because they them-selves are part of the era they are studying. "In each period there is a general form of the force of thought; and like the air we breathe, such a form is so translucent, and so pervading, and so seemingly necessary, that only by extreme effort can we become aware of it."[2] In this general and comprehensive form, the so-called prevailing movement and the counter-movement or movements take their place not as organic

[1] Cf. T. E. Hulme's observations on Byzantine art in *Speculations* (1924).

[2] A. N. Whitehead, *Adventures of Ideas*, p. 14.

elements of the pattern. Even when we have dismissed the notion that nineteenth-century England was exclusively an age of progress, optimism and "respectability", there is still a sense in which it may accurately be labelled "Victorian".

The conclusion at which we arrive, therefore, is that history consists not of well-defined movements but of movement itself: a complex of forces which, though separately incompatible, are collectively compatible, just as the grips of two wrestlers become the "holds" whereby they preserve a precarious balance. Thus it is a serious error to regard freedom, for instance, as a kind of gift or talent which a society either possesses or does not possess according to whether it is "authoritarian" or "democratic". Freedom might be defined as the health of society: and we know that good health is not a static condition which we either possess or do not possess, but the product of the successful functioning of a complex of bodily processes. And just as these processes are functioning either well or badly, so the general health of the body-politic is constantly undergoing modification. There are some people who declare that they are never ill; others insist with equal force, and sometimes with hardly less gusto, that they are never well. But in reality we are always either getting better or getting worse. If we are well, that means that we are better than we were; if we are ailing, that means that we are worse than we were. In other words, good health is that which is at every moment being either preserved or undermined. And precisely the same is true of the health of the body-politic. Liberty is that which is at every moment being either preserved by the vigilance of the few, or undermined by the apathy of the many. A perfectly free society and a perfectly enslaved society would have this much in common, that they would be essentially static; and a static condition of freedom would have as little to recommend it as a static condition of oppression—in fact, there would be some difficulty in distinguishing one from the other.

I V

Hegel and the Rise of the Historical Consciousness

The Nature of Presuppositions

Before we undertake a review of the thought of Hegel—to which the concluding paragraphs of the last chapter, with their insistence upon the dynamic character of historical development, are intended to form a kind of prolegomena—we must do something to resolve certain doubts that may be circulating in the reader's mind as to the exact nature of the "presuppositions of science" about which we have been speaking. If, as we have insisted, all historical movements are engaged in constant struggle with counter-movements, with the result that the pattern of civilised life in any age is a dynamic pattern; and if this pattern of civilisation is a pattern of presuppositions entertained by the mind—what, it may well be asked, is the guarantee that these presuppositions that we hold, even if we do not consciously realise that we hold them, are valid? Out of the complex of presuppositions that have been held in the course of history, which should we select as most reliable? And finally, if presuppositions *qua* presuppositions are the foundation upon which our science is built, how can they be justified, seeing that science, by presupposing them, is automatically ruled out as an arbiter?

These questions are extremely pertinent and, before going farther, we must acknowledge the fact by advancing at least tentative answers to them.

To point out that a presupposition is of such a nature that

it cannot be justified by the science that presupposes it is perfectly correct. What is incorrect is to conclude, as many enquirers have concluded, that it therefore cannot be justified at all. Let us take as an example the presupposition involved in the statement that there is a world of nature which obeys rational and uniform laws. Although this is a presupposition accepted by western science—and, incidentally, a presupposition entailed by an acceptance of the Christian revelation—no one has ever been able to prove it from experience, since any such proof would be based upon its prior acceptance. It may be objected that the Greeks, and especially Aristotle, thought otherwise: they believed, in other words, that the existence of the natural world was something that can be deduced from experience. Now the reason why Aristotle held this view was that he entertained a notion of God's activity which, as we saw in Part II, was incompatible with the notion that He created the world. To us it may seem strange that Aristotle should have believed that the world created itself out of its own resources; that the movements and activities of this world happened of themselves and by themselves; and that such rationality as these movements possessed was due to a striving on the part of nature to attain to that absolute rationality which God, in communing with the world of Forms, embodied in Himself. But such a view of God and the world, besides being in harmony with Greek traditional thought, represented one of the few alternatives to which a philosopher, finding no reason to believe the world to have been the direct creation of any supernatural power, might be expected to have recourse. It does not follow that the view was coherent, the presupposition sound: and Aristotle, though he may not have realised its unsoundness, failed to show how, assuming its truth, we are made aware of the existence of nature from experience. The Christian philosophers, claiming that they were in possession of a more intelligible account of the relations between God and nature, pointed out that an acceptance of God entailed the belief that nature, being His creation, was something given anterior to experience. For what did they mean by an "acceptance of God"? They meant a belief that God exists; and since this God had not merely created the world but sealed His union with His creatures by taking human form at a particular moment of time (such temporal manifestation being the only way in which this could be done), a belief that God exists entailed a belief in the existence of every manifestation of His activity, including nature. Now the belief in a creative God was a matter of faith; consequently a belief in this particular manifestation of His creativity was a matter of faith, too.

No doubt it will be suggested at this point that such "naïve" faith, while necessary and even to be encouraged at a "primitive" period, is today no longer required. We can prove these matters scientifically. But can we? The existence of a world of nature obeying rational laws is as much a presupposition today as it was when it was first presupposed.[1] If it is not, that is not because it has been proved to be false—for a presupposition, as we have said, is neither true nor false—but because it has been replaced, or at least countered, by another presupposition equally supported by faith.[2] The important thing is that we should know what the faith is, and what an acceptance of it implies. The first of these tasks is fulfilled by religion (sometimes appropriately called Faith for short) and

[1] Cf. Whitehead: *Adventures of Ideas*, Part II, Chapter 8.

[2] Cf. Max Planck: *Where is Science Going? passim.* Nevertheless, the prevalent talk among scientists about "statistical laws" and "principles of indeterminacy" need not necessarily be taken to mean that nature is a realm of imprecision. "Heisenberg now makes it appear", says Sir James Jeans, "that nature abhors accuracy and precision above all things"; but as Professor Stebbing has pointed out in her *Philosophy and the Physicists* (p. 183), it is incorrect to suppose that "the uncertainty relations show that there is anything *indeterminate* in nature, or that science has now become inaccurate. . . . Granted that in a given case the initial conditions are determined as precisely as the Principle of Uncertainty permits, then the probability of all subsequent states is determined by *exact laws*. . . . There is nothing *lawless* in *quanta* phenomena".

nurtured by the institutions that religion bring into being; the second by metaphysics. And without metaphysical enquiry, science will have to do the work of metaphysics on its own.

When, therefore, it is declared that every society must have its religion, this can only mean that every society, in order to sustain the presuppositions upon which it is based, must have some means of confirming its members in a belief in them. Every powerful political movement, once it claims to regulate the lives of the people, partakes of the nature of a religion, promulgating its dogmas that may not be questioned. Consequently, such a movement must have its forms of ritual, its rallies, its orations, and above all its solemn trials of heretics and apostates. There is no faith without ritual. Those churches which reduce all outward show to a minimum, even to the extent of dispensing with a proper order of service, cannot abolish ritual altogether. The requisite emotions are aroused in other ways; and the preacher who inveighs against incense will all the time be drowsing his congregation with the censer of his pungent eloquence.

We are now able to see more clearly why metaphysics, even —and perhaps most of all—to those who know very little about its object and procedure, has been associated in the past with the discussion or promulgation of the Eternal Verities, such as Kant's God, Freedom and Immortality. The Eternal Verities, apart from their reference to the characteristics of honest thought itself, are and can only mean the basic presuppositions of the civilisation to which we belong. For we must not interpret their eternal nature in a temporal sense, meaning that such truths have always been entertained by the best minds of every epoch. Clearly they have not. While much of the ethical content of Christian civilisation is in harmony with the Greek view of life, much of it was so utterly new that the apostle was not guilty of exaggeration when he declared that to the Greeks it must represent the extreme of "madness". As a great scholar has pointed out,[1] the Greek mind would not have understood the Beatitudes. Furthermore, this tendency to associate metaphysical speculation with Eternal Truths in the old sense is not incompatible with the notion that it has to do with something as devoid of character as Pure Being. Human nature abhors a vacuum; and the existence of an empty abstraction is a standing invitation to the imagination to fill it with picturesque and exalted images. In this way Pure Being becomes identified with God, the Absolute, Nirvana, Mana, or the Life Force—whatever cannot be defined in human terms, and by whatever name the indefinable happens to be known in each generation.

Hegel and the Idea of History

That we should end this section of the book with a chapter on the philosophy of Hegel is fitting, because it is in Hegel that we find not merely an attempt to sum up the whole history of metaphysical thought but an attempt to interpret reality in the dynamic manner referred to in the last chapter. The reputation of Hegel has suffered of late years for two main reasons: first of all, the idea has got about that he is an unspeakably abstruse and "heady" thinker, and secondly, he is thought to be in many ways responsible for the development of ideas which, on the political plane, have brought untold misery upon Europe and the world. With regard to the first point, there is no denying that Hegel makes difficult reading, though not perhaps such difficult reading as some of Kant; and with regard to the second, it is true that his followers, developing certain aspects of his thought at the expense of others, have suggested that he was nothing but an apologist for oppression and violence. It is equally true, however, that these same philosophical doctrines have given birth, by way of reaction, to ideas diametrically opposed to those preached

[1] Sir Richard Livingstone in *Greek Ideals and Modern Life*.

H

by so-called "Fascist" thinkers. A man whose thought has occasioned such diverse reactions ought clearly to be studied.

The most important fact to be borne in mind in approaching the philosophy of Hegel is that it is permeated with an idea which is not merely absent from the work of Kant but foreign to its character. This is the idea of history. To say that Kant and his predecessors paid no attention to history of a kind would be untrue. Hume, among others, was a historian. He wrote both a history of religious belief and a very popular history of England: to his contemporaries, indeed, he was more celebrated for his historical writings than for his philosophical. Kant, likewise, interested himself in history, as he interested himself in so much else; and in Kant's time, as we shall see, his own countrymen were making discoveries in this field which were to be of permanent importance. Nevertheless, Kant's world is the world of Newtonian science; his attention was concentrated upon the success of physics and the methods by which it had achieved success, rather than upon the new attitude to historical studies. Hegel, on the other hand, was heir to these new ideas; consequently his approach to the problems of the present and the past is altogether new.

It has been observed that the most convincing criticism of the cosmopolitan rationalism of the eighteenth century was the rise of modern nations; and the modern nation, as Dupont White has said, is something dating from the time of the French Revolution. Certainly, the intense nationalist spirit which flared up in the early years of the nineteenth century particularly in countries like Germany,[1] was different in kind from that which followed the Renaissance. The great revolution in thought which is summed up in the word Renaissance—and all great historical movements are primarily revolutions in thought—constituted a victory above all for the scientific spirit. Consequently, the nationalism of the era

[1] German nationalism, it will be remembered, helped to overthrow Napoleon.

preceding the French Revolution, though strong, was tempered by the vague cosmopolitan outlook to which we have referred. Reason was King, whatever Louis XIV might say. And in the atmosphere of this period the word Reason fulfilled a function similar to that fulfilled in the nineteenth century by the word evolution; it represented, in the words of Josiah Royce, "a sort of general comforter of all those who felt puzzled and longed for light".[1] Now it is true in the main that the world of the eighteenth century was, as regards its thought, a static world. The *savants* of the eighteenth century believed themselves to be not partially but wholly enlightened; and if you believe yourself to be in complete possession of the truth it is impossible to move forward and sheer perversity to move back. Voltaire wrote his *History of the Reign of Louis XIV* to prove that the eighteenth century was the summit of civilisation. He evinced slight interest in other epochs since, in his view, the only interest other epochs could possibly possess was that of being precursors of the eighteenth century. The past, in other words, was essentially a dead past, a past of darkness and supersition, a past to which no civilised person could possibly wish to return, and for this reason a past of which no writer would wish to write, and no reader would wish to read, the history.

Now if the Renaissance may be said to have resulted in a victory for science, the French Revolution may be said to have resulted in a victory for history. The rediscovery, or rather the conscious discovery, of nationality was a historical act: the national consciousness so clearly observable in the famous Addresses to the German Nation of the philosopher Fichte, was above all a consciousness of the nation's past. Thus, the most significant aspect of the Romantic Revival was not so much the efflorescence of poetry as the preoccupation with history: a preoccupation which is manifested in intellectual achievements as diverse as Savigny's researches into law,

[1] *Lectures on Modern Idealism*, 1923, p. 65.

Scott's historical novels, Herder's virtual creation of the science of anthropology, Winckelmann's attempt to write the history of Greek Art, and above all Hegel's historical approach to philosophy. And this preoccupation with history is something that we observe to increase in range as the century proceeds. It is at the root of Marx, who is concerned (in the first volume of *Capital*, for instance) to trace the origins of capitalist society; it pervades the thought of Cardinal Newman, especially the *Essay on the Development of Christian Doctrine*; it informs the author of *The Origin of Species*; it is the inspiration of that last nineteenth-century *savant* Renan. The latter, indeed, never spoke more truly than when he observed: "*l'histoire est la vraie philosophie de la 19ème siècle*". When nineteenth-century philosophy is divorced from history we get great learning and immense bulk but complete sterility; in short, we get Herbert Spencer. And it might be added that when nineteenth-century "history", rejecting the new historical vision, endeavours to retain the old eighteenth-century methods, we get the nineteenth-century equivalent of Montesquieu, Buckle.

The Hegelian Dialectic

Those for whom the very word Hegelian signifies "abstraction" will no doubt wonder how its originator should be concerned with so concrete a thing as history. Admittedly, the notion of abstraction is one with which Hegel is much occupied; but he uses the term in a particular way, and it is our business, before protesting that we cannot follow him, to discover what this way is.

Whether he is acquainted with the method of philosophy or not, everybody is aware of the existence of a number of "opposites" in both thought and life: truth and falsehood, love and hate, beauty and ugliness, and so on. He is likewise vaguely aware that one of the tasks of philosophy or metaphysics is to show how these pairs of opposites can be reconciled, though he is not always certain of the extent to which this reconciliation has been accomplished. It may readily be admitted that, in trying to effect this reconciliation in the sphere of theory, metaphysics has often tended to employ a form of dodge. One of the terms of the "dualism", as it is called, is shown by an act of prestidigitation to be a form or disguise of the other. We are told, for instance, that all our actions are motivated by selfishness, so that the idea of disinterested or virtuous action turns out to be an illusion; or that the æsthetic pleasure that we derive from art is merely the rationalisation of some natural instinct, such as sex. Such philosophies enjoy a transient vogue, usually on the morrow of some social upheaval in which baseness and cruelty, treachery and vice, have obtruded themselves with more than their usual abandon; they satisfy neither the instincts nor the intellect.

Instead of attempting to deny the existence of these so-called "irreconcilable" opposites, Hegel claims that they form the very stuff of reality. We must not dismiss them, or one of them, as illusions; we must not endeavour to keep them apart or to treat them separately; we must resolutely match one against the other, jam their heads together, and observe what issues from such violent concussion. For it is Hegel's contention that while the "opposites" may be opposed one to another in abstraction, living—as it were—by mutual hostility and committed to destroying one another or at least "buying one another out", they are not opposed to the unity which issues from their actual coming to grips. Set over against each other, they represent alien immobilities; locked in struggle, they generate movement and dynamic change.

Thus Hegel arrives at two main conclusions: first, that the essence of reality is opposition, and secondly, that such opposition is the cause of all movement and development. This movement, this development, this "becoming", *is* reality; indeed, it is life itself.

In expounding his doctrine of opposites, to which he gave the name Dialectic, Hegel claimed to be trying to solve a problem raised by Plato and taken up by Aristotle. As we have already seen, the chief criticism to which Aristotle subjected the Forms of Plato was that they were too static to account for movement and change in the world. Hegel, on the other hand, maintained that the world of Forms was itself a dynamic world; that reality consisted of the development of what he called, in the singular number, the Idea; and that in the logical development of the Idea both nature and mind took their place as phases or "moments". He is careful to point out, however, that this process is not a temporal but a timeless one.

Taken by itself, each "moment" of the process formed an abstraction. The negation of one abstract concept by its opposite, however, gave rise to a synthesis which was not abstract but concrete. To recognise the original opposition was the work of the intellect; to achieve the "concrete universal" by overcoming this original opposition was the work of reason. Thus in Hegel the word reason carries much the same meaning that it does in the latter part of *The Critique* of Kant. He even speaks of the "cunning of reason" (*die List der Vernunft*) much as a theologian would speak of Providence.[1]

There is still another respect in which Hegel starts where Kant left off. In defining the "thing-in-itself", Kant makes it clear that such knowledge as we possess of this "thing" is not to be regarded as scientific knowledge. Except in so far as we can grasp its reality in moral exertion or action, it remains totally unknowable. Hegel denied this. There is no difficulty, he declared, in getting into contact with the thing-in-itself. The truth is that we are always in contact with it. We brush with it at every moment of time. As to whether we know much

[1] Hegel's view of the working of Reason in history was anticipated in many ways by Vico (1668-1744), the first discoverer of the *Zeitgeist*. Cf. H. P. Adams: *The Life and Writings of Giambattista Vico*, p. 157.

about it, that is another matter. To know a thing implies that there is something substantial to know. The thing-in-itself is not easy to know because there is next to nothing about it to be known. This is because the thing-in-itself is nothing more nor less than Pure Being.

Of the traditional association of metaphysics with the idea of Pure Being we spoke in the last chapter. There we pointed out, in anticipation of Hegel, that Pure Being was not so much the goal of metaphysical enquiry as the mirage in lieu of a goal that flickers on the horizon of the process of abstraction. When we think we are coming upon it we find there is nothing there. In his *Logic* Hegel makes much the same point. Pure Being, he says, is difficult to distinguish from nothing simply because it possesses scarcely any characteristics to distinguish it therefrom. When we try to conceive it we come as near to thinking of nothing as we can manage. How is this? Does it mean that Pure Being and Nothing are the same thing?

To this question Hegel replies in the negative. The difficulty of distinguishing Pure Being from Pure Nothing, he says, is due not to the two being identical but to the one being meaningless except when taken in conjunction with the other. Directly both are grasped in combination, the contradiction between them is found to generate a third concept, in which they are able to live in harmony: this third concept is Becoming—the movement which constitutes reality. The first "triad" of the Dialectic is therefore: Being, Not-Being, Becoming. The first two "moments" are abstractions because, though the intellect can separate them, they are unable to live apart from each other. The third, Becoming, being the work of reason, is what Hegel calls a concrete universal.[1]

The Hegelian Attack on Abstractions

Having arrived at this "first concrete concept", Hegel

[1] This is Hegel's version of Kant's *a priori synthesis*.

shows that we cannot stop there. The dialectic goes on, impelled by a force or urge planted inside itself; and this process of opposition overcome by synthesis must continue until all opposition is "taken up" into the highest form of synthesis. Anything that falls outside the synthesis is not true reality but abstraction. To those who would obtain a kind of specious unity by disguising the opposition at the nature of things, Hegel replies that unity without opposition is impossible. And for this reason he describes the logical "law of identity" (i.e., that a thing cannot both be and not be) as "the law of the abstract intellect". To preserve unity by cancelling the reality of opposition is an occupation in which the abstract intellect is continually indulging; for the abstract intellect is the enemy of true philosophy, which is concerned with the concrete universal. In other words, Hegel, seemingly one of the most abstract of philosophers, is in reality the great opponent of abstractions.

Borrowing a phrase from Goethe, Hegel defines reality as that which has neither nut nor shell. Here again he is tilting at abstractions. His objection to materialism, for example, is that it tries to live by cancelling its opposite, spirit. Materialism maintains that the only true realities are phenomena, matter, and that which is finite; all else must be "illusion". But such concepts as phenomena and matter remain, as Hegel points out, inconceivable without their opposites, by and through which they live. Are self-declared materialists nothing but liars, then? No: but they are not above inventing the props upon which their doctrines, to be coherent, must rest. Needing an infinite to match their finite they make this finite spin infinity out of its own bowels. The finite material thereby becomes a "creative" thing, the source of everything in existence, producing other finites *ad infinitum*:[1] and so in time we arrive at such bastard productions as Dialectical Materialism,

[1] Cf. Benedetto Croce: *What is Living and What is Dead in the Philosophy of Hegel* (translated Ainslie, p. 52 *et seq.*).

the invention of one who, having been trained in the Hegelian school, ought to have known better and thought he did. So, too, as Hegel had pointed out, we arrive at the Kantian division of reality into phenomenon and noumenon. For although Kant finds no room for the "thing-in-itself" in his system, he is obliged to postulate its existence: a world of phenomena subsisting in the void is inconceivable.

Hegel therefore believes himself to have disposed once and for all of the distinction between two worlds of reality, one subjective and the other objective, one internal and the other external, as if the first somehow confronted or stood over against the second. Convex is not "over against" concave; it is correlative with it. To confront each other one would have to reverse and in so doing would drag the other with it, like a cat trying to confront its own tail, leaving the problem still to be solved. Nevertheless, Hegel does believe in something called an external world, but it is external in a new and important sense, hereafter to be described.

The Hegelian View of Nature

If reality consists of the logical development of a world of Forms, operating outside time but providing the ground for all that occurs in time, how do we account for the existence of mind and nature? Some commentators have given the impression that the Idea of Hegel is identical with mind: if it is identical with anything, it is identical with God, being a kind of blue-print of his self-revelation. As God, the world of Forms gives rise to nature, and nature in turn gives rise to mind. The world of nature is therefore a presupposition to mind. And this is not the least of Hegel's reversals of currently held doctrine: for most philosophers before him had argued that mind, instead of being the child of nature, was the source of it. Hegel was reverting to orthodoxy.

Now since nature represents the stage in a process—a stage

H*

that must pass over into the next, and is always so passing over—it is at any one moment incomplete, unfinished, truncated. Therefore, all its characteristics and components are infected with the same limitations. The world of Forms seeks embodiment in nature but never satisfactorily attains it. Nothing in nature succeeds in being precisely what we would expect it to be; everything seems to be engaged not so much in bettering itself as in trying and failing to live up to its own standard. Plato noticed this characteristic of things in nature and Hegel tries to account for it by a similar, but more dynamic, theory of Ideas. Natural things are imperfect, he says, because nature is an abstraction. It is part of a process of which the whole includes its turning into mind. Take or abstract the part from the whole and you get something incomplete and contradictory. But why contradictory? Because as we have seen, the Forms, failing to be embodied to perfection in natural things, introduce an element of contrast between that which is and that which ought to be.

According to Hegel, this contrast or contradiction is real not illusory: it is the real and unavoidable state of affairs prevailing in a sphere that has not yet turned into something else. Opposition, here as everywhere in Hegel's system, signifies neither muddle nor illusion but simply incompleteness.

In addition to its incompleteness and instability, the realm of nature is distinguished from any other by a characteristic which has often been attributed to it, but in an ambiguous fashion. Philosophers of the past, and especially the empiricists, had been in the habit of referring to nature, or the objective world, as the "external" world. Precisely what they meant by the word "external" was not clear. Some of them undoubtedly meant external in the sense in which popular writers on astronomy refer to "the universe around us": all of them seem to imply by it the world external to our bodies or at least to our sense-organs. To Hegel this picture of the mind as a box-camera located somewhere in the body and looking out on an alien environment is a false picture. When he speaks of an external world he is referring to a world external neither to our bodies nor to our minds, nor to any mind-body complex such as we mentioned in Part I: he is referring to a world wholly composed of mutually external objects. And by mutually external objects he meant objects which, in order to become identified as objects, must be spread out both in space and in time. Nature, therefore, is an external world in the sense that it is a world which is distributed simultaneously in all the so-called dimensions, and cannot exist save by such distribution. To ask what the external world is "external to" is to reply that it is external to itself.[1]

The Abuse of the Dialectic

The notion of objects as external both to their own elements and to other objects, and the further notion that such objects require a certain minimum time in order to realise themselves —for their special distribution in time necessitates this—is one that has been revived, often without acknowledgment to Hegel, by some modern philosophers of physics. Hegel, without anticipating Darwin in any way, thus lays the foundation of a new view of nature.[2] On the one hand, he puts an end to the rationalist-empiricist controversy by showing that nature is permeated but not possessed—soaked but not saturated—with mind; and on the other hand, he claims to have solved the problem of God's relation to both mind and nature by showing that the latter are two phases in an ideal process which, taken in its entirety, is God Himself.

While Hegel rejects the possibility of the evolution of

[1] Cf. R. G. Collingwood: *The Idea of Nature*, p. 126, and the same author's *Principles of Art*, p. 166.

[2] See Part IV.

species in nature[1], he is vitally concerned with development
of another kind, namely, that which takes place in history.
Hegel's view of history has been ridiculed because, as a result
of the strict application of the Dialectic, he is led into committing himself to a number of conclusions that, however
plausible they may have seemed in his own time, strike us to-
day as ludicrous. He takes the Oriental World, negates it
with the Classical World, and makes out of the opposition a
synthesis to which he gives the name of the Germanic World.
In the first, only one man is free—the despot; in the second,
some only are free, since there is a vast slave population; in
the third, all are free.[2] The same triadic form is clamped
down upon almost every other subject, astronomy, physiology,
biology, and so on, until the habit of dialectical manipulation
becomes a kind of mania, and Hegel, like Charlie Chaplin in
Modern Times, runs amok outside his proper sphere, screwing
up everything with which he comes into contact.

It is one thing to say that philosophy embraces both art and
religion: it is another thing to say that apart from philosophy
art and religion represent errors. Yet that is the conclusion
to which the dialectic of opposites, wrongly or indiscrimin-
ately applied, leads. Each "moment", taken separately, is an
abstraction. The second negates the first; and the third,
negating a negation, produces for the first time something
concrete. Thus Hegel is led to propounding a theory of the
State which is frankly absolutist and totalitarian. He takes
the family as his thesis: he negates it by what he calls civil
society, which is his antithesis; he unites the two in the State,
which is his synthesis. It follows that only the State possesses
concrete reality, and that the rights of the family and those of

---

[1] There is an interesting footnote in the *Encyclopædia of the Philosophical
Sciences* (*Philosophy of Nature*, Part II, paragraph 299), in which Hegel
says: "Misty representations . . . such as the birth of animals and
plants from water or of more developed animal organisms from lower,
etc., must be entirely excluded from philosophical consideration."

[2] Hegel's *Providence*, it will be seen, is somewhat pro-German.

social life are to be subordinated to those of statecraft.[1] For some reason best known to its advocates this theory is known, both in Germany and abroad, as the *Metaphysical Theory of the State*[2]: a better name would be the unmetaphysical theory. Some people have expressed surprise that in Germany a tradition of pedantry and a tradition of militarism and dictatorship should have existed and even flourished side by side. The reason is simple: the pedants were tolerated because they were preaching, right down to our own day, precisely what the militarists wanted them to preach. The two classes understood each other perfectly. The professors were militant in their pedantry; the generals were pedantic in their militarism. Their combined efforts cost them two wars.

The Value of Hegel's Philosophy

Although the dialectical method is put to such misuse by Hegel, and to still further abuse by his disciples, both of the Left and of the Right, and although the preposterous conclusions at which he arrived have brought discredit upon his whole philosophy and more than one catastrophe upon his nation, it does not follow that we can dismiss him as an obscurantist fraud, as some "realist" philosophers and political theorists have done, or regard him as one among the ghosts but lately standing trial at Nuremberg. He was a serious and profoundly original thinker, whose speculations in more than one field are worthy of the most careful attention. For it must not be forgotten that the point at which a man goes astray is still situated on the right path. And we can follow him for a great deal of the way, even if not all the way. His own defection provides a warning of which he himself enjoyed no equivalent benefit.

[1] Cf. Berdyaef: *Spirit and Reality* (p. 47): "According to Hegel, history is the self-revelation of development of freedom; but that freedom is independent of ours, it is not for us."

[2] Cf. the work of Bernard Bosanquet of that title.

To return to his view of history. If the creation of nature represents that phase in the manifestation of spirit in which the Idea "externalises" itself, the transition from nature to mind represents a process which Hegel, employing the kind of terminology which has perplexed and irritated his students, describes as "the return of spirit upon itself ". Let us try to understand exactly what Hegel means by this, for it will not do to suppose that he is merely indulging in a series of intellectual conjuring tricks. He was trying to explain something. What was it, then, that he was trying to explain?

He was trying to reinterpret, in the light (or darkness) of modern issues, the old problem of the relation between God and the World—in short, the problem of which we spoke in Part II. Being a historian, or at least a man with a keen historical sense, he was not trying to "begin all over again", except in so far as every original thinker, faced with a major problem, is obliged to begin all over again; he was trying to rethink the problem in all its aspects from the time of the Greeks, through the early Christian and mediæval period, up to his own day. He was trying to integrate modern philosophy into the tradition from which, since the time of Descartes, it had shown a tendency to stray. No doubt for this reason Hegel has been described as the Aristotle of the modern world; at least as regards the scope of his work, this description is not inept. We cannot understand the course of modern philosophy, or even (as we have hinted) the tendencies of modern physics, unless we make some attempt to grapple with the problems attacked so energetically and with such a mixture of insight and obtuseness by Hegel. When he wrote the *Phenomenology of Spirit* (1807), his first important work, he was doing something which had not been done since the time of St. Thomas Aquinas; he was undertaking a "voyage of discovery" (his own phrase) from the most elementary forms of sense perception to the knowledge of absolute spirit. That Kant had contemplated such a voyage we have already seen; but he set out upon it too late, and left merely a bundle of notes on soundings. Hegel was the first modern philosopher to demonstrate not merely that the problem of perception leads on inevitably to the problem of metaphysics, as we have tried to indicate in Part I, but that the problem of metaphysics is in reality the problem of cosmology, understanding that term to include both the order of nature and the order of civilisation.

The transition of nature to mind is, in Hegel's view, the transition of science to history. Since the underlying presupposition in Hegel's thought is that the Idea experiences the need to pass through various stages in order to fulfil its purposes, first taking outward shape in nature and then assuming a new inwardness in history, he regards the development of social institutions, of moral law, and of states as direct manifestations of the spirit. In nature, as we saw, the objects are not merely external to each other; they are composed of parts which are themselves mutually external. In history there are no objects but only events; and the reality of these events, the significance they possess, is not an external significance but an "internal" one—that is to say, their significance lies in the thought that gave rise to them. Whereas we can be said to "understand" a natural process, such as a chemical change, by observing the law to which it conforms (without which observation we cannot understand it at all), we can be said to understand a historical process, such as the French Revolution, only by penetrating through the various events to the thoughts and motives of those concerned in them.

Nevertheless, opposition is as much a characteristic of history as of everything else; indeed, it is in the historical process that the function of opposition as a stimulus to thought and action is most apparent. In other words, Hegel's view of history is a dynamic view: he never sees a great movement but he detects its antithesis shadowing it, and thereby thrusting it into relief. The contradictions and clashes on the historical plane are real things, to be faced up to as such; and their resolution is always giving place to still further contradictions in an endless dialectic. For this reason Hegel exalts the influence of great men in a manner which the nineteenth century made familiar; a great man, to Hegel, is one who "tells the time what it wills and means and then brings it to completion".[1] For the same reason Hegel's philosophy can be invoked as the justification of either conservatism or revolution; for in declaring that "the real is the rational and the rational is the real", he laid himself open to contradictory interpretations. The conservatives understood him to mean that rationality lies in that which prevails at the moment; the radicals understood him to mean that rationality must be imposed upon a reality that showed itself recalcitrant. The first, identifying the State with "the progress of God in the world",[2] maintained that the Idea must be regarded as arranging all things for the best; the second, interpreting the Idea in a purely material sense, maintained that the convulsions of history were social stresses, in which classes struggled for domination, were in time themselves overthrown by more organised groups, and finally gave place to a society from which the class element was wholly eliminated. Both the right-wing and the left-wing Hegelians were unorthodox in one respect; they both regarded the historical process as soon about to come to an end. Whereas Treitschke conceived the culmination of history to be the apotheosis of the German State, Marx conceived it to be the enthronement of the liberated proletariat. It is true that at the conclusion to his *Philosophy of History* Hegel declared: "knowledge has reached this point in its development". But he did not imply that his successors might not carry the development a stage, or several stages, farther. Indeed, it was his repeated view that while the Idea manifested itself in a series of external forms which

[1] *Philosophy of Right*, Trans. S. W. Dyde (1896), p. 325.
[2] *Op. Cit.*, p. 247.

developed and passed away again, this process of development and passing away never itself developed or passed away. Thus Hegel did not envisage a time when nature should have completely turned into mind; but neither did he envisage a time in which it should cease to try to do so[1].

The Rôle of Philosophy

It must not be supposed, however, that according to Hegel's view of history the mind of man exhausts its energies on the purely political plane. It cannot by its very nature be satisfied with such practical activities; it craves, as it were, to be alone with itself and with its own products. And the realms of art and science, religion and philosophy are those in which it finds such solace. Nevertheless, these realms, like all the others, are related one to another dialectically, so that the highest, philosophy, is to be regarded as the final synthesis of human thought. We have already pointed out that owing to his abuse of the dialectic, Hegel is led to the conclusion that the first two "moments" of the triad are abstractions and therefore, if considered apart from the final synthesis, errors: and this implies that art, science and religion are forms of thought which, considered in themselves, are shot through with falsity. As Croce has indicated in the book on Hegel to which we have already referred, this conclusion is arrived at by a confusion between "opposites" and "distincts", so that religion is made the negation of art, whereas the former is in fact implied by the latter, and so on. Similarly, Hegel arrives at a serious misunderstanding concerning the nature of language, which he defines as "organised contradiction". But the rejection of language as an imperfect means of expression can only be done in the name of a language purged of

[1] The contrast between Hegel's method, according to which nothing in the world is perfect but only *becoming* or trying to become perfect, and his doctrine of the perfection of the Prussian State, was undoubtedly largely responsible for the rift among his disciples.

these defects, and this Hegel is unable to provide. In the next chapter we shall have occasion to treat of a similar attitude to language displayed by a school of thinkers very different in inspiration from Hegel, but in this respect at one with him.

In dividing his philosophy into three parts, the Logic, the philosophy of Nature and the Philosophy of Mind (a trilogy which forms his *Encyclopædia of the Philosophical Sciences*), Hegel, himself an orthodox Christian, was aiming at a metaphysical transcription of the Christian doctrine of the Fall, the Incarnation and the Redemption. The *Logic*, written between 1812-16, is in fact a treatise on the nature of the Logos; the *Philosophy of Nature*, an account of the manifestation of the Logos in material form; the *Philosophy of Mind*, an account of the return of nature to the Spirit which created it. In short, Hegel's metaphysics is nothing more nor less than a theology; and in identifying one with the other he was returning to the tradition of Aristotle and making way for the modern philosophers of nature and spirit in which the so-called old, but in fact comparatively recent, quarrel between Science and Religion is healed.

PART IV

The Present Situation

The Present Situation

The Positivist Attack on Metaphysics

In the course of Part III we have made a general survey of the thought of some of the greatest names in philosophy, with special reference to their attitude to metaphysics. We observed, as time went on, a gradual widening of interests. First, the question to which philosophers addressed themselves was that concerning the reliability of our impressions or ideas. Then, after Hume's destructive analysis, an attempt was made by Kant to settle once and for all the status of metaphysical enquiry—an attempt about which the fairest thing we can say is that it failed magnificently. Finally, Hegel, taking a synoptic view of philosophy, originated a system which, in spite of the obscurities of its exposition, straddles modern thought like a colossus: so that whatever attitude we may finally choose to adopt towards it, we cannot deny that it raises a number of profound problems, and that it provides a formidable challenge to those who dismiss metaphysics as mere obscurantist mumbo-jumbo. In this final section we shall be concerned with the state of philosophical enquiry at the present time. As this is a task requiring great condensation, we shall inevitably be obliged to omit reference to many names of deserved importance. But all the while we shall be bearing in mind the main currents of European thought, and the general attitude, whether friendly or otherwise, assumed towards metaphysics. And there is one school of thinkers to which we shall be paying particular attention, because its adherents have waged unceasing war upon metaphysics for almost a century: this is the school of Positivism. Positivism, which is the form taken by the *anti-philosophia perennis* at the present day, represents perhaps the most resolute attack upon metaphysics that has ever been launched.

The Positivist school was established by the French philosopher, Auguste Comte (1798-1857), who expounded his views on philosophy at length in a work called *The System of Positive Polity* (1851-4).[1] Now, although Comte was an avowed enemy of metaphysics, if not perhaps so extreme an enemy as some of his present-day disciples, he realised clearly enough with what kind of subject-matter metaphysics is, or believes itself to be, concerned. *The System of Positive Polity* is a treatise on the origins and nature of civilisation; and in attacking metaphysics Comte recognises that civilisation and metaphysics are somehow intimately bound up the one with the other. He therefore sets himself the task of discovering, by means of an enquiry into the past history of civilisation, precisely at what point the two have become associated, and why. And in so doing he covertly reveals his awareness of another characteristic of metaphysical thought: namely, that the way to discover what it is, is to institute a historical enquiry. As we shall see again later, Comte "tracked down" metaphysics to where it belonged more successfully than most opponents of this subject, and with a great deal more insight than the majority of his self-styled followers.

The objection advanced against metaphysics by Comte is not so much that it is false as that it is an anachronism. That a metaphysical view of the world was both possible and legitimate, he was disposed to admit; but it was possible, he contended, only to a people whose mentality was at a fairly rudimentary stage of development. *The System of Positive Polity* provides, among other things, a wealth of information concerning man's sojourn at this particular stage, and also at the stages anterior and superior to it.

[1] This was preceded by a *Course of Positive Philosophy* (1830-42).

Although Comte died two years before the publication of *The Origin of Species*, his work bears numerous traces of the conflict already in progress between science and religion. It is this conflict that he hopes to resolve. Nor does he confine his attention to the purely practical aspects of it; he believes that the upheavals of society are directly attributable to the no less disturbed intellectual atmosphere. Although science has largely caused the trouble, science can cure it. Whereas many nineteenth-century thinkers advocate a return, even at the expense of destroying the new machinery, to the pre-industrial or pre-scientific age, Comte urges his contemporaries to go on to consolidate the victories of science, realising that in science we have an instrument that not merely takes the place of all other systems of thought, but is heir to their great emotional influence over mankind. In the work of Comte, then, we observe very clearly the tendency, already noted as being characteristic of the competitors or metaphysics and religion, to attribute to science the functions and privileges of a complete system of beliefs. Science seeks to end the conflict between itself and religion by taking over the functions of religion. Science is the "receiver" of the emotional assets of its bankrupt adversary.

The solution, then, is to give free rein to the scientific spirit, to allow science to remould society according to its own laws; and in this way to evolve a new kind of scientific study—the study of society or Sociology. True science, in other words, is applied science: not science applied to this or that aspect of social life, but science applied to society as a whole. Comte's conclusions were characteristic of the France of his time: for it was in Revolutionary and post-Revolutionary France that the first concerted effort was made to apply Reason to society, of which the introduction of the metric system is but a minor example.[1] And the successors of Comte in the field or

[1] What capital but Paris has an underground station called "Art et Métiers"?

Sociology, above all Tarde and Durkheim, are aiming at the same thing.

But why, we may well ask, did this conception of the function of science appear no earlier, and why is it even now denied general acceptance? The answer is that it is the conception of the future, the future that must and will come, almost the immediate future. For, according to Comte, the age which is dawning is the truly practical or positivist age; and the age which is passing into it and therefore passing away is an age of abstraction and vagueness. To this latter age Comte gives an interesting name: he calls it, for reasons which we shall examine, the "metaphysical" age.

Now, the metaphysical age, the age in which abstractions dominate men's minds—albeit abstractions that men endow with force and vitality, such as souls or essences—is itself preceded by an age even more primitive in character. This is the theological age, the age in which men think anthropomorphically and populate the nature world with living gods and spirits. Of all the ages or stages of civilisation, this is the most primitive, and consequently that in which the major part of mankind tends to remain longest.

The Positivist Conception of Civilisation

The idea of civilisation as evolving in stages, usually three in number, was by no means new. It had been put forward with striking effect by Giambattista Vico at the beginning of the eighteenth century, though Vico's work did not become known until a much later time.[1] It found expression likewise in the work of Lessing (1729-81), who, in his remarkable essay entitled *The Education of the Human Race*, portrays history as

[1] Not really until our own time. His fellow-countrymen, Benedetto Croce and Giovanni Gentile, have done most to popularise his ideas. Today it is Vico's cyclic view of history that has chiefly attracted attention. James Joyce, for instance, claimed Vico as one of his many "influences".

the unfolding of a religious revelation in three general stages, of which the last and most complete, the so-called Age of Reason, is that in which man becomes completely conscious of himself and of his power to organise the world according to his highest desires. Incidentally, Comte was at one time associated with a group of Saint-Simonians[1] who sponsored a translation of this essay: and although he broke loose from the group as his studies took a more practical turn, he retained unmodified the idea of a progressive revelation of reason. Similar theories of progress were advanced by Fichte, Schelling, and Hegel himself.

Now just as society undergoes development according to a law of rational revelation, so likewise does the form of thought which is the motive power behind its unfolding. Thus we have theological science, metaphysical science and positivist science. By an elaborate and ingenious classification of the individual sciences, Comte demonstrates that each one develops logically out of the other, so that the last (that of positivism) logically presupposes all the rest. Paradoxically, the simplest of the sciences are also the most positive, and *vice versa*. Thus mathematics has never been a discipline about which men have entertained superstitions to the point of praying for a suspension of its laws. Although they have regarded certain specific numbers, or combinations of numbers, as being endowed with magical significance, they have never prayed for the kind of miracle in which two and two ceased to make four, or the angles of a triangle no longer added up to 180 degrees. In the case of a science like astronomy, however, superstition still takes the form of seeking for a change, however temporary, in the prevailing order of nature. For while we may have ceased, except in some quarters (such as the corners of certain newspapers) to believe that our destinies are controlled by the position of the heavenly bodies, we still deem it not unreasonable to offer up

[1] Followers of Saint-Simon, the 19th century sociologist.

prayers for rain; so that our attitude to meteorology is still several stages behind our attitude to the rest of astronomy. As for chemistry and physics, they are (or were in Comte's day) in some ways even less advanced on the road to positivism than astronomy. And sociology, the rational ordering of science as a whole, though clearly the *science de nos jours*, had been invested with all kinds of unnecessary obscurities and absurdities (especially by such "reactionary" thinkers as De Maistre and De Bonald), which, in Comte's view, had seriously held up the advance of the human race.

In his *Autobiography* John Stuart Mill describes how, having begun as an enthusiastic admirer of Comte, he became less and less disposed to accept the tenets of the positive philosophy as the successive volumes of the *System* made their appearance. The reason for Mill's gradual disillusionment was that Comte, though a thorough-going empiricist at the start, began to change his tune as the argument unfolded. For although Comte did his best to show that the proper development of civilisation is a development from theological conceptions, through metaphysical conceptions, to positivist conceptions, he could not resist a *dénouement* in which religion and to some extent metaphysics stage a dramatic "come-back", though in suitably altered guise. Driven to explain how man's technical ability is to be guided and tempered by his emotions, and how a harmony between the "reasons of the abstract intellect" and the "reasons of the heart" (to adapt Pascal's distinction) can be achieved, Comte introduces the notion of a new and highly sophisticated form of faith called the Religion of Humanity, whence the New Man of the positivist society is expected to derive sufficient uplift to carry him through mundane and mechanical routine of a technological existence. We have said that this reintroduces both the religious and the metaphysical mode of thought: and indeed the Religion of Humanity, about which Comte tells us very little that is definite, is almost more metaphysical than it is religious, for

its god is a highly abstract entity and its faith is a vague faith
in the future perfectibility of the human race.[1]

Modern or Logical Positivism

This paradox at the bottom of Comte's thought has been
responsible, like the similar paradox at the bottom of the
thought of Hegel, for a rift among his disciples so extreme as
to make it very difficult for the two schools to recognise their
common parentage. The label "positivist" has been adopted
by a modern school of philosophers who have concentrated
chiefly upon Comte's attack upon metaphysics. For reasons
which we shall endeavour to make clear, this school has
prefixed the term with the word "logical". Another group of
thinkers, of whom the most celebrated and in some ways the
most vilified was the French Royalist leader, Charles Maurras,
inherited quite another aspect of Comte's thought, concentrating chiefly upon his crusade against traditional religion.
With the latter group, which consisted of a number of people
too diverse to constitute a group save by reason of their
common antipathy to the Christian Faith, we are not here
concerned. With the former we are very much concerned,
since Logical Positivism, as it is called, has won many converts
in the present century, especially among the younger philosophers at our universities.

It should be stressed at the outset that while the Logical
Positivists derive their title and much of their general manner
from Comte, they are in the habit of claiming spiritual descent
from a much less constructive philosopher than Comte,
namely, Hume. It is not so much that they disagree with
Comte's attitude to metaphysics as that they claim for Hume
a more thorough-going scepticism and more professional

[1] The Religion of Humanity has its apostles today. Mr. Middleton
Murry is preaching such a religion when, in his book, *The Necessity of
Communism*, he writes: "What is the difference between believing in God
and believing in man—in the unknown, the future?"

working out of its implications. We have seen reason to believe that Hume, for all his "remorseless logic", was not perhaps so thorough-going as is sometimes supposed: Kant, as we
noted, showed that his line of argument could be "paid out" a
great deal farther, with not uninteresting results. And while
the Logical Positivists may admire Hume's dismissal of the
supernatural as a "plaything", so different from Comte's
final surrender to a numinous anthropolatry, they are not
altogether free from faith-mongering themselves, witness the
Free Man's Worship of Earl Russell, one of the foundation-
members of the Logical Positivist Metaphysical Liquidation
Board, and the political fervour of more than one member
of the same institution. For the moment, however, we
are concerned with the specific arguments advanced by
the Logical Positivists against metaphysics in general and
with the reasons for their choice of the prefix "logical" to
distinguish their method from that of any other sect of
positivist thinkers.

No discussion of these questions can be undertaken without
some preliminary reference to another preoccupation of
Logical Positivists, namely, their contribution to the theory
of Language. At first glance, it may not be easy to understand
why, in directing their attack upon metaphysical thought, the
members of this school should pay particular attention to the
nature of language; but it must not be forgotten that the
primary aim of a Logical Positivist is to apply positivism to
logic, and above all to demonstrate that logic, after two
thousand years of Aristotelean domination, needs a thorough
overhaul if it is to be of service to modern science. Thus the
title of one of the works of a modern Logical Positivist is aptly
worded: *Language, Truth and Logic.*

To enter into the history of the modern attitude to logic
would be outside the scope of this chapter. Suffice it to say
that the relation of logic to language has been the subject of
much attention of recent years, chiefly owing to the brilliant

studies of Earl Russell.[1] If metaphysics and kindred subjects like theology are to be regarded as thoroughly outmoded, the question that naturally arises is how we are to regard the statements of metaphysicians and theologians: do they mean anything at all and, if so, how much do they mean, or are they just groups of high-sounding words, which, though individually significant are collectively meaningless? This is an important point, because if once we are obliged to admit that at least some of the metaphysical statements of metaphysicians and theologians are significant, then this is surely the thin end of the wedge and we must finally acknowledge that metaphysics has some sort of *raison d'être*. If, on the other hand, we are driven to the conclusion that the statements of these persons are utterly devoid of meaning, then it is difficult to see how mankind should have persisted in imagining that, in using such statements, they were talking sense and, further, how they could possibly have derived comfort and knowledge from their repetition.

The explanation advanced by the Logical Positivists, and by those who, like I. A. Richards, accept certain tenets of Logical Positivism, is a plausible one. Language, they hold, is a general term covering two distinct media of communication. On the one hand, there is referential language, which is the language of science, and on the other hand, there is emotive language, which is the language of metaphysics, theology, poetry and anything you happen to regard as nonsense. The first is logical and rational; the second is illogical and irrational. The first means something; the second means

---

[1] On the Continent the chief advocates of the new attitude were Wittgenstein and Carnap. To Wittgenstein, the meaning of a proposition about the world was the means of its verification, and the unit of significance was the "atomic" proposition. Carnap drew the distinction, later to be developed by Messrs. Ogden and Richards in their book, *The Meaning of Meaning*, between the "formal" mode of speech, consisting of definitions and tautologies, and the "material" mode of speech, consisting of empirical or verifiable statements.

nothing. In short, the first contains thought; the second contains merely feeling.[1]

Now it must be noted that this distinction between scientific and emotive language begins by being a distinction *within* language; but this distinction is so radical, and cuts so deep, that we soon find language coming to pieces in our hands. As a result, the two separate halves begin to assume an independent existence, each endeavouring to render itself completely free of the other. In other words, we are back again at the old distinction between two different kinds of reality, one objective and scientifically measurable and the other subjective and susceptible to no scientific apprehension of any kind. Logical Positivists and their disciples (who sometimes call themselves "philosophical analysts") are applying to language what the Cartesians and their successors applied to perception. The rift has spread from nature to our way of talking about nature. The cleavage has become a cleft of our tongue.

Having isolated a certain type of language as being "scientific", the Logical Positivists proceed to reduce this medium to a number of units of significance called "propositions". A proposition is the result of fining down language to its irreducible minimum of sense; and the test of a valid proposition is simply whether or not it is capable of experimental verification. An experimentally verifiable proposition is called in the Kantian terminology synthetic. Certain propositions, however, are not synthetic in this sense. They are analytic, which means that, in analysing them, we arrive at a tautology. (In the proposition "bodies are extended", for instance, the word "extended" tells us nothing that we did not know already about bodies; therefore the statement is tautologous.) If a

---

[1] Cf. I. A. Richards: *Principles of Literary Criticism* (1926), chapter XXXIV, p. 167: "A statement may be used for the sake of the reference true or false, which it causes. This is the scientific use of language. But it may also be used for the sake of the effects in emotion and attitude produced by the reference it occasions. This is the emotive use of language."

proposition cannot be shown to fall into one or other of these categories, then it is not a proposition at all. It is simply nonsense masquerading as sense; and the skilful analyst will soon expose it as the fraud that it is. Give us time, say the Logical Positivists, and we shall be able to show you "beyond question" that the propositions advanced by metaphysicians, theologians, poets and indeed any persons who put forward statements, or claim to assert knowledge "transcending the world of science and common sense", are pseudo-propositions and therefore nonsensical.

Nevertheless, as we have already pointed out, it must be admitted that the pseudo-propositions of metaphysics, theology, and poetry have exerted, and still exert, a powerful influence over the mind of man; and there are some among the Logical Positivists who are themselves not indifferent to the charms of creative writers who, from Logical Positivist standards, are engaged in the production of sheer undiluted nonsense. Such writers, it is held, are concerned with that which, while being devoid of literal significance, may well possess "emotional significance"; and so, as we foresaw just now, the thin end of the wedge is delicately, and even a little archly, inserted, and we are invited to believe, if only for pragmatic reasons, that significance may attach to other forms of language than purely scientific language, and that the poet, the artist, and even possibly some few metaphysicians are not the complete charlatans that we imagined them to be, but men who in their way can contribute to the mental welfare of the human race. What is this but a re-enactment of Comte's remarkable tergiversation whereby traditional religion was banished only to reappear later on in a more rarefied form as the "Religion of Humanity"?

Positivism Loses its Nerve

If we examine the statements of the analytical philosophers

more closely we notice that their definition of scientific language undergoes a certain degree of modification as the
argument proceeds. Having begun with the assertion that
"a sentence *says* nothing unless it is empirically verifiable"[1] in
experience (that is, by reference to observed facts), Mr. Ayer
(whom we take as our representative of the school, at least in
its English form) startles us with the admission that no
empirical proposition can be more than probable. This, of
course, is tantamount to saying that all empirical propositions
are hypotheses; and as Mr. Ayer has reminded us, "a hypothesis cannot be conclusively refuted any more than it can be
conclusively verified". That is true; but what, we may well
ask, has now become of the author's proud claim to be able to
demonstrate conclusively that metaphysical statements, or
indeed any statements concerned with a reality "transcending
the world of science", are utterly meaningless? "The traditional disputes of philosophers", he has announced in his
first paragraph, "are for the most part as unwarranted as they
are unfruitful. The *surest* way to end them is to establish
beyond question what should be the purpose and method of
philosophical enquiry. And this is by no means so difficult a
task as the history of philosophy would lead one to suppose.
For if there are *any* questions which science leaves it to philosophy to answer, a straightforward process of elimination *must*
lead to their discovery" (my italics). After this clarion call to
action the rest of the book dies away rather faintly. For not
merely are we deprived of any certain criteria in our search
for true knowledge (note that it is knowledge itself and not
merely metaphysical knowledge that is in jeopardy), but, as we
have observed, we find that empirical knowledge has to be
eked out with other sorts of apprehension, be they ever so
vague and evanescent.[2] Once it is admitted that so-called

---

[1] A. J. Ayer: *Language, Truth and Logic.*

[2] In his book, *Illusion and Reality,* Christopher Caudwell, a young
Marxist critic, who was killed in the Spanish war, observed shrewdly
that "positivism is always dishonest, and from the start smuggles another

emotive statements have a certain "significance", then the door is ajar for those philosophies in which truth and certainty are held to reside in intuition alone. One extreme generates another. And so we may say without exaggeration that the thorough-going empiricist of today ends up, though with becoming reluctance, by flirting with the Kantian view that true knowledge—i.e., knowledge of what truly is—derives not from the world of experience but from a world behind experience. That the Logical Positivists should admit this in so many words is not to be expected; but it is clear that the extraordinarily dogmatic character of their work is due, not to any rational objection to metaphysics, but to an emotional prejudice—a prejudice which leads Mr. Ayer, in his chapter entitled "A Critique of Ethics and Theology", to commit himself to some supposedly facetious remarks about the nature of religion which class him with the band of soap-box orators.[1] In short, the positivist attack upon metaphysics and theology is an attack upon absurd caricatures of these things: and therefore it is not the metaphysician or the theologian who is made to look ridiculous, but the positivist who, by tilting at windmills, imagines himself to be engaged in a noble crusade in defence of reason and enlightenment.

Of the modern tendency to endow something called Science with the attributes both of religion and of philosophy, we have spoken already. Practical science (called by Comte Sociology) is for many people today the universal provider, the universal solace, of which everything is to be expected; the scientist, a man in whose words most people put implicit, if somewhat bewildered, trust. Science is the magic of democracy. And the criterion of science is not whether a thing is true but whether it is useful. Our positivists are quite clear in their

reality (usually the mind) into the system of appearances in order to organise it and provide some standard of validity. This reality will be concealed under some such name as 'convenience' or 'probability' ". From such a source these words are worth pondering.

[1] *Language, Truth and Logic*, p. 139. Since the present work went to press, Mr. Ayer has reissued his book with a new preface.

I

own minds about this. "We trust the methods of modern science", says Mr. Ayer, "because they are so successful in practice". And in another place he asserts that the object of scientific propositions is to minister to our "simplest desires, including the desire to survive".[1] Since these words were written we know a little more about the capacity of science to minister to our desire to survive. And the experiments at Nagasaki and Hiroshima, as also those at Bikini Atoll, have taught us something of what is meant, in the sphere of science, by "success in practice". Meanwhile, those whose business it is to state precisely what the "methods of science" are, have moved on to an altogether less concrete position. Eddington, for instance, while agreeing that "the whole of our physical knowledge is based on measures", proceeds to the view that "the physical world consists, so to speak, of measure-groups resting on a shadowy background that lies outside the scope of physics";[2] and later that "the whole subject-matter of exact science consists of pointer-readings and similar indications".[3] This "shadowy background that lies outside the scope of physics" is, of course, identical with the "world transcending science and common sense" which, according to Mr. Ayer, cannot in the nature of things exist. Eddington goes even farther: "The essential point is", he writes, "that although we seem to have very definite conceptions of objects in the external world, these conceptions do not enter into exact science and are not in any way confirmed by it".[4] Here is the "world of common sense" crumbling about us: for the positivists presuppose an array of "facts" against which every proposition must be measured as a means of verification. If it does not fit them, either directly or "in principle", it is meaningless; but now the standard measure is itself discredited—not by some

[1] Language, Truth and Logic, p. 139.
[2] The Nature of the Physical World (1925), p. 152.
[3] Op. cit., p. 251.
[4] Ibid., p. 252.

"enemy of science", such as a metaphysician or a theologian, but by a respected member of the profession.[1] This is really too bad.

In admitting that emotive language has its uses, especially of a therapeutic kind,[2] the positivist thinkers do not succeed in showing how the two forms of language are related, and indeed their logical theories forbid them to do so. This is due primarily to a failure to realise that the logical "proposition" of which they talk so freely is an abstraction. Now there is nothing wrong with an abstraction as such. What is wrong is to treat it as if it were something concrete. And that is what science, claiming to deal in "brute facts", has an ineradicable habit of doing. The logical proposition is an abstraction *from* language; it is the scientific or logical aspect of language considered apart from the emotive "nest" in which it has been reared. In actual fact, no one ever talked in the form of pure propositions, any more than any army launched a tank-attack in the form of a series of blue-prints. There is no thought apart from emotion: and the emotion, if we are thinking properly, is not that which interferes with or obfuscates thought, but that which feeds it and sustains it. Language, even when most logical, is always expressive. What is logical and "scientific" in language is something that "grows up", and can only grow up, in an atmosphere of expressiveness. To attempt to dispel this atmosphere, this ambient breath, would be to leave logic high and dry, like a fish out of water. Language begins, in other words, by being chiefly the expression of emotion; only slowly, as we see in the case of the child, does it become articulate and "transparent" to thought. And at its most

[1] Cf. Earl Russell, *The Scientific Outlook*, p. 88: "It is a curious fact that, just when the man in the street has begun to believe thoroughly in science, the man in the laboratory has begun to lose his faith."

[2] I. A. Richards's *Principles of Literary Criticism* is a brilliant statement of the view that art, though concerned with pseudo-statements, is a necessary aid to mental health and balance: it refreshes the sensibility by means of a process of "synæsthesis". See also L. K. Ogden and I. A. Richards, *An Outline of Æsthetics, passim.*

transparent pitch, the emotional charge is not less strong, but merely purer, than at lower levels. Consequently, the idea that emotion or expressiveness is something *added* to thought, as a decoration or fancy wrapping, and therefore as easily removed, is a fallacy. Behind such prefabricated forms of language as Basic English or Professor Hogben's *Interglossa*, lies the false assumption that by abstracting from living speech a series of verbal counters, language can be manufactured in a pure state. The purity of such language resembles the dry whiteness of a skeleton.[1]

Positivism the Enemy of Science

These modern theories of positivism are evidence of the bankruptcy of a tradition of thought originating with the rationalist-empiricist dispute of the seventeenth century. That century began with a belief in the universal applicability and efficacy of mathematico-physical science. It imposed its own terms; it declared its own policy; it went straight ahead without looking back. However strenuously the philosophers tried to come to terms with it—and the greatest single effort was that made by Kant—the negotiations usually resulted in nothing more satisfactory than a concordat, against which the scientists jibbed as soon as it was drawn up, and which they finally repudiated. But the greater and more spectacular the victories won by science, the more territory it succeeded in overrunning, the weaker became its own foundations: until by the time its conquests had extended over all reality and it was about to gather in the harvest, it found to its dismay that the crops had strangely withered and the fields lay barren

---

[1] It is important to distinguish such a view of language from that which was put forward in the early works of Croce, above all in the famous *Æsthetic*. Croce's "pure intuition" is very properly regarded as logically prior to thought; but its very purity prevents it from ever giving rise, except by a miraculous "jump", to the stage of conceptual thinking. This error is to some extent repaired in the *Breviary of Æsthetic* and the *Logic* (1909).

at its feet. The "universe of science" proved, by the admission of its own creators, frankly unacceptable. Whitehead has summed up the position in a famous passage: "Each molecule blindly runs. The human body is a collection of molecules. Therefore the human body blindly runs, and therefore there can be no individual responsibility for the actions of the body. If once you accept that the molecule is definitely determined to be what it is, independently of any determination by reason of the total organism of the body, and if you further admit that the blind run is settled by the general mechanical laws, there can be no escape from this conclusion".[1] Science has drained the world of all significance.

To maintain that the scientific account of the world, however plausible and triumphant, met with complete and universal acceptance would be not merely untrue but incompatible with all that we have said about the dialectical nature of movements of thought in general. It was constantly being challenged. There were many who, within a few years of Bacon's eulogies of the possibilities of mechanical invention in the *Novum Organum* and the *New Atlantis*, expressed scepticism as to the benefits of the new inventions that promised to revolutionise the world. In his *Religio Medici* (written 1635-6) Sir Thomas Browne declares that "of those three inventions in Germany, there are two which are not without their incommodities, and 'tis disputable whether they exceed not their use and commodities".[2] But apart from this distrust of innovation, which is a feature noticeable in every age among certain sections of the community, signs of growing revulsion against the scientific point of view appeared in the next century not merely within the Church and its nonconformist outriders (Wesley started in 1739), but among the writers and artists. The Romantic revival—which, as we have seen, was

[1] *Science and the Modern World*, Chapter V.

[2] The "three inventions" were printing, guns and the mariner's compass, the first two being of doubtful value.

concerned with new attitudes as much to law and history as to poetry—was Europe's first concerted reaction against scientific mechanism and abstractionism. And it is not without significance that the English Romantic writers, though rarely on the best of terms with the ecclesiastical hierarchy, tended as time went on to ally themselves with the Church: Wordsworth died within its bosom, Coleridge became suffocated by its vestments,[1] and Southey wrote his *Colloquies with Sir Thomas More* to demonstrate the superiority of the idea of Christendom over modern secularism. In France the alliance was declared more openly still. Whereas Shelley had been sent down from Oxford for writing a tract on *The Necessity of Atheism*, Châteaubriand made his name by a voluminous work entitled *The Genius of Christianity*, and ended up as an ambassador.

Up to the middle of the nineteenth century the foundations of the mechanist view of the world, though subjected to strain in the way we have described, were still firm. Even the influence of Kant and Hegel did not prevent the rise in England of the new empirical school of the "philosophical radicals", James Mill, Stuart Mill and Bentham. Indeed, James Mill, who declared with an unusual show of confidence that he "saw only too clearly what poor Kant was about", proceeded to write an *Analysis of the Human Mind*, in which he sought to make the human mental processes "as clear as the road from Charing Cross to St. Paul's". It is not agreed that he succeeded. English philosophy up to the time of T. H. Green and F. H. Bradley suffered from the effects of the erosion of experience for which the philosophical radicals were largely responsible. Well might Newman declare "Let Benthamism reign if men have no aspirations!" It is clear

---

[1] Although Coleridge's addiction to German philosophy, especially that of Schelling, has often been ridiculed, and although he was incapable of systematic thinking (his treatise on *Church and State* is the only one that he really completed), he did succeed in grasping, though not developing, the idea that the rise and fall of civilisations has something to do with metaphysical presuppositions.

that you cannot long continue to believe in materialism without modifying to some extent your thoughts and even your
habits in conformity with the beliefs that you hold. If, for
example, you sincerely believe that your own mind is no more
than a machine, your thinking will *tend* on the whole to become
mechanical: or, to put it more accurately, those faculties
which, in the light of your philosophy, are either non-existent
or largely irrational—such as imagination—will tend imper-
ceptibly to atrophy. The modern world, with its pyrrhonist
tendency or what it calls its broadmindedness, has come to
lose sight of the really terrifying truth that error, even trivial
error, does corrupt. Moreover, an age which, like the nineteenth century, is influenced, albeit unconsciously, by mechanistic theories, will in all probability be one in which the people
as a whole receive a pretty raw deal. For if you assume that
men are at bottom machines, you will have no scruples in
putting them to work.

Whereas the early Romantic revival was a revolt against
mechanistic materialism, the outburst of imaginative literature
that marked the mid and later Victorian period was a revolt
against biological materialism. Darwin was no philosopher:
and to say that a man is no philosopher is to say not that he
accepted no philosophy at all but that he accepted his
philosophy at second hand. The theory of Evolution had to be
integrated into man's world-view; and as the prevailing
theology showed itself unwilling to accommodate it, the
philosophy to which the scientists had recourse was the arid
rationalism of their time.[1] Nevertheless, material and technical advance had generated its own religion; and Evolution,
in so far as men understood it, was thought by many to provide

[1] The rationalists were as mistaken in accepting it as the theologians
were in refusing it, for, as Jacques Maritain has rightly said, "The
Christian idea of man and of human personality which is founded on
revealed dogma was in no way imperilled by Darwinism; but the
rationalist conception of human personality received a mortal blow".
(*True Humanism*, 1938, p. 21.)

uncontrovertible scientific evidence of the idea of automatic Progress. In the work of a poet like Tennyson, however, the idea of Progress is regarded with a mixture of exultation and suspicion; and it will not do to lump Browning along with the "progressives" on the strength of a line here or there, such as "the best is yet to be". There is nothing in English nineteenth-century literature to compare with Victor Hugo's *Légende des Siècles*,[1] and a poem such as "The City of Dreadful Night" knocks the bottom out of the idea that the Victorian Age was an age of irrepressible optimism. Someone has to keep the conscience of mankind; and if the philosophers will not do it the imaginative writers must.

The Reaction against Positivism

The influence of Hegel upon his philosophical contemporaries and successors was enormous, and, as we have seen, the extreme complexity of much of his thought did not prevent it from being translated into social and even political terms. Nevertheless, it was not until comparatively recently that the relevance of much of Hegel's thought to the view of Nature outlined by modern physicists was perceived.[2] Meanwhile, another thinker of extraordinary originality had launched an attack upon materialism, both mechanistic and biological: this was Henri Bergson (1859-1941). And now that the "vogue" enjoyed by the Bergsonian philosophy has largely died down,[3] it may be possible to distinguish the grain from the chaff, the genuine metaphysician from the purveyor of Couéistic propaganda.

That the philosopher who defines life as the "perpetual

[1] *The Torchbearers* of Alfred Noyes is a late and none too successful essay in this *genre*.

[2] Cf. R. G. Collingwood, *The Idea of Nature*, p. 127.

[3] Raissa Maritain in her book of memoirs, *Les Grandes Amitiés*, Vol. 1, gives a vivid picture of the exhilarating effect of Bergson's early lectures upon students oppressed with the materialistic ideas of the time, even though his thought soon failed to satisfy her and her philosopher husband.

gushing forth of novelties", and to whom the human intellect is simply the instrument which cuts across and arrests this pyrotechnical discharge, should be counted as the arch-enemy of the abstract scientific spirit, is not surprising. For although Bergson's intuition is not quite the same as that of Descartes, he does—at any rate in his earlier work—regard the intuitive faculty as having greater contact with reality than the intellectual. Matter, however, exists and exists to be acted upon, and the intellect, in apprehending Matter, per-forms the indispensable function of enabling us to live. To maintain that Bergson's "message"—by which we mean the popular view of his philosophy—is that we should renounce the use of our intellects and plunge into the torrid stream of intuitive life, it is not therefore so true as is commonly sup-posed. Matter, in spite of a few typical but misleading Bergsonian metaphors (and few of his metaphors, brilliant though they are, lead him quite where he wants them to), cannot be regarded merely as dead intuition, to be cut away or swept up like refuse; it possesses something more than negative value. Here, in other words, is an "arrest" or hitch in Bergson's own thinking; and since the instrument by which such arrests are made is, in his view, the intellect, it is clear that the Bergsonian counsel to follow our instincts is an intellectual counsel. As we pointed out in the Introduction, if we were really in the habit of following our instincts we should obviously not need to be told that we did so, for we should do so—instinctively.

How are we to account for this intellectual rift through the philosophy of one of the most popular of the apostles of flux? We can do no more than hazard an explanation. That life is the product of matter is a proposition which, taken literally, does not commend itself to most minds; but that matter—that is to say, the entire inorganic world—is the product of so localised a burgeoning as life, will strike most people as pre-posterous. If Bergson were right, life would have to be a great

I*

deal more autonomous than even he is willing to allow. To picture life as a perpetually flowing river is to invite us to fill in the details of the picture for ourselves; and once we begin to do this we arrive at the view of a river flowing through natural countryside, whose contours provide precisely those obstructions the existence of which Bergson has always acknowledged. Such obstructions cannot be inherent in life, for life as such is without inhibitions, nor can they rightly be conceived as the inert deposit which life, in the course of its flowing, leaves behind—for such deposit, once relinquished, could hardly be *encountered*. They are simply the result of something other than life, something but for whose presence life would never have taken the course that it has. Hardly a metaphor employed by Bergson fails to point, in some way, to this other principle. "Duration", he says, "is the continuous progress of the past which gnaws into the future". Here we have a picture of life not as "bodying forth", as Bergson so often conceives it, but as making progress by wresting it, as it were, from some peculiarly stubborn barrier. Life, it seems, must work for its living; and it could not keep its teeth sharp unless there were something substantial to work against.

Of Bergson a modern writer has said that "he is throughout recommending capitulation to the material *in struggle against which the greatest things in the world have been constructed*".[1] But as we have seen, the philosophy of Bergson is not committed to the overthrow of intellect. His celebrated intuition, like that of Croce, is not able to stand by itself. Granted that to cut up or classify reality is merely to manipulate it and not in the true sense to know it, can we be said truly to know reality by means of intuition. Intuition, unlike thought, is immediate; and stretch the term as we may, we can never get it to mean much more than feeling. Knowledge, in short, is a form of cognition to which neither intellect nor intuition, in the Bergsonian sense of these terms, can be said to correspond.

[1] P. Wyndham Lewis: *The Art of Being Ruled*, p. 390.

Neither to "grasp" nor to "dissect" is identical with the unique operation summarised in the words "to know". Now we have already stated that intuition is not quite so independent a faculty as Bergson appears to think. The intellect, in spite of his efforts to disparage it, has obtruded itself to the detriment of its more volatile senior partner. It has "cornered" a section of reality to which intuition, hitherto regarded as holding a complete monopoly, is unable to penetrate. It seems, in other words, as if the enemy of everything for which the intellect stands is nothing but an intellectualist *malgré lui*.

No one has ever succeeded in being a complete revolutionary; and sometimes the greatest innovators in one sphere remain die-hard conservatives in others. Bergson's emphasis upon the concept of life was most salutary, and he developed his theme with highly plausible illustrations and arguments. But whenever he contrasts the concept of life with that of matter, the matter to which he refers is the hard and opaque substance of which the nineteenth-century physicists spoke: whereas by the time that Bergson had produced his great works the physicists had begun to abandon this view in favour of one altogether less "materialistic". "Brute" matter was debrutalised; the hard, billiard-hall type of atom was analysed into components less susceptible to spacial description; new notions of force and energy were being entertained; and the nineteenth-century world of nature began to dissolve into "waves of probability" strung across a nexus of mathematical equations.

The New Synthesis

With the highly complex ideas entertained by modern physicists about the nature of the universe we are not here concerned. Theories that cannot be expounded without recourse to difficult and specialised terminology by their originators are not in a condition to be summarised by the layman in the space of a few paragraphs. Recent events, however, have shown that the abstract speculations of some modern mathematicians are no parlour or laboratory game. They are capable of application. They promise to revolutionise not merely our view of the world but the world itself. Philosophers, therefore, cannot pretend to ignore them. In so far as they can be grasped by philosophy, they must be assessed by philosophical canons.

Among modern philosophers two names stand out by reason of the profundity and originality of their thought upon metaphysical questions. These are S. Alexander and A. N. Whitehead. Our sketch of modern thought closes with a brief survey of the philosophy of these two men, both because they represent modern thought at its most cultivated level and because they sum up, each in his way, the tradition of speculation which dates from the time of Descartes. Unlike the analytical or "minute" philosophers of the last fifty years or so, Alexander and Whitehead take a synoptic view of experience. They are concerned not with a partial aspect of reality but with the whole of reality. For them, metaphysical thought is something free and unfettered. Their outlook is not provincial but universal; not local but cosmological. At no point in their argument do they stoop to engage in the acrimonious polemics that deface the work of writers of a lower order. In respecting the integrity of all men of good will they do no violence to truth.

An additional reason why we conclude upon this noteworthy theme is that it links up conveniently with the chapters on the theory of perception which formed the first part of this book. It will be recalled that, as our argument proceeded, we arrived at the view that perception, while affording us a certain kind of knowledge, represented but a means to an end. We are now to consider a theory of nature in which the function of perception is placed in due perspective, and in which the knowledge that it provides is shown to serve a more transcendent faculty, which is mind operative at its highest level. At the same time, and for the same reasons, we shall represent this view of nature as one in which "realist" and "idealist" elements, though discernible, are held, as it were, in equilibrium; where the empirical and rationalist tendencies of modern philosophy are shown to consist chiefly of differences of emphasis; and where, finally, the two parties agree to work in coalition for the sake of meeting the onslaught of an irrationalism that threatens them both in equal measure.

To expound in detail the elaborate argument of Alexander's huge, but exceedingly readable work, *Space, Time and Deity* would take us too long: we are concerned here with as bare an outline as that which we gave of the philosophy of Bergson. Briefly, Alexander sets out to trace the development of the cosmic process from its origins to its highest development: for Alexander, in common with Hegel and with writers such as Lloyd Morgan starts from the view that mind is somehow an "emergent" from nature.[1] At the base of the hierarchy is a four-dimensional continuum called space-time, which Alexander insists upon regarding not as a temporary grand alliance between separate dimensions but as a single principle, almost a personality, of which (to use his own metaphor) space is the body and time the mind.[2] Thus the simplest components of reality are neither "points" in space nor "moments" in time, but spacialised moments or "point-instants"; and each successive emergent is due to the arrangement of these point-instants in a determinate pattern. A particular pattern of point-instants forms the electron; a particular pattern of electrons forms the atom; a particular pattern of atoms forms the molecule, and so on. Moreover, as each pattern is formed, it generates a new quality. Just as the quality of the electron-pattern is physical, and the quality of the atom-pattern is chemical, so the qualities of the patterns higher up in the

[1] The term "emergent evolution" was first employed by Lloyd Morgan in 1912.

[2] *Space, Time and Deity*, Vol. II, p. 39.

scale of nature are of the kind which Galileo called "secondary", e.g., colours, sounds, etc. In short, quality depends upon structure; and what is called evolution is simply the emergence of new patterns and patterns of patterns in a cosmos which is urged onwards towards ever greater feats of organisation.

By tracing the successive realisation of new structures and therefore new qualities, Alexander shows how natural organisms, though themselves composed of pieces of matter, derive their quality of being alive from a certain distribution of these material elements. What, then, of the higher order of minds? These likewise are the result of new patterns, but patterns of which the elements are vital. Just as life is the particular way in which matter is organised, so mind is the particular way in which life is organised. But life and mind are not capable of being resolved into, or explained by, their material or vital components: once the particular pattern is established it assumes the independence and autonomy of a new emergent. To quote the author himself: "Ascent takes place, it would seem, through complexity. But at each change of quality the complexity, as it were, gathers itself together and is expressed in a new simplicity. The emergent quality is the summing together into a new totality of the component materials".[1]

Have we any reason to suppose that the emergence of mind represents the final stage of cosmic evolution? Alexander would say no. Each stage of evolution is permeated with a desire to pass over into the next (again the resemblance to Hegel may be noted); and where such a desire or *nisus* is present the evolutionary process is seen to be incomplete. Is such a "nisus" felt at the stage of mind? It most certainly is. Not merely is the stage of mind that in which the urge to greater perfection, greater freedom and greater achievement is most acutely felt; it is the stage at which the desire or nisus becomes fully conscious of itself and of its former efforts.

[1] *Space, Time and Deity*, Vol. II, p. 70.

At lower stages of evolution nature yearned for greater freedom, as a tree stretches its branches and roots to the limit; at the stage of mind this blind yearning becomes self-conscious will. Mind has its ideals and its aims; and therefore mind, though the highest entity of nature, is perpetually engaged in an effort to transcend itself.

Towards what, we may ask, is mind evolving? Alexander's answer is somewhat startling. It is evolving, he says, into Deity. God is that to which the evolutionary process has had an urge from the beginning: but—and here Alexander's thought takes a peculiar turn—God is not the end "to which the whole creation moves", but the process itself in its upward movement. God is the creation of the world, and not *vice versa*.

Now Alexander would be perfectly entitled to conceive of God in this manner if, at the beginning of his book, he had not insisted so strongly that his method was purely empirical and descriptive. He is not out to upset men's conventional assumptions about the world; merely to analyse them. Philosophy, he says, must not argue; it must describe. But it would take a good deal of argument to convince the ordinary man that his conventional idea of God must be altered to the extent of being completely reversed. Modern man, whether or not he personally "believes in God", admits that if there is a God He must be the creator of the world. To conceive of God as being the end of creation rather than the beginning is to conceive of a God who cannot be worshipped. The "Ancient of Days" is a legitimate object of reverence; the Unformed of To-morrow is a figment. There is a sense in which one can worship one's remote ancestors—in fact, the more remote the better; there is no sense in which one can worship one's remote successors.

Whitehead

In the work of Whitehead, some of these difficulties are cleared up. Whitehead's approach to the problem of nature is primarily that of a mathematician, and consequently his thought tends to take a rationalist direction. But being a mathematician with an extraordinarily broad outlook, his contributions to philosophy are marked by precisely that "balanced development", the absence of which he deplores among his contemporaries. "Each theorist", he writes,[1] "makes progress, but in his own groove". Whitehead has endeavoured to achieve a synthesis of thought of the kind that St. Thomas Aquinas produced in the thirteenth century. For the last three hundred years the sciences have run riot, each claiming to provide a complete "view of the world", and denying the right of others to legislate upon ultimate matters. The time has therefore come for serious stocktaking: and few thinkers are better equipped than Whitehead to undertake it.

As a result of his mathematical training, Whitehead is more attracted to the thought of Plato than to that of Aristotle: and in the course of his early works he emphasises the degree of resemblance between Plato's view of matter and that of modern physics.[2] It was Plato's contention, for instance, that the structure of objects depended upon the form of their atoms—those of the earth were cubical and those of fire pyramidical: and this emphasis upon form and structure is as important for Whitehead as it is for Alexander. Like the latter, he holds that the natural world is made up of dynamic patterns which pervade all time and space. Nature, indeed, is an organic process in which there are not so much "things" as "occasions" (Alexander's "point-instants"). What the materialists call "things" are in reality "fields of force" which act all over the universe. There is therefore no such thing as "nature at an instant"[3]: and for the same reason there is no such thing as "cause" in the old sense of that highly ambiguous word. To maintain that a thing or an event occupies a

---

[1] *The Concept of Nature* (1926), p. 17.

[2] *Op. cit.*, p. 17.

[3] *Nature and Life* (1934), p. 48.

definite space and a particular time is to fall into what White-head calls the "fallacy of simple location".[1] At the end of Part I, it will be remembered, we referred to Field-Marshal Smuts's conception of the "fields" or penumbra surrounding natural events. Whitehead has developed this idea to the point at which the "field" of any one event becomes equivalent to the whole universe. Incidentally, Smuts also draws attention to the resemblance between Whitehead's view and that of Leibnitz.[2]

This new view of the natural world may strike many people as unusually difficult: but it is difficult not so much because it is inherently abstruse as because it takes getting used to.[3] In *Science and the Modern World* Whitehead shows convincingly how the conventional view of nature as an "external world" was built up, or bolstered up, by the scientific discoveries of the seventeenth century. To the seventeenth-century philosophers the relation between mind and nature was conceived in terms of the relation between body and mind. Whitehead points out that all the popular conundrums about perception are the result of this "bifurcation". In reality, the mind-body unity which perceives and the object which is perceived are two elements within a single society; and in consequence it is a mistake to place the secondary qualities of colour or sound in one or the other element (the "fallacy of simple location"), since these qualities are the result of the kind of *collaboration* of which we spoke earlier. The emergence of mind, like the emergence of subordinate entities, confers upon the universe new qualities: and thus the universe is impelled by a *nisus*

[1] See *Science and the Modern World*, Chapter III.

[2] *Holism and Evolution*, p. 16.

[3] Cf. Whitehead: *Adventures of Ideas*, Chapter IX, Section 7: "Newtonian physics is based upon the independent individuality of each bit of matter." For modern physics, however," there is a focal region, which in common speech is where a thing is. But its influence streams away from it with infinite velocity throughout the utmost recesses of space and time. . . . For physics, the thing itself is what it does, and what it does is this divergent stream of influence".

towards the realisation in itself of characteristics which formerly existed only potentially (see Part I, Chapter III).

Not merely did these characteristics exist potentially; their constituents were scattered. Mind, in its lower aspect as sentience, fuses together in unity that which was previously disparate. It liberates qualities by gathering up the heterogeneous into new patterns. Mind in its higher aspect is the focus whereby the universe achieves what Alexander would call self-enjoyment. Qualities such as redness or blueness, sonority or odoriferousness and, at a higher stage, beauty, truth and moral virtue—none of these would exist without mind, and all of these live in and through mind. Thus, in mind, the externality characteristic of nature in its lowest forms gives place to greater and greater integration, until, after the last barrier is down, one mind learns to know another mind, and—as the mysticism of religion teaches—finite and infinite are resolved.[1]

This mysterious resolution of mind with that which is above itself is something so rare and fleeting that there are many who deny its possibility. But unless we are to go back we must go forward; we must either be naturalists or supernaturalists.[2] It is, in fact, an anticipation. The stage of mind with which we are familiar, and with which we are likely to remain familiar, is that in which mind is free to exercise its powers only in a physical or natural world. The mind that we know is rooted in nature. The mind that truly knows itself, on the other hand, seems to give promise of an existence altogether higher in quality, in which such natural trappings are shed and thought issues forth new-born into a world subject to neither inhibition nor limitation. Those experiences in which the mind finds itself projected into another and loftier sphere are the true "intimations of immortality", of which Words-

[1] Cf. M. C. D'Arcy, *The Spirit of Charity*, p. 9: "The Lover has all the virtues and the Beloved is perfect, and so the Beloved and the Lover are one."

[2] Cf. T. S. Eliot, *Second Thoughts on Humanism* ("Selected Essays").

worth spoke both in the poem of that title and in *Tintern Abbey*:

> "That serene and blessed mood,
> In which the affections gently lead us on,
> Until the breath of this corporeal frame
> And even the motion of our human blood
> Almost suspended, we are laid asleep
> In body and become a living soul."

Experience brings to everyone at some time or other the sensation of being lifted on a wave of passionate enquiry, whether induced by æsthetic contemplation or by the more exalted forms of human contact, with its inevitable recession into apathy and weariness: the repetition of which suggests that, in our present "human condition", we can hope merely to glimpse the promised land but never actually to tread its paths. Nevertheless, once the vision has been attained, mind cannot reconcile itself to its immediate environment, but must strain at its mortal reins until the latter snap or wear out, dissolving an uneasy partnership at the moment when it seemed capable of yielding the ultimate fruits of vision:—

> "An aged man is but a paltry thing,
> A tattered coat upon a stick, unless
> Soul clap its hands and sing, and louder sing
> For every tatter in its mortal dress,
> Nor is there singing school but studying
> Monuments of its own magnificence;
> And therefore I have sailed the seas and come
> To the holy city of Byzantium."[1]

Whitehead's cosmology is expounded at great length in a work which, in spite of its extreme difficulty, has become a landmark in modern metaphysics: *Process and Reality* (1929). Here we find an answer to the question which Alexander, clinging loyally to the empiricism with which he started out, leaves inconclusive and frankly unsatisfactory. Whereas Alexander fails to explain why each stage should lead inevitably to the next—or indeed why there should be any process at all—Whitehead, adhering to the orthodox Christian

---

[1] W. B. Yeats, *Sailing to Byzantium*.

tradition, maintains that the processes in nature are not merely impelled forward by *nisus* but "lured" forward by something standing outside the process. That which acts as a "lure" is an Eternal Object; and the infinite Object, the Monad of Monads, to which all creation and creating are directed, is God. Thus metaphysics returns, by a devious route, to a conception of the order of nature as being the creation of an infinite God and therefore the presupposition of all science. And in his later works, particularly that from which we have often quoted, Whitehead explicitly declares that the function of metaphysics is to elucidate precisely such presuppositions as we have mentioned. He goes even farther. The absolute presuppositions with which metaphysics concerns itself are, in his view, the binding-chains of social order. "Apart from metaphysical presupposition there can be no civilisation".[1]

Conclusion

One question remains to be tackled. Is it possible, the reader may ask, that the abandonment of metaphysical thought would bring about that continually anticipated event, "the collapse of civilisation"? And, if so, what would happen? Are we sure that there is sufficient metaphysical thinking being done at the present time to prevent the return of chaos in our age? And, further, what ought we to do to prevent this sort of cataclysm? Ought we not to launch an immediate appeal for funds to endow as many chairs of metaphysics as possible at our universities? Shall we organise intellectual working-parties, start study-circles, finance an intensive advertising campaign to make people "metaphysics conscious"? Give us some practical suggestions and we will do our best, ill-equipped and ignorant as we may be, to help stop the rot.

To answer these questions without descending to the

[1] *Adventures of Ideas*, Chapter VIII, Section 4.

depths of bathos is not easy. But they remain questions which, frivolity apart, are urgently in need of a reasoned reply. Let us take them in a somewhat different order.

First of all, would the complete abandonment of metaphysical thinking entail the collapse of civilised society? Theoretically, yes—if such an abandonment of constructive thought were at all possible. Fortunately it is not. As we have said earlier, the repudiation of metaphysics (in the sense in which we have been employing that word) is a metaphysical act: a treacherous act, no doubt, but then even the traitor must, if he persists in his subversive conduct, display qualities of steadfastness and courage which distinguish him from a monster. Disloyal to one cause, he is loyal to another. His betrayal is not purely wanton, or, ceasing to be a traitor, he would become an irresponsible lunatic, not even capable of consistent treason. The Quislings of the late war preserved a loyalty *à rebours* to the country they tried to "sell" above the heads of their compatriots. They sought not so much to ruin their country as to save it on the cheap: forgetting that true salvation is possible only to those who are prepared to sacrifice even that which they wish to preserve. In other words, treachery to metaphysics is fifth-column treachery. The positivists who attack metaphysics do not wish to destroy science: they wish to preserve it. But in attacking that which forms the base (metaphysics) and the walls (religion) of science, they are engaged in a form of warfare which is incompatible with its preservation as an ordered and disciplined form of thought. It is not so much that they wish to eat their cake and have it, as that they wish to eat and have their cake in spite of having scorched the earth that yields its ingredients.

Nevertheless, even if it is pretty well inconceivable that our civilisation is to be utterly destroyed, there is nothing to prevent that civilisation from being subtly transformed into something which, once they realise that a change has occurred (a realisation that may not dawn on them for a long time), men find themselves heartily disliking. And that is a situation in which mankind—and European man in particular—is only too likely to find itself. It is not a case of waking up one morning and finding civilisation gone; it is a case of lying down one night and finding the will to live, and therefore to enjoy wholesome repose, strangely and almost inexplicably impoverished. The choice before man is not between civilisation and barbarism, but between a civilisation that on the whole satisfies his deepest needs and a civilisation which, after due trial, is found to leave him restless yet impotent, exasperated yet powerless, to assert his will. It is then that the so-called "revolutions" occur; for revolutions are made not by the massed action of whole communities (as they are in fairy tales, especially the fairy tales called historical textbooks), but by the action of shrewd and calculating individuals who know how to mobilise a people's sullen discontent with what it has in support of changes that, by superficial comparison, it can be persuaded into believing that it would prefer. If disillusion follows, that is much to be regretted; but —*tu l'a voulu, Georges Dandin.*

How can we tell precisely at what stage in the transition we have arrived? That is not at all easy. "This is an age of transition" is a common trope; as Dean Inge used to say, the phrase was first used by Adam to Eve as they evacuated the Garden of Eden. But today we have good reason to believe that the direction in which civilisation is going is a dangerous one, if only because technical science appears to be making discoveries in the wrong order.[1] It is quite obvious that if reason does not exert control over science, unreason will. And it is of little use complaining of the waywardness of physical science if we have not some means of showing that the heritage of science is dependent upon more ultimate forms of thought,

[1] This point was brought out very well in a commentary published in the *New English Weekly* (August 30th, 1945) after the dropping of the atom bomb in Japan.

and if we do not realise that the idea that science is the only form of enquiry free from superstition, is the greatest superstition of all. As Remy de Gourmont has said: "Physiology was long unknown while human curiosity was preoccupied with monsters". Science may stumble upon the means of destroying the universe before it has learned to understand a tenth part of that which it has learned to destroy.

At the present time, therefore, we are in a position to appreciate the fact that wisdom, far from being innate in man, is rather an endowment which he can either inherit to the full or unthinkingly repudiate. "The truth is", as Bergson wrote in his last book,[1] "that if civilisation has profoundly modified man, it is by accumulating in his social surroundings, as in a reservoir, the habits and knowledge which society pours into the individual at each new generation. Scratch the surface, abolish everything we owe to an education which is perpetual and unceasing, and you will find in the depth of our nature primitive humanity, or something very near it". In the preceding pages we have expressed our conviction that the "habits and knowledge" which are poured into the individual at each new generation are preserved in the religious institutions of society, beginning, of course, with that institution which our present economic and social order threatens more than any other, in spite of hysterical injunctions to increase the birth-rate, namely, the family. The family, we may say, is the cradle of values; and family education, as every mother knows, is essentially religious education.

To specify what other measure may be necessary to the preservation of civilised life would take us too far afield. Nevertheless, as we have been emphasising all along the necessity of maintaining a tradition of metaphysical thought, we must dwell briefly upon the kind of social organisation that is necessary for the cultivation of the so-called higher forms of enquiry. An attempt to discuss this question at a

[1] *The Two Sources of Religion and Morality* (Trans. 1935), p. 105.

period somewhat similar to our own was made after the first great war by the French critic, Julien Benda, in his book *La Trahison des Clercs*. Benda recommends the isolation of a super-class of intellectuals whose function is to look after the "eternal verities" while the ordinary man gets on with his mundane employment. This is an attractive suggestion, though not perhaps to the taxpayer; but it has serious drawbacks of another kind. For one thing, it calls to mind the statement of a member of the Abuan tribe of Southern Nigeria: "It is for this reason our people chose an Ake-Abuan that he might be holy on our behalf, keeping all the laws that ordinary people have no time to remember because of their regular work".[1] Every society must have its intellectual class engaged in pure research, whether scientific or philosophical; but a society in which there are two classes, one of pure researchers and the other of toiling millions, between which there exists a yawning gulf, is already on the way to disintegration. For the defect of such a society is that it presupposes not so much a swollen proletariat of workers as a wilting proletariat of intellectuals—or rather, that it envisages the existence of two proletariats functioning side by side, without any natural commerce between the two. Social critics have, in the past, spent much energy in deploring the existence of a class of pure manual workers, without realising that there is equal danger in the emergence of a class of pure brain-workers. "It is not 'Alas! poor Yorick', but 'Alas! poor Hamlet'."[2]

Perhaps the most serious objection to an exclusive class— or, in other words, a caste—of pure intellectual workers, is that it tends, like all castes, to conduct its studies and researches in a language unintelligible to all but its members. Hence the impression is given that a subject like metaphysics must remain for ever a closed book to the ordinary unpreten-

[1] See Talbot, *Southern Nigeria*, iii, p. 606.
[2] M. C. D'Arcy, *The Nature of Belief*, p. 64.

tious man in the street. That the technical aspect of any subject is bound to be mystifying to the layman is obvious; but this is not because the layman is stupid but because he does not happen to have been instructed. Today, as every student of philosophy knows, it is not the upholders of metaphysics who are anxious to cultivate a private jargon of their own, but the attackers of metaphysics: so that we have the strange and somewhat ludicrous spectacle of logicians protesting that they do not understand ordinary propositions unless they are "translated into scientific language". The adoption of such jargon is the first step in the organisation of a conspiracy not merely against metaphysics (which may disturb few) but against common language (which should disturb us all). To combat this new species of pedantry is the duty of everybody; and in combating it a blow will have been struck in defence of that form of enquiry to which this book is intended as a modest introduction.

Index of Proper Names

270

Subject Index

IT might justly be said that most people go for their philosophy to almost every place save philosophical textbooks; and that is not necessarily an unhealthy sign. The seeker after truth and certainty wants a living system of belief, a faith that works, rather than a collection of dead precepts, a charnel house of wisdom. But there is danger in this increasing neglect of the actual work of philosophical writers. Philosophy comes to be identified with specious profundities or portentous maxims, to be culled from the pages of highbrow or middlebrow novelists, from leather-bound poets, or even from the smart aphorisms of columnists. From the historical development of philosophical thought little is expected. The purpose of this book is to provide a necessary corrective to this common attitude. It is designed to send the ordinary reader to the study of the actual works of philosophical writers.